Leo Strauss:
The Early Writings
(1921–1932)

D1610110

SUNY series in the Jewish Writings of Leo Strauss
Kenneth Hart Green, Editor

Leo Strauss

The Early Writings
(1921–1932)

translated and edited by
Michael Zank

State University of New York Press

∧00580076

Published by
State University of New York Press

© 2002 State University of New York

For information, address the State University of New York Press,
90 State Street, Suite 700, Albany, NY 12207

Marketing by Patrick Durocher • Production by Diane Ganeles

Library of Congress Cataloging-in-Publication Data

Strauss, Leo.
    [Selections. 2002]
    Leo Strauss : the early writings, 1921–1932 / Leo Strauss ; translated and edited by
Michael Zank.
        p. cm. — (SUNY series in the Jewish writings of Strauss)
    Includes bibliographical references and index.
    ISBN 0-7914-5329-4 (alk. paper) — ISBN 0-7914-5330-8 (pbk. : alk. paper)
        1. Philosophy, Jewish. 2. Zionism. 3. Spinoza, Benedictus de, 1632–1677—Views on
Biblical interpretation. 4. Bible. O.T.—Criticism, interpretation, etc. I. Zank, Michael. II.
Title. III. Series

BM755.S75 A25 2002
181'.06—dc21
                                                                                2002017627

10 9 8 7 6 5 4 3 2 1

Sarah Shenitzer
July 31, 1929 – March 9, 2002
in memoriam

Contents

Preface

The writings included in this volume are unfamiliar, if not completely unknown, even to the growing number of American students of the work of
Leo Strauss, nor is the relation of these early writings to Strauss's later work
immediately evident or easily understood. The present volume is therefore
intended as a contribution to the study of the origins of the political philosophy of Leo Strauss.

Not only are the writings themselves quite foreign to most readers of
Strauss, but we are largely unacquainted with the intricacies of their original
setting in the intellectual and political climate of the German Jewish community of the 1920s. The purpose of the introduction and of the notes to the
translations is to provide the early writings with the necessary background
and context.

Within the German Jewish community of his time Strauss relates to two
seemingly opposite trends, namely, to the academic institutions of the liberal
European Wissenschaft des Judentums and to the Zionist youth movement
calling for an exodus from Europe. His affiliation with the elite of European
Jewish scholarship is evident from the context of his first scholarly works.
Strauss submitted his 1921 dissertation to Ernst Cassirer, who, at the time,
was known as the foremost student of the Jewish neo-Kantian philosopher
Hermann Cohen; in the years 1925 to 1928 Strauss produced a monograph
on Spinoza as a fellow of the Akademie für die Wissenschaft des Judentums;
and in 1935 he applied for a position in Jewish philosophy of religion at the
Hebrew University of Jerusalem, to which he submitted a set of studies on
medieval Jewish philosophy under the title *Philosophy and Law*, published by
Schocken in Berlin. However, neither the affiliation with Cassirer, nor the
relation with the director of the Berlin Akademie, Julius Guttmann, nor the

Jerusalem candidacy was easy and simple. Contrary to Cassirer's levelheaded interest in the "problem of knowledge," Strauss's dissertation celebrated Friedrich Heinrich Jacobi's critique of Enlightenment rationalism; the monograph on Spinoza focused on his critique of religion instead of, as the fellowship mandated, on his biblical scholarship; and the candidacy in Jerusalem was torpedoed by the introduction to *Philosophy and Law,* where Strauss disparages both Orthodox faith and the Zionist project and associates himself with the "honest atheism" of Heidegger. While thus working in the midst of the synthesis of Jewish and humanist *Bildung* that was typical of nineteenth-century liberal German Jewish scholarship, the institutions of which continued to operate until the 1930s, Strauss also distanced himself from this tradition and, along with others, challenged its synthetic assumption on the basis of the experiences and concerns of a generation disenchanted by the failure of social integration and troubled by the universal crisis of values precipitated by the World War. To be sure, this uneasy bedfellow of the increasingly apologetic trend of German Jewish scholarship is not a naive proponent of the neoromantic "renaissance" of German Judaism either.

In his early political writings Strauss contributes to debates among the youngest generation of German Zionists on the spiritual orientation of their movement, which, to them, concerns the future of Judaism as a whole. Publishing in major Zionist venues and speaking to federal assemblies of midstream youths associated strongly neither with the Left nor with the Right, Strauss carried his theoretical concern with the post-Enlightenment fate of religion onto the platform of discussions on the post-Balfour state of political Zionism. His theoretical insights compelled him to reject the two most accepted combinations of the political secularism of Herzlian Zionism with traditional Judaism, namely the cultural Zionism associated with Ahad Ha'am and Martin Buber and the religious Zionism of Mizrahi. While the sophistication of his essays initially attracted the attention and support of the leadership of the mainstream Zionist students' organization, his outspokenly negative analysis of both cultural and religious Zionism was eventually rejected as politically inopportune when the forging of practical alliances began to take precedence over the "honesty" of the intellectual stance.

A study of a major figure in the differentiated world of the German Jewish renaissance of the 1920s would be incomplete without a consideration of the outside forces at play in his intellectual and political choices. It goes without saying that these outside forces were as complex in themselves and as driven by unresolved conflicts as those experienced by the Jewish minority. The scholarship of early-twentieth-century cultural Protestantism *(Kulturprotestantismus),* for example, was itself an uneasy amalgamation of classicist, humanist, and Teutonic sources. The peak of the achievements of this tradition impressed itself on the mind of the young Strauss in the work of Max Weber, Ernst Troeltsch, Rudolf Otto, and Edmund Husserl. But there were also such cultural pessimists as Friedrich Nietzsche, Paul de Lagarde, and Oswald Spengler whose perspective on politics, religion, and society was in fact much more congenial to the cultural analysis of Zionism than the new social, religious, and philosophical approaches developed in the schools of Göttingen, Heidelberg, and Freiburg. Furthermore, the influence of the established masters was gradually eclipsed by Martin Heidegger, the rising star of the younger generation who, all dressed in black, was to declare the death of Wilhelminian bourgeois philosophy in a single theatrical stroke taken utterly seriously not only by himself but by his otherwise perfectly reasonable admirers, among them the circle of Strauss's philosophical intimates: Hans-Georg Gadamer, Karl Löwith, Gerhard Krüger, and Jacob Klein.

To be sure, it would be overly simplistic if we assumed that Heidegger's gesture affected only the outside and not also the inside of the German Jew. The very dichotomization between such an "outside" and an "inside" was perpetually in question: in fact, it was the essence of the German Jewish question. Strauss certainly perceived any distinction between a solidly Jewish and a solidly German context—whereby if one lived in a land between two rivers, one could choose one's spiritual nourishment from either and mix it according to taste—as unrealistic, and any premature claim to authenticity as inauthentic. He was not alone in this perception. The creativity of the small elite of German-Jewish renaissance intellectuals was driven by the realization of the utterly hybrid nature of each and every aspect of their lives. Put in the terms of Zionism, the question was this: How was a return to Judaism possible if the world of the ghetto was irretrievably lost, while modern Judaism (even if transported to Palestine) was inextricably European? This question is the point of departure for the early writings of Leo Strauss.

* * *

For the purpose of orientation, the following bibliography lists the texts included in this volume[1] (indicated in boldface) in the context of the larger body of Strauss's early writings. The titles appear in the order of their date of composition, when that is known, or else in the order of their date of publication.[2] The list includes all known publications and manuscripts,[3] covering the years 1921 to 1932, including two previously unknown essays, first published, respectively, in 1925 and 1928 in *Der jüdische Student*.[4] Not listed, for reasons of simplification and clarity, are eight brief introductions to volumes

2 and 3, pt. 1, of Mendelssohn's philosophical and aesthetic writings, which Strauss produced in 1931 and 1932 for the Mendelssohn *Jubiläumsausgabe* of the Akademie für die Wissenschaft des Judentums.[5]

I. Philosophical dissertation (1921)

"The Problem of Knowledge in the Philosophical Doctrine of Friedrich Heinrich Jacobi." Inaugural dissertation. University of Hamburg, 1921.

The Problem of Knowledge in the Philosophical Doctrine of Friedrich Heinrich Jacobi.
Extract from the inaugural dissertation, originally published in 1921.

II. Zionist writings (1923–25)

Response to Frankfurt's "Word of Principle"
Originally in *Jüdische Rundschau* (Berlin) 28, no. 9 (30 January 1923): 45–46.

The Holy
Originally in *Der Jude: Eine Monatsschrift* (Berlin) 7, no. 4 (April 1923): 240–42.

A Note on the Discussion on "Zionism and Anti-Semitism"
Originally in *Jüdische Rundschau* 28, nos. 83/84 (28 September 1923): 501.

The Zionism of Nordau
Originally in *Der Jude: Eine Monatsschrift*, vol. 7, no. 10/11 (Oct./Nov.), Berlin: 1923, pp. 657-60.

Paul de Lagarde
Originally in *Der Jude: Eine Monatsschrift*, vol. 8, no. 1 (January), Berlin: 1924, pp. 8-15.

Sociological Historiography?
Originally in *Der Jude: Eine Monatsschrift*, vol. 8, no. 3 (March), Berlin: 1924, pp. 190–92.

Review of Albert Levkowitz, *Contemporary Religious Thinkers: On Changes in the Modern Views of Life*
Originally in *Der Jude: Eine Monatsschrift* 8, no. 7 (July 1924): 432.

On the Argument with European Science
Originally in *Der Jude. Eine Monatsschrift* 8, no. 10 (October 1924): 613–17.

Comment on Weinberg's Critique
Originally in *Der jüdische Student* 22, nos. 1 and 2 (February 1925): 15–18

Ecclesia militans
Originally in *Jüdische Rundschau* 30, no. 36 (8 May 1925): 334.

Biblical History and Science
Originally in *Jüdische Rundschau* 30, no. 88 (10 November 1925): 744–45.

III. Historical-philological writings on Spinoza (1924, 1925–28)
Cohen's Analysis of Spinoza's Bible Science
Originally in *Der Jude: Eine Monatsschrift*, 8, nos. 5 and 6 (May/June 1924): 295–314.

On the Bible Science of Spinoza and His Precursors
Originally in *Korrespondenzblatt des Vereins zur Gründung und Erhaltung einer Akademie für die Wissenschaft des Judentums* 7 (1926): 1–22.

Die Religionskritik Spinozas als Grundlage seiner Bibelwissenschaft: Untersuchungen zu Spinozas Theologisch Politischem Traktat. Series: Veröffentlichungen der Akademie für die Wissenschaft des Judentums, Philosophische Sektion, Zweiter Band. Berlin: Akademie Verlag, 1930.

IV. Reorientation (1928–32)
Sigmund Freud, *The Future of an Illusion*
Originally in *Der jüdische Student* 25, no. 4 (August 1928): 16–22.

"Der Konspektivismus" (1929). First published by Heinrich Meier in *GS*, 2:365–75. A review of Karl Mannheim, *Ideologie und Utopie.*

Franz Rosenzweig and the Academy for the Science of Judaism
Originally in *Jüdische Wochenzeitung für Kassel, Hessen, und Waldeck* 6, no. 49 (13 December 1929).

"Religiöse Lage der Gegenwart" (1930). First published in *GS*, 2:377–91. A "lecture, to be held on Dec. 21, 1930 at the federal camp of *Kadimah* in Brieselang, near Berlin."

"Cohen und Maimuni" (1931). First published in *GS*, 2:393–436. Draft of a lecture, 4 May 1931, at the Hochschule für die Wissenschaft des Judentums in Berlin.

"Maimunis Lehre von der Prophetie und ihre Quellen" (1931) = "Die philosophische Begründung des Gesetzes," in *Philosophie und Gesetz: Beiträge zum Verständnis Maimunis und seiner Vorläufer*, 87–122. Berlin: Schocken, 1935. The manuscript for this essay was completed in July 1931 and was supposed to be published in the *Korrespondenzblatt für die Akademie des Judentums*, which was, however, discontinued in 1931.[6]

Review of Julius Ebbinghaus, *On the Progress of Metaphysics*
Originally in *Deutsche Literaturzeitung* 52 (27 December 1931): 2451–53.

"Die geistige Lage der Gegenwart" (1932). First published in *GS*, 2:441–64. The original is a twelve-page lecture manuscript, dated 6 February 1932.

"Anmerkungen zu Carl Schmitt, *Der Begriff des Politischen*." *Archiv für Sozialwissenschaft und Sozialpolitik* (Tübingen) 67, no. 6 (August–September 1932): 732–49.

The Testament of Spinoza
Originally in *Bayerische Israelitische Gemeindezeitung* 8, no. 21 (1 November 1932): 322–26.

The early writings may be divided into four phases coinciding with four distinct but related preoccupations, namely,

    I. the dissertation on Friedrich Heinrich Jacobi (1921),
    II. Zionist writings (1923–25),
    III. work on Spinoza's critique of religion (1924, 1925–28), and
    IV. writings from a phase of reorientation (1928–32).

This division shows a predominance of scholarly preoccupations for the entire decade (I and III; also IV, especially if one adds the Mendelssohn introductions), with the exception of the years 1923–25 when Strauss wrote mostly on political Zionism (II, aside from the 1924 essay on Cohen and Spinoza, which, for thematic reasons, is here listed under III). The years 1928-32 (IV) are distinguished by a mixture of pursuits and venues, as well as by the fact that much of what Strauss wrote during these years was not published immediately.[7] Some of the essays written during this period (IV) were eventually combined into what became one of the best-known works of Strauss, namely, *Philosophie und Gesetz: Beiträge zum Verständnis Maimunis und seiner Vorläufer*, published in 1935, a work whose interpretation has been notoriously elusive. It is thus a further purpose of the introduction to examine what we can learn from the early writings about the character of this crucial phase in the work of Leo Strauss.

NOTES

1. The scope of this volume is limited to the shorter early publications from 1921 to 1932, excluding the full text of the dissertation and the Spinoza monograph, as well as manuscripts not published during this period. Also excluded is the 1932 review of Carl Schmitt, *Der Begriff des Politischen*, which has been available in Heinrich Meier, *Carl Schmitt and Leo Strauss: The Hidden Dialogue. Including Strauss's Notes on Schmitt's Concept of the Political and Three Letters from Strauss to Schmitt*, trans. J. Harvey Lomax, foreword by Joseph Cropsey (Chicago: University of Chicago Press, 1995).

2. The texts translated in this volume are given with English titles. For the original titles and further bibliographic information see the unnumbered source notes to the translations at the beginning of the endnotes.

3. A number of hitherto unknown manuscripts from the early period as well as the full text of the 1921 dissertation of Jacobi have been made available by Heinrich Meier, with the editorial assistance of Wiebke Meier, in Leo Strauss, *Gesammelte Schriften*, vol. 1: *Die Religionskritik Spinozas und zugehörige Schriften* (Stuttgart and Weimar, 1996), J. B. Metzler, and vol. 2: *Philosophie und Gesetz: Frühe Schriften* (Stuttgart and Weimar (J. B. Metzler, 1997). These important texts are extensively referenced below, and an English translation is in planning.

4. "Comment on Weinberg's Critique" (1925) and a 1928 review of Freud's *The Future of an Illusion* were brought to my attention by Professor Eugene Sheppard, who discovered copies of the original publications in the Scholem archive at the National and University Library Givat Ram, in Jerusalem. The texts were included among notes Scholem put together upon receiving notice of Strauss's death, presumably for an obituary. I am grateful to Professor Sheppard for sharing this material with me so generously.

5. For a complete listing of these introductions and Strauss's important later contributions to the Mendelssohn edition, see the notes below.

6. Cf. *GS*, 2:xiif.

7. The lectures are, of course, a form of public utterance. Not unlike other political movements of the time, however, the Zionist students' movement had a policy of secrecy and distinguished between publications restricted to its membership and publications open to the public. This policy of secrecy, first introduced during World War I, seems to have been suspended for most of the 1920s, but was reintroduced in the early 1930s, that is, exactly at the time when Strauss, the Zionist, spoke to Zionist audiences without publishing his lectures, and when Strauss, the philosopher, rediscovered the principle of the exoteric! More on this in the introduction, below.

Acknowledgments

Working on translating, annotating, and introducing the early writings of Leo Strauss, I incurred a debt of gratitude to a number of individuals and institutions whom it is my pleasure to acknowledge. Kenneth Hart Green invited me to contribute this volume to the SUNY Series in the Jewish Thought of Leo Strauss on the recommendation of Professor Marvin Fox, of blessed memory, who was *Doktorvater* to both of us. Ken Green accompanied the growth of this book from the first draft of the translations to the completion of the manuscript with unwavering dedication and sustained commitment to the making of a first-rate edition. If the work comes even close to such a standard it is not in small measure due to the attention of the series editor to each aspect and every turn of phrase in the oeuvre of Leo Strauss. The remaining shortcomings are, of course, my own responsibility.

As a non-native speaker of English, I repeatedly relied on the linguistic advice of my in-laws, veteran translators Abe and Sarah Shenitzer. Others also helped with problems of language, research, or content, among them most notably Laurence Berns, Aaron Garrett, Abigail Gillman, Tomás Kalmar, Deeana Klepper, Miriam Shenitzer, Hartwig Wiedebach, Matthias Wismann, and Martin Yaffe. My sincerest thanks to all. Thanks also to Professors Rémi Brague and Stanley Rosen, who kindly read and commented on various drafts of this volume.

Special mention must be made of Eugene Sheppard, who brought two hitherto unknown publications by Strauss to my attention and provided me with initial copies of the texts. Professor Sheppard has been a wellspring of information, an attentive and critical reader, and a delightful colleague.

In 1998/99, the Humanities Foundation at Boston University, directed by Katherine T. O'Connor, kindly provided me with a junior fellowship that allowed me to return to my work on Strauss, which I had begun in 1994. Thanks to the fellows who provided important suggestions for improving the introduction to this volume, especially to John Clayton, James Schmidt, and Steven Scully.

In the summer of 1999, when I enjoyed the privileges of the Martin Buber Visiting Professorship in Jewish Philosophy of Religion at the Johann Wolfgang Goethe Universität in Frankfurt am Main, I discovered volumes 1 and 2 of Heinrich and Wiebke Meier's edition of Leo Strauss's early writings, along with Heinrich Meier's other contributions to the study of Leo Strauss. Without what I learned from Meier, this work would not be what it is.

For help with research I am indebted to the staff at Boston University's Mugar Library, to Frau Rachel Heuberger at the Städtische und Universitäts-bibliothek Frankfurt, to Jim Rosenbloom and Dr. Charles Cutter at Brandeis University, and to the staff at the library of the Hochschule für Jüdische Studien in Heidelberg.

Finally, thanks to Joseph Cropsey, the literary executor of Leo Strauss, for the permission to make these early writings of Strauss available in this edition.

Abbreviations

EJ   Cecil Roth and Geoffrey Wigoder, eds. *Encyclopaedia Judaica.* Jerusalem: Keter Publishing House, 1966–.

JS   *Herman Cohens Jüdische Schriften.* Mit einer Einleitung von Franz Rosenzweig herausgegeben von Bruno Strauß. 3 vols. Series: Veröffentlichungen der Akademie für die Wissenschaft der Judentums. Berlin: C. A. Schwetschke & Sohn, 1924.

GS   Leo Strauss. *Gesammelte Schriften.* Edited by Heinrich Meier, with the editorial assistance of Wiebke Meier. 2 vols. Vol. 1: *Die Religionskritik Spinozas und zugehörige Schriften.* Stuttgart and Weimar: J. B. Metzlar, 1966. Vol. 2: *Philosophie und Gesetz: Frühe Schriften.* Stuttgart and Weimar: J. B. Metzlar, 1997.

RGG   *Religion in Geschichte und Gegenwart.* Edited by Kurt Galling. 3d, unabridged edition. Tübingen: C. B. Mohr (Paul Siebeck), 1986.

Editorial Note: Endnotes are by the editor, and are numbered with arabic numerals. Strauss's own notes to the treatises are given as page-end footnotes with lowercase roman numerals. His marginal remarks are indicated by asterisks.

Part I
Introduction

A GERMAN JEWISH YOUTH

When Leo Strauss died in 1973, he did not leave an autobiography, and a scholarly biography on this major political philosopher has as yet to be written.[1] But Strauss left us with a number of autobiographic fragments, and what else we need to know in order to approach the writings assembled in this volume is easy enough to ascertain.[2]

Strauss was born 20 September 1899, to an Orthodox Jewish family living in the rural town of Kirchhain (Hesse), just ten kilometers northeast of the university town of Marburg. He shared this rural rather than urban background with the majority of German Jewry; in fact, he shared it with most Germans of the time. Strauss grew up, as he once described it, in an atmosphere of strict observance yet with "very little Jewish knowledge."[3] Influenced by the typical humanistic *Gymnasium* education of his day, he "formed the plan, or the wish, to spend [his] life reading Plato and breeding rabbits while earning [his] livelihood as a rural postmaster." He describes the estrangement from his Orthodox home as a gradual and nonrebellious movement that culminated in his "conversion," at the age of seventeen, "to simple, straightforward political Zionism." The group he joined was the Jüdischer Wanderbund Blau-Weiss.[4]

While the history of Blau-Weiss as an independent organization was relatively short-lived, it exerted a significant influence on the German Zionist youth movement as a whole.[5] A group by this name was first constituted in Breslau in 1907, as a Jewish counterpart to the influential German Wandervogel. The Wandervogel movement had existed since the 1890s when a group of youngsters came together in Steglitz under the leadership of Karl

Fischer.[6] What united these youths was their contempt for modernity, for urban civilization, and for the materialism of adult society. The early Wandervogel was inspired by the Teutonic mysticism of Friedrich Ludwig Jahn,[7] Paul de Lagarde,[8] and Julius Langbehn,[9] and its majority espoused a more or less de-Christianized Lutheran spirituality. Only a minority embraced the neopaganism of the Far Right or the radical utopianism of the Far Left. Clad in short pants and open-neck shirts, such bands of "perpetual adolescents"[10] would hike through the German countryside, singing folk songs and debating the inspired poetry and social criticism of the day (such as the writings of Stefan George, Rainer Maria Rilke, and Hermann Hesse). Although the youngsters were not committed to any party or any ideology, they were unanimous in the assumption that Jews could not well or sincerely be part of their movement.[11] Lagarde and other favorite authors associated the Jews with the urban materialism so viscerally rejected by this new generation, and it seemed doubtful to them that Germans and Jews could share the real inner communion and feeling of commonality that was the hallmark of this movement. Most constituents of the Wandervogel considered themselves "a-Semitic" rather than anti-Semitic, regarding the alienness between the two nationalities as a fact of nature and life. The nonchalance by which they were excluded from this German *völkisch* renewal precipitated a quest among young Jews to experience the irrational grounds of commonality among their own. To them the most appropriate and dignified answer to this experience of exclusion presented itself in a German-Jewish Zionist youth movement.[12]

Blau-Weiss established itself as an alternative to the German youth movement, and it modeled itself on its ideals and practices.[13] Its rhetoric was a form of heightened speech that, in hindsight, may appear quaint and makes all analysis of its content rather difficult.[14] The membership consisted of high-school-age children and university students (i.e., ages fifteen to twenty)[15] who acted without adult supervision[16] and who rejected anything on principle that smacked of politics and political organization. Countering the Protestant Germanism of the Wandervogel with a corresponding "German Jewish" orientation, Blau-Weiss provided a haven for the assimilated and alienated Jewish youths who enjoyed the sense of belonging provided by the uniforms and pins and who thrived on the ritual of marching through the streets, returning the German "Heil!" with a self-assured Jewish "Shalom!"[17] Hiking across the German countryside was a novel expression of Jewish communal life, and it was perceived as such. The Wanderbund provided "instant movement and action . . . in the course of which they hoped to achieve their human and Jewish substance."[18] Like its German counterpart, Blau-Weiss was decidedly middle-class[19] and hence recruited more successfully among those who were like themselves, that is, among assimilated Western Jews, and much less successfully among the Eastern European Jewish proletarians who were more strongly attracted by the socialist *haluts* movement (which, of course, also had its German counterpart in the socialist Arbeiterjugend). As in the case of their German peers who, at the 1913 Hohe Meissner meeting, called for "inner truthfulness" as the hallmark of their *völkisch* renewal,[20] the enthusiastic rhetoric of Blau-Weiss often covered up for a pervasive lack of concrete content. In the case of Blau-Weiss with its highly educated, liberal, and assimilated constituency, this meant most often a pervasive lack of Jewish knowledge. Affiliation with a Zionist youth organization meant for many to find a place where they could study Jewish history (from a Zionist perspective) and Hebrew for the first time in their lives.

In contrast to the *haluts* movement and the association of Zionist fraternities—the Kartell jüdischer Verbindungen, or K.J.V.—the Wanderbund Blau-Weiss was initially rather lukewarm when it came to the question of settling in Palestine.[21] This changed under the post–World War I leadership of Walter Moses (1922–26), who completely reorganized Blau-Weiss, briefly united it with K.J.V., and managed to establish a German-speaking settlement in Palestine.[22] When this experiment collapsed, however, the Wanderbund was dissolved (1926), a setback that affected the entire German Zionist youth movement.[23]

Leo Strauss had first joined Blau-Weiss with the enthusiasm of a convert to a movement whose very purpose was the encounter *(Erlebnis)* of a deep commonality between its members. Yet this enthusiasm gave way to a "spirit of sobriety." In his very first Zionist essay, "Response to Frankfurt's 'Word of Principle'" (1923), Strauss admits to his earlier "confusion" in a phrase that echoes Nietzsche's confession of having temporarily been afflicted with the disease of anti-Semitism.[24]

> It was thought that by heaping upon us for years, to the point of nausea, "personal encounters" [*Erlebnisse*] and "confessions" [*Bekenntnisse*] one could make us forget that there is such a thing as critique. *We ourselves were temporarily confused*, but now we unambiguously profess the spirit of sobriety as opposed to that of pathetic declamation. "Belief" may still be decisive, yet belief is no oracle but is subject to the control of historical reasoning. (See below, p. 66. Emphasis added.)

By invoking the "spirit of sobriety as opposed to that of pathetic declamation," Strauss distanced himself not only from his earlier self but also from a new Blau-Weiss, whose covenant had been issued in 1922 by Walter Moses in Prunn. While he was certainly not alone in criticizing Blau-Weiss, he was not ready to accept the alternatives proposed by other, no less vocal critics. Instead, he performed a careful dance of distinctions in which he distanced himself from virtually all contemporary trends. Strauss's very first intervention was thus characterized by a keen ear for false rhetoric and by an insistence on arguments that can be defended with the force of "intellectual probity."[25] Strauss, the Zionist, was after all—a philosopher.

As Strauss honed his literary skills as a Zionist writer, he also informally continued the philosophical studies that he had formally concluded in 1921 with his dissertation on the problem of knowledge in the work of Friedrich Heinrich Jacobi (1743–1819). In the curriculum vitae that was part of the "extract" from his dissertation, Strauss indicates that, after having completed his secondary education at the humanistic Gymnasium Philippinum in Marburg (1912–17), he had served in the German army for seventeen months before returning to Marburg as a student of "philosophy, mathematics, and the sciences." In the typical fashion of the time, Strauss had then attended four universities in only four years before graduating with a doctorate from the newly founded University of Hamburg. Aside from the convenient proximity to his hometown, what had initially attracted Strauss to Marburg was the reputation of Hermann Cohen (1842–1918), founder of the Marburg school of neo-Kantianism, spiritual leader of German Judaism, and a profound inspiration to aspiring Jewish philosophers. Strauss never personally met Hermann Cohen who, after moving to Berlin in 1912, no longer taught in Marburg on a regular basis. By the time Strauss returned from the war, Cohen had passed away.[26] The decision to continue his studies under Ernst Cassirer, who was then still in Berlin, may also have been inspired by Strauss's regard for the work of Cohen. Cassirer (1874–1945) had been Cohen's master student, the stellar representative of the younger generation of neo-Kantians; his appointment to a full professorship was delayed by a governmental policy of discrimination that, despite legal emancipation, prevailed throughout the Wilhelminian era. Jews were prevented from taking higher positions in the military, in the court system, in the administration of the state, and other key areas, such as the discipline of philosophy proper (in contrast to disciplines that then also fell under the heading of philosophy, such as mathematics and the sciences). Hermann Cohen had been the notable exception to this rule. After the demise of the Second Reich, Cassirer finally received a call, and Strauss followed him from Berlin to Hamburg.

Initially quite loyal to Cassirer, Strauss nevertheless found no congenial mind in the philosopher of "symbolic forms." The content of the dissertation indicates that his agenda was sharply at odds with that of his advisor. While the title and research question of Strauss's dissertation superficially conform to Cassirer's interest in the "problem of knowledge,"[27] the substance of the work describes and, more importantly, defends Jacobi's philosophy as a counterposition to the methodological rationalism of the Kantian tradition maintained by Cassirer. When he wrote his dissertation, Strauss was influenced by a different group of thinkers. Among the theorists of religion and philosophers Strauss acknowledges in his dissertation are Ernst Troeltsch, Max Weber,[28] Max Scheler, and Rudolf Otto. The methodology of "description" that Strauss applies to Jacobi's concept of "belief" *(Glaube)* is the methodology of the phenomenological school of Edmund Husserl. Yet this affiliation alone would not have pressured Strauss into opposing Cassirer.

What is most striking about the dissertation is its celebration of "belief" at the expense of critical reason. In light of this fact, the above-cited "confusion" with respect to "belief" from which Strauss had recovered by 1923 emerges as a pervasive condition that involved not only his political but also his philosophical views. Be that as it may, in 1923 we see Strauss defending the values of critique and argument against belief and enthusiasm. One might say that the philosophical career of Strauss began only after he had completed (and rejected) his philosophical dissertation. Hence it is not surprising to see Strauss, now a young doctor of philosophy and freelance Zionist writer, continue his studies, first in Freiburg, and then back in Marburg. Strauss went to Freiburg to hear Edmund Husserl, the founder of the phenomenological school, but instead he came under the influence of Martin Heidegger, whom he henceforth regarded as the most important philosophical voice of his time.[29] He followed Heidegger back to Marburg, where he befriended the new crop of students of philosophy, among them most prominently Hans Georg Gadamer and Karl Löwith.[30]

Despite his newfound "spirit of sobriety," Strauss's distance from Cassirer prevails unabatedly and becomes explicit in "The Argument with European Science" (1924). Yet his critique of Cassirer does not entail a distancing from Hermann Cohen. Rather, Strauss distinguishes between the thoroughly idealist presuppositions of Cassirer's work on religion, which he continues to reject, and the presupposition in the philosophical work of Hermann Cohen of a concept of religion that is rooted in the religion of the Hebrew prophets. According to Strauss, the flaw of Cassirer's concept of religion derives from the assumption that what we call religion is located on a developmental continuum with the mythological phase of the cultural consciousness.[31] In contrast, Cohen's concept of religion derived from the assumption that the transcendent God of the Hebrew prophets cannot be understood on the basis of a continuous development but only on the basis of a radical rejection of its mythological predecessors.[32] Following Cohen, Strauss asserts against Rudolf Otto that the religion of the Hebrew prophets is no less rational for being "uncanny." Rather (and this is what, according to Strauss, Cohen was after), the rational core and the resistance to myth of the biblical prophets could be understood only if they were recognized as mutually constitutive aspects of a profoundly rational religion. In this way, Cassirer is distanced from Cohen, who himself, as Strauss saw it, had always maintained a critical distance from many of the views held by the other representatives of the Marburg school.[33]

It was this aspiring philosopher who raised his voice among other sophisticated young Zionists. What kind of a Zionist was this philosopher? Was he lukewarm about making converts for the movement, as one anecdote seems to suggest,[34] or was he an engaged and productive *alter Herr* (as postgraduate members of students' corporations were called)? The latter is supported by the fact that, in 1924, Strauss was invited by the board of the K.J.V. to give a keynote lecture at a retreat, which he defended against a critic in the 1925 "Comment on Weinberg's Critique." Here Strauss also mentions his repeated participation in recruitment events (in the language of the students: *Keilerfahrung*).[35] Furthermore, the lecture manuscripts recently published by Heinrich and Wiebke Meier show that the Zionist student organization continued to provide him with an audience for his ever more theoretical ruminations on the modern predicament.

Strauss's highly academic and intellectualist Zionism is not unrepresentative for the German Zionist youth movement of the early 1920s, but it seems somewhat out of step with the general developments in the second half of the 1920s and the early 1930s.[36] This may explain why Strauss's participation in the Zionist debates declined after 1925. While he made a transition from Blau-Weiss to K.J.V., the latter was not an ideal venue for the discussions on the theoretical matters Strauss was most interested in, such as the relation between Judaism and European culture, religion and Zionism, and so on. While these topics could still be debated, the student organization was primarily interested in practical questions, such as recruitment, ideological education, and preparation for immigration to Palestine. Given its very moderate recruitment successes, K.J.V. also showed increasing interest in the new "science" of propaganda.[37] In the second half of the 1920s, the few attempts at theoretical debates were eclipsed by the practical concerns of the movement: German Zionist settlements in Palestine, Jewish-Arab relations, and, last but not least, the deteriorating political, social, and economic situation in Germany. There is no trace in Strauss's lectures and essays of interest in these practical questions.

In terms of its social and economic ideals, the Zionist movement was a microcosm of the political world of the 1920s, which was divided between the proponents of socialist and capitalist blueprints for the future of society. In addition, beginning in 1929, the representative parliamentary democratic aspects of the Weimar constitution began to lose out to its more popular presidential aspects. While Strauss does not speak to the socioeconomic question of the time directly, his affinity with the revisionism of Jabotinsky (see below) may put him in the camp of the supporters of a capitalist economy in Palestine, while his 1932 review of Carl Schmitt's essay "Concept of the Political" may put him in the camp of the foes of political pluralism.[38] Yet, trying to judge the politics of the philosopher, one must keep in mind that his political Zionism was of a "formal" rather than practical nature, a tendency very much in the tradition of the youth movement that he had originally joined and that, in a sense, he never outgrew. The intellectualist bent of Strauss's Zionism is documented in the following anecdote in which he recalls an exchange he had with the Zionist leader, man of letters, and founder of the Jewish Legion, Vladimir Jabotinsky (1880–1940),[39] whom he met on several occasions.[40]

> I was myself . . . a political Zionist in my youth, and was a member of a Zionist student organization. In this capacity, I occasionally met Jabotinsky, the leader of the Revisionists. He asked me, "What are you doing?" I said, "Well, we read the Bible, we study Jewish history, Zionist theory, and of course, we keep abreast of developments, and so on." He replied, "And rifle practice?" And I had to say, "No."[41]

In sum, the very absence in the early essays of any acute political content and their ultramoralistic concern for a truthful statement of principles makes these writings typical of the middle-class intellectualism of the German Zionist youth movement of early 1920s. The early publications and lectures place Strauss squarely in the society of the German-Jewish cultural renaissance of the 1920s,[42] which was widely sustained by university students and graduates, their informal circles, and their organizations. Within this renaissance culture, Strauss is most closely associated with the Frankfurt circle of young intellectuals against whom he polemicizes in his very first essay.[43] This circle included the future educator and cofounder of Brith Shalom, Ernst Simon, the sociologist Leo Löwenthal (who, like Simon and his friend Gerhard Scholem, came from a highly assimilated background), and the psychologist and later Trotskyite Erich Fromm.[44] Fromm and Löwenthal were connected with the Frankfurt Institute of Social Research. The members of this circle also had in common that they were admirers of the Frankfurt rabbi Nehemia

Nobel, himself an *Alter Herr honoris causa* of K.J.V., and that they all lectured at various times at the Freies Jüdisches Lehrhaus founded by Franz Rosenzweig, as did Leo Strauss.[45]

Strauss's early writings appeared in some of the most important organs of the Jewish culture of renewal, namely in *Der Jude*,[46] in *Die jüdische Rundschau*,[47] and in *Der jüdische Student*.[48] As a Zionist and a *Bundesbruder* (member of the brotherhood of Zionist students), he articulated what he saw as the short-comings of political, cultural, and religious Zionism. By articulating his concerns as forcefully and honestly as he did, Strauss followed the maxim of the 1913 Hohe Meissner assembly of the German Wandervogel, the demand of "inner truthfulness."

Strauss returned to his philosophical pursuits more formally in February 1925, when he accepted a fellowship from the Akademie für die Wissenschaft des Judentums. Its academic director, Julius Guttmann, had read Strauss's essay "Cohen's Analysis of Spinoza's Bible Science" (1924) and encouraged Strauss to pursue his research on Spinoza further. Over the course of the next three years, Strauss wrote his first monograph, in which he examined not only the "Bible science" *(Bibelwissenschaft)* of Spinoza and his predecessors, as mandated by his fellowship, but Spinoza's critique of religion, a shift in topic that caused a rift between Strauss and Guttmann. The Akademie für die Wissen-schaft des Judentums had been initiated in 1917 by Franz Rosenzweig and Hermann Cohen[49] with the aim of stimulating a culture of study that was to bridge the gap between the academy and the Jewish community. For this purpose, the fellow was to combine his or her[50] research and writing with a period of residence and teaching in a provincial Jewish community. Strauss's agreement with Rosenzweig's innovative approach to Jewish adult educa-tion[51] may be evident from the fact that he not only accepted the Academie's funding that allowed him to pursue his research but also took on the peda-gogical responsibility that came with the fellowship, spending time as a scholar-and lecturer-in-residence in Kassel. As far as we know, he was the only fel-low to do so.[52] On the other hand, Strauss's radical intellectual curiosity and the independence of his philosophical mind seem to have put him at odds with an academy that, at the time, may have been guided more by apologetic than by scholarly concerns.[53] After completing *Spinoza's Critique of Religion*, whose publication was delayed because of the previously mentioned disagree-ment with Guttmann, Strauss went on to produce a number of introductions to volumes 2 and 3, pt. 1, of Mendelssohn's philosophical and aesthetic writ-ings, published by the Akademie in 1931 and 1932 as part of its jubilee edi-tion of the collected writings of Moses Mendelssohn.[54] Strauss's association with the Akademie lasted until 1931, when, after twelve years of operation, it encountered financial difficulties that forced it to dismiss its employees. Among those dismissed was Leo Strauss.[55]

While writing on Mendelssohn, Strauss was working on Thomas Hobbes as well as on the political philosophy of the medieval Jewish and Muslim traditions. On the strength of his studies of Hobbes, Ernst Cassirer, Carl Schmitt, and Julius Guttmann[56] recommended Strauss to the Rockefeller Foundation, which provided him with a grant allowing him to pursue his studies, first in Paris (from October 1932 until December 1933), and then in London (1934).[57] Unemployed and with his fellowship due to run out by October 1934, Strauss—by now in effect an expatriate on the move—searched for academic employment outside of Germany. He repeatedly turned to Carl Schmitt, asking him for letters of introduction to contacts in France and the United States. Schmitt, however, who by then had thrown in his lot with the National Socialists, no longer answered Strauss's letters.[58] At the same time, Strauss pursued a position in Jewish philosophy at the Hebrew University in Jerusalem. In order to boost his candidacy, Strauss combined several essays on Maimonides and medieval philosophy into one volume, published by Schocken Verlag in Berlin under the title *Philosophie und Gesetz*.[59] None of these attempts came to fruition, and it was not until 1938, when he relocated to the United States, that Strauss was able to put an end to this period of itinerancy that affected not only himself but also his immediate family. The career of the American political philosopher began at the New School for Social Research in New York.[60]

In the United States, Strauss went on to become a widely read, highly respected, and deeply influential author and teacher. Among the major works he came to produce are *On Tyranny: An Interpretation of Xenophon's Hiero* (1948), *Persecution and the Art of Writing* (1952), *Natural Right and History* (1953), *Thoughts on Machiavelli* (1958), *What is Political Philosophy?* (1959), *The City and Man* (1964), *Socrates and Aristophanes* (1966), *Liberalism Ancient and Modern* (1968), *Xenophon's Socratic Discourse* (1970), *Xenophon's Socrates* (1972), *The Argument and the Action of Plato's Laws* (1975), and *Studies in Platonic Political Philosophy* (1983), to name just those mentioned by Hilail Gildin in his *Introduction to Political Philosophy*.[61]

Strauss's own reminiscences suggest that his career as a political scientist began about at the time when the political Zionist fell silent—at a time, that is, when Strauss returned, by way of Maimonides, to the love of his high school years, Plato. Whether this reorientation constituted a change of mind or merely a privileging of the theoretical work Strauss had been pursuing all along, even under the guise of a rather "formal" political Zionism, cannot be decided without a further look at the early writings.

"CHANGE IN ORIENTATION"

The earliest text included in this volume is an extract from the 1921 philosophical dissertation on Jacobi. The latest one is a piece from 1932, published on the occasion of a Spinoza jubilee, in which Strauss bids a Zionist farewell to the author of the *Theological-Political Treatise* without, as a philosopher, taking leave of the philosopher Spinoza.[62]

The entire collection of early writings allows us to take a closer look at the "young Jew born and raised in Germany" whom Strauss describes in the preface to the English edition of his *Spinoza's Critique of Religion,* adding that, at the time, he found himself "in the grips of the theologico-political predicament."[63] The later texts included in this edition provide us with material from a time when Strauss began to articulate the means by which to extricate himself from this very "theological-political predicament." At that point, the predicament in question was widened into one that concerned not just the German Jew but modern man in general. Yet it was also one that no one perceived as clearly and as unsettlingly as did the German Jew.

In the preface to *Spinoza's Critique of Religion,* which "comes as close to an autobiography as is possible within the limits of propriety,"[64] Strauss speaks of a "change in orientation which found its first expression"[65] in the critical review of a book by the German political philosopher Carl Schmitt entitled *The Concept of the Political* (1932).[66]

The essay to which Strauss refers as containing "the first expression" of his "change in orientation,"[67] then, is a review of the work of another author. This characteristic would not by itself make the essay exceptional among Strauss's writings. From early on and throughout his career, Strauss's writings are reviews of the writings of others. With the exception perhaps of his dissertation (which he later called "a disgraceful performance"),[68] even his earliest essays show him not only as an attentive reader who is interested in tracing the thought of others to its (usually either unadmitted or unconscious) ultimate presuppositions but also as a thinker preoccupied with the relation between reading and writing. One of the maxims, formulated in 1931, in which Strauss articulates the means by which we are to extricate ourselves from the crisis of modernity, is "learning through reading" *(lesendes Lernen).* Strauss recommends a conscious and vigorous return to the "old tome," or to the "old books," that must again be opened. This recommendation is first expressed in—a book review ("Review of Julius Ebbinghaus, *On the Progress of Metaphysics*"). Strauss taught others how to read more carefully by examining the reading habits of the great authors for clues as to the way in which they constructed their own texts.[69]

Strauss's predilection for the form of the review is not an indication of modesty, if by modesty one understands a kind of softness that in the world of letters may arise from the realization that, given the historical relativity of all knowledge, no point of view can be superior to any other point of view. The very opposite is the case with Strauss. The modesty he praises is the rather immodest modesty of Socrates who, when entering the marketplace to inquire into the pursuits of his fellow Athenians, did so with the perplexing knowledge of an ignorance that was surpassed only by the ignorance of those who failed to realize their ignorance. Strauss learned from Socrates and Plato about the "natural difficulties" of philosophizing that the moderns must first relearn, since modern ignorance is more profound than the ignorance addressed by Socrates and Plato. But it was from Maimonides that Strauss learned in what respect and due to what event our modern, artificial ignorance surpasses that of the Platonic cave dwellers. This realization is first expressed in an unpublished lecture draft, written in 1930.[70]

In our search for indications of a "change of orientation" we have been moving backward from the date given by Strauss himself, 1932, to 1930. This should not come as a surprise. Strauss must evidently not be taken too literally when he cites his review of Carl Schmitt as the first expression of a change in orientation that led him beyond the position of *Spinoza's Critique of Religion*. In 1962, when Strauss wrote the preface to *Spinoza's Critique of Religion*, it was merely the most widely accessible place to which Strauss could point in order to make sure his American readers would not take it as a binding or valid statement of his current views. It seems more accurate to speak of a series of discoveries that precipitated, "changes in orientation"— perhaps not just one but several—or perhaps a change in stages.

Based on Strauss's own understanding, which of course is echoed in the literature on this matter, the writings before us may therefore be divided into those written before the "change in orientation" (up until the completion of *Spinoza's Critique of Religion* in 1928), and those that point to this change in orientation. Yet what surfaces in the published writings is insufficient to explain the nature and extent of the reorientation Strauss was undergoing in the late 1920s and early 1930s. The very fact that Strauss left several rather important lectures and manuscripts unpublished at the time may indicate that he was no longer certain that what he had to say benefited the Zionist audience to which he had immediate access. Similarly, it is highly unlikely that Strauss would have published *Philosophy and Law* in the form he did had it not been for the pressure on him to come forward with a Judaic publication that would make him a plausible candidate for a position in medieval Jewish philosophy at the Hebrew University in Jerusalem. In fact, one does not need to be a trained psychologist to see how Strauss's ambivalence about his own candidacy may have induced him to add a last-minute introduction to his more or less traditional interpretations of Maimonides in which he adumbrates a position that was inevitably misunderstood. Whether one mistook him for a *hozer bit'shuvah* (someone who reverts to Orthodoxy) or an atheist—both interpretations were as likely as they were inaccurate (as will be shown more broadly below)—neither of these readings would have endeared him to those making the decision on his candidacy.

If we are not mistaken, the basic observation that emerges from the early writings may be described as follows. Strauss identifies with neither one of the extreme, absolute, and diametrically opposed positions that he diagnoses as the prevailing forces of the time. He is neither Left nor Right, but wishes to reach beyond—that is, "before"—the division between Left and Right. By the same token, he is neither Orthodox nor atheist, but seeks to reach beyond—that is, "before"—the division between Orthodoxy and atheism. He pushes the prevailing positions to the extremes of their fundamental, irrational motives and assumptions, and points out the irrational first assumptions of seemingly rational positions (a method already present in his dissertation and even more so in his early work on Spinoza). Conversely, he argues that there are rational implications to the seemingly irrational *mysterium* of the transcendent God of prophetic religion that cannot be captured even using Rudolf Otto's assumptions about the historical development of perceptions of the sacred. The last word of the early writings invokes the maxim engraved on Spinoza's signet ring, *caute*, which Strauss renders as a call for "independence" *(Unabhängigkeit).*[71]

These concerns are present throughout the early Zionist and philosophical-historical writings. With these concerns, Strauss finds himself in the company not just of the fellow Zionists he addresses, nor just of Jews, but also of his philosophical friends and contemporaries. It is typical for the atmosphere of the time that what seems a parochial and limited Jewish venue (after all, was not Zionism all about overcoming the humanism of the reform generation, and about a return to cultural inwardness?) is in fact a highly public and hybrid enterprise where all kinds of young intellectuals find one another through the deeper, ultimately universal issues, even though these issues may be articulated in terms of irreconcilable differences. The seemingly straightforward political movement of Zionism served Strauss and others as a forum for the discussion of profound matters of political, religious, and philosophical orientation. Thus the sophisticated readers and fellow authors of *Der Jude* understood Strauss quite well when he wrote about the end of *galut* (exile) and the inextricable indebtedness of modern Jews to European "content"; about traditional religion, the Enlightenment critique of religion, and the pseudoreligion of an atheistic theology; about the problem of the rationality of transcendence; about typologies of thought (Max Weber); about the atheism of modern biblical theology; about the inverted affinities between Zionism and anti-Semitism (Paul de Lagarde); and always about Spinoza. The thread running through all the early writings is the attempt to determine, from history, one's place in history. Yet it became increasingly clear to Strauss that the effort of deriving a philosophically ("scientifically") sound imperative from historical existence was ill conceived. At a time when political theologies began, not only in theory but also increasingly in practice, to displace the culture of argument and critique, Strauss turned away from the present altogether. The great urgency with which his later political philosophy is invested bears the mark of the hour of its birth.

When, in 1935, Strauss described a "Jew who cannot be orthodox and who must consider purely political Zionism, the only 'solution to the Jewish question' possible on the basis of atheism, as a resolution that is indeed highly honorable, but not in earnest and in the long run, adequate,"[72] it seemed to many that he was describing himself. But surely one could not be an atheist and an Orthodox believer at the same time! Could there be a synthesis of revealed religion and modern historical consciousness? Strauss's answer is: No. But there should be such a synthesis! Strauss's answer is: such a synthesis can only exist at the expense of the truth of religious belief. It would be atheism in disguise. Can one not be a Jew in the full sense, just by virtue of seeking the well-being of the Jewish nation? Strauss: but is not nationalism a modern European rather than a truly Jewish value? So what is a Jew to do? In the statement cited above, Strauss formally ends his association with the Zionist movement, and he does so at the very moment when the Jewish state had become a matter of greater urgency than ever before.[73] But he also formally acknowledges that he can no longer be Orthodox. What is left for him to choose? This is the point at which Strauss turns to Maimonides, to his Muslim predecessors, and to Platonic political philosophy.

In order to get a sense of the relation between the various writings from the early period and the overall agenda of Strauss's thought that may have been in the making at the time, we need to return, for a moment, to the figure of a "change in orientation," mentioned in the autobiographic preface to *Spinoza's Critique of Religion*. Strauss dates it—not too precisely as we saw above—as taking place around 1932. What is he referring to, and what do students of Strauss mean when they refer, in this context, to a "turn" (Meier)[74]

or a "return" (Green)[75] to Maimonides that is variably dated as having occurred around 1932, or between 1928 and 1932, or even as beginning in
earnest only in 1936?

Some caution may be advised when it comes to the interpretation not
only of the date but also of the rhetorical figure of a "turn" itself. German
intellectual history of the interwar period and German Jewish intellectual
history of the same period are all too replete with "turns," "returns," and
other forms of conversion to be comfortable with this cluster of metaphors
when used to describe the intellectual biographies of what seems an entire
generation of converts. Martin Heidegger, whom Strauss heard first in Freiburg
and later in Marburg and whom he greatly admired (although only up to a
point), is perhaps the most famous case of a philosopher who encountered a
turnaround *(Kehre)*. The word *Kehre* scarcely hides the religious underpinnings of this trope: *Kehre* is short for *Umkehr*, that is, repentance. Of course,
in Heidegger's context the reference is more immediately to movements of
the sort Plato expects the dwellers of his cave to undertake. Yet again, the
religious underpinnings of the metaphor are such that the whole thing may
be suspected of an unclear mixture, an internalized "Jerusalem" encroaching
on an "Athens." If so, to speak of *Kehre* accomplishes the very obfuscation of
difference that Strauss sets out to overcome from early on.

There are other pertinent cases. The key date in the hagiography of Franz
Rosenzweig, whom Strauss knew and admired no less than he knew and
admired Heidegger,[76] is a turn from the baptismal font that inaugurated and
determined the direction of his return to Judaism. Similarly, Hermann Cohen
was likewise credited (not accidentally by Rosenzweig) with having experienced a "return to Judaism" that is supposed (by Rosenzweig) to have occurred in his old age. To be sure, these are only superficial remarks on a single
rhetorical figure that enjoyed a certain currency in Strauss's youth, and that
he seems not to have been beyond applying to himself. Of course, the phrase
of a "change of orientation" that Strauss uses to describe what occurred after
the completion of his book on Spinoza may simply mean that Strauss turned
"backward" in history, doing what was generally considered the impossible
by "returning" to pre-Enlightenment thought, more precisely by seeking in
a renewed study of ancient Greek and medieval Jewish and Muslim sources a
way out of the modern predicament, that is, out of the "theologico-political
predicament."

What this means for the present volume is the following. As much as one
may be convinced of the descriptive value of metaphors such as "turning"
and "returning," these metaphors clearly put greater emphasis on what is
being turned to than on what prepares the ground for such turning. The

metaphor makes the latter appear as a mere precondition, usually a negative precondition, a "no-thing," as it were, that precedes the real thing. But we should not judge before the fact, and in any case it is a good thing to distrust overused characterizations such as the metaphor of a "turn."

To be sure, convenient generalizations are not easily disposed of, nor are they without utility. As just noted, the figure of a turn is characteristic of early-twentieth-century Continental discourse, and Strauss shares it with many of his contemporaries. This observation may not indicate much about the substance of the philosophical moves that are characterized by it. Yet it articulates a common concern of the younger generation of the time. This generation consisted of those who had seen their peers perish in the merciless trenches of the First World War, a war that had been waged in the name of culture, civilization, and progress, and that had turned culture, civilization, and progress into doubtful propositions. War, revolution, economic hardships, and a foundering democracy made it impossible for the younger generation to naïvely subscribe to the wisdom of their elders, a wisdom that had turned out to be folly. Thus, at least, we may account for the eagerness of that generation to articulate radical solutions to problems that were not only of a theoretical nature but were eminently political. Suspicious of liberalism and humanism, and nauseated by the sanctimonious cultivation of vast theoretical solutions to concrete practical problems, they sought to break out of the ivory tower and participate in life. Some of the philosophers of the time, such as Margarete Sussmann, spoke of an "exodus out of philosophy."[77] A response to the situation generated by the First World War that was commensurate with it had to entail a clear "turn" away from the values, ideas, notions, systems, and so on, that had sustained the ill-conceived notions that had led to the war itself.

Strauss himself was fully aware of this mood and deeply suspicious of its allure. While he was sympathetic to this kind of analysis, he felt that such shared sympathy does not prove the legitimacy of a standpoint.[78]

Around 1929, Strauss realized that the true problem consists in the expectation that any answer directed only at the present could claim validity or necessity.[79] Strauss's earliest Zionist writings still assume that historical reasoning will provide the right answer to the problems of the time. In the writings dating from 1929 and onward, however, Strauss articulates the insight that the *proton pseudos* resides precisely in this presupposition. He realizes that the quest for the right position in history raises more questions than it answers. What begins as the Jewish quest for historical orientation in a new situation ("How are the people to live now?") turns into the question of whether it is possible to recover the timeless problem of the right life.[80]

POLITICAL EXISTENCE AND RELIGION

The early essays document Strauss's gradual shift from political Zionism to
the eternal problem of the political itself, from the question, "How are the
people to live now?"[81] to the question: "How is one to live?"[82] This reorientation does not necessarily constitute the displacement of one cause by another, yet it entails the expression of a resignation, of a loss of political faith.
In the transition from one question to the other, however, concern with
political existence prevails, especially with political existence in relation to
religion. The relation between religion and politics—a central issue also in
Strauss's early scholarly work—is no more fundamental to the Zionist writer
than to the genealogist of political philosophy. While the phase of reorientation is characterized by a withdrawal from political participation for the sake
of retrieving the classical political philosophy of the Platonic tradition, his
earliest essays are permeated by the no less Platonic hope that Zionism might
afford one of those rare moments when the philosopher might be king. To
put it somewhat paradoxically, then: If there is a turn in the writings of the
early Strauss, it is one from Plato to Plato.

In his 1923 "Response to Frankfurt's 'Word of Principle,'" Strauss positions himself firmly between all established ideologies, a strategy that was to
remain one of the hallmarks of his authorship. While he defends the values of
liberalism against the authoritarian trends of the new Blau-Weiss,[83] he also
rejects the Frankfurt circle's demand for "Jewish content." While "Breslau"
(i.e., the original, religious Zionist, pre–Walter Moses Blau-Weiss) may not
yet have found its "word of principle," "Frankfurt" (the cultural Zionist circle
including Ernst Simon, Leo Löwenthal, Erich Fromm, Fritz Goithein, and
Erich Michaelis) was relying on surrogate stuff: it merely countered the new
"pagan-fascist" rhetoric of Walter Moses with the rhetoric of "mystical-hu-
manitarianism." Strauss diagnoses that both of these attempts at extricating
oneself from modernity/Europe/Christendom were essentially indebted to
modernity/Europe/Christendom in that they themselves were nothing but
expressions of the modern self-consciousness. Antimodernism, he states, is
itself profoundly modern and anything but a safe and certain return to Jewish
"content." The essay is as sharp a critical analysis of early-1920s German
Zionism as exists. Yet, unlike other critics of Blau-Weiss (e.g., Scholem),
Strauss despairs of practical solutions to a theoretical problem, that is, he
avoids suggesting action, practical work, and immigration to Palestine as solutions to what he regards as a theoretical problem.[84] Instead, he holds up the
standard of "critique" and "historical reasoning" and thus opposes the Zionist

rhetoric of his time that privileges belief and affirmation over doubt and argumentation.

State and religion, and hence Zionism and the problem of Jewish "content," are to Strauss two separate concerns, and the cultural Zionist attempt to mix the two seems to Strauss an ill-conceived undertaking. What is passed off as religion seems to Strauss to deny the fundamental doctrinal assumption of revealed religion—namely, the existence of God, understood as preceding all human concerns. Instead, what prevails is the modern humanistic theology of Martin Buber and others that, as he writes, had attained "canonical" status among many Zionists, and that Strauss diagnoses as incongruent with the dogmatic presuppositions of the Bible and of Jewish prayer.

> Take, for example, Buber's thoroughly immanentist interpretation of religion. If God is "later" than the religious experience [*Erlebnis*] of the individual or of the people (and this is Buber's doctrine), then the trajectory toward absolutizing "the human" is already determined. (It is of lesser concern whether one thinks of the human more in terms of the heroic or of the Hasidic.) ("Response to Frankfurt's 'Word of Principle'," p. 67)

Strauss asserts that it is this dogmatic presupposition of a humanistically reinterpreted religion rather than the values of argumentation and critique that he advocated that is to blame for the general "anarchy of standpoints" lamented by the Zionist leadership.

The Zionist pursuit of a state, on the other hand, seems to Strauss a sober and realistic expression of the normalization of the Jewish people, not—as in the period of assimilation—regarding individuals, but regarding the people as a whole. Overcoming the dream- or ghostlike existence in the exile (*galut*), Zionism has the mandate of accomplishing the Jews' return to reality. Strauss speaks here, somewhat artificially, of *Einwirklichung*, that is, a kind of adaptive process aiming at overcoming the status of *Entwirklichtheit* that characterized the *galut*.

In order to develop the resolve that was needed for the Zionist pursuit of the state, the basic presupposition of *galut* had to be overcome. This presupposition is the Orthodox religious faith, and it was essentially overcome in the Enlightenment struggle against all fundamentalism. Among the Jews of the period of Enlightenment and emancipation, however, the space that was emptied of traditional faith was filled not with Jewish "content" but with German "content." What Strauss's intervention aims to point out above all is the futility of denying this. The atheistic faith that is rooted in the Enlightenment critique of religion must not be passed off as religion, and certainly not as identical with biblical religion.

Several further observations can be made on the basis of Strauss's first Zionist essay. While Strauss hints, in good liberal fashion, at the deep congruence between biblical religion and the modern state (as mediated by Spinoza), he clearly wishes to distinguish in no uncertain terms between modern humanistic theologies and religion in a pre-Enlightenment sense. Strauss describes as a kind of atheism the modern theological position that seeks a synthesis between biblical faith and modern humanism. Thus he writes in 1925 that

> the atheism of present-day Bible science is evident. If it is not so evident that everyone can grasp it, this is due to the accidental fact that this science happens to be predominantly in the hands of professors of theology; that the inclination to react to "God," implanted in the human heart from time immemorial, cannot be uprooted overnight; that no atheist emerges unscathed from reading the Psalms and the prophets; mostly, however, that this science has its seat in Germany, the land of "reconciliations" [*Versöhnungen*] and "sublations" [*Aufhebungen*]. ("Biblical History and Science," p. 133)

Strauss continued to maintain the impossibility of reconciling traditional religion and the modern atheistic belief in the sufficiency of human reason.[85] Yet, in 1924 and 1925, the focus of his critique shifts from the "Left" to the "Right," a shift by which he aims to bring about what he believes is a long overdue realignment within the entire German Zionist movement.

> In order to make my intention as clear as possible I shall proceed from its practical-political effect. I believe that the grouping of German Jewry into parties no longer corresponds to the spiritual situation of our generation. The alliance of Zionism and Orthodoxy will have to be replaced by the alliance of Zionism and liberalism. Today, the enemy is on the right! ("Comment on Weinberg's Critique," p. 118)

With greater involvement in the Zionist students' organization K.J.V., Strauss shifts his attention to a new enemy. Having settled the question of cultural Zionism to his satisfaction, Strauss turns to an issue that he regards as an even greater threat to the pursuit of a Jewish state, namely, the alignment between Zionism and Orthodoxy; Strauss attacks the religious Zionist organization Mizrahi. His thesis is that state and religion—that is, Jewish state and Jewish religion—cannot be aligned with one another. This is so because classical Jewish religion is fundamentally apolitical, whereas the modern state rests on self-determination and the dignity of man, values alien to traditional Judaism. Again, therefore, Strauss criticizes a contemporary movement, in this case the Orthodox religious Zionism of Mizrahi, for sailing under a false flag. What

Mizrahi aspires to cannot be justified on the basis of pre-Enlightenment religion, and since, in case of a conflict of interest, Mizrahi is more Orthodox than Zionist, the entire alliance can only be to the detriment of the project of a political movement based on self-determination and dignity. Strauss made this argument for the first time in a lecture to the members of the Kartell jüdischer Verbindungen assembled in the walled town of Forchtenberg in Hohenlohe. The board of directors of the K.J.V. had invited him to address the "burning issue" of Zionism and religion. On this occasion, Strauss was so much the spiritual leader of the entire assembly that he was even put in charge of speaking the commemorative words at the Herzl celebration concluding the retreat.[86]

Oddly enough, some of his comments, of which we have only an indirect summary, invited the conclusion that Strauss was not only not on principle averse to a return to Orthodox faith, should that be possible, but that he himself enthusiastically embraced it. This, at least, is what his critic Hans Weinberg insinuates in his response to Strauss's Forchtenberg lecture.

> Concerning the *content* of the lecture, Strauß [*sic*] has only done half the job. He declares his intention to merely wish to show the dualism [*viz.*, of Zionism and religion] but to be incapable of resolving it; nevertheless he already makes a decision, and an emotional one at that, in favor of Orthodoxy. Here I simply do not understand Strauß. Either one regards nationalism and religion in most perfect harmony with one another, as one used to see it until now, or one recognizes the dualism, in which case it is, at least, premature—and it perhaps testifies to honest enthusiasm but certainly not to mental power—if one daringly leaps across such concerns and lands very comfortably at the desired result.[87]

Strauss, of course, strongly rejects the insinuation of a thoughtless, emotional decision in favor of Orthodoxy.

> I do not know how Weinberg comes to impute to me a decision in favor of orthodoxy, and to impute it to me, outrageously, as a decision "from honest enthusiasm." I trust that the *Bundesbrüder* who heard my Forchtenberg presentation will agree with me when I conclude that there was no trace of "enthusiasm" to be found in it. As concerns my "decision for Orthodoxy," this anticritique will not leave any remaining doubt and thus may serve as an example [of my true position]. However, if what I am being reproached for is my understanding that there are things in the Jewish tradition that are essential and obligatory for us, then I am being reproached for not being a perfect horse. ("Comment on Weinberg's Critique," p. 120)

The ambivalence toward religion in Strauss's Zionist presentations and writings may derive from his distinction between biblical religion, on the one hand, and its modern distortions, on the other, of which the Orthodoxy of Mizrahi is no less guilty than the Bible science of modern theologians. Neither cultural Zionism nor the religious Zionism of someone like Isaac Breuer[88] (see "Ecclesia militans") may claim to be in genuine agreement with biblical religion, or with religion in the pre-Enlightenment sense (cf. "Biblical History and Science"). The entire political rhetoric of Orthodoxy against secular Zionism is criticized as largely disingenuous, and the only basis on which Strauss (referring to "Zionism," but meaning himself) is ready to argue with Orthodoxy is the basis of the European critique of religion (see "On the Bible Science of Spinoza and his Precursors"). While political Zionism is defended against the discontents uttered by the cultural Zionism of the Frankfurt circle and the religious Zionism of Mizrahi, Strauss denies that the "deeper spheres of spiritual man"[89] can be fully satisfied by the political dimension of Zionism. Strauss is careful to distinguish between the spiritual trappings of nationalism, which he believes are not the issue, and the legitimacy of the political will of a people, as articulated by the political Zionism of Herzl. Nationalism, cultural or religious, may well fill the background left vacant by sober political Zionism, but it is hardly a genuinely Jewish sentiment, one congenial with the pre-Enlightenment sources of Judaism. Rather, it is Europe's parting gift to the Jews. The political will of the Jewish people leaves the "deeper spheres of spiritual man" empty; yet Strauss is far from ready to say how this void may be filled. Where he proposes a solution, it is—unsurprisingly—"rather negative."[90]

While the 1925 Forchtenberg lecture gained Strauss the accusation of performing a leap of faith into Orthodoxy, his last Zionist publication—the 1928 review of Freud's *Future of an Illusion*—gained him the charge of being an atheist.[91] The prominence that the refutation of Strauss's position received in volume 25 (1928) of *Der jüdische Student*[92] may indicate a desire on the part of the Kartell jüdischer Verbindungen to mend the fences with the religious Zionists. Strauss's honest yet politically incorrect attack on an important ally in the Zionist struggle does not seem to have caused a permanent rift between himself and the leadership of K.J.V.; at least, he was invited on a further occasion to address one of its federal retreats.[93] Yet the strong rejection he experienced in connection with the Freud review may have triggered a number of important new considerations. First of all, it may not be coincidental that Strauss henceforth ceased to publish in the Zionist press.[94] It may indicate a growing skepticism on his part as to whether the intellectual was able to exert a direct and meaningful political influence.[95] And it may have

compelled him to search for a clearer articulation of the way out of the impasse
he had diagnosed, one that reached beyond the flawed alternative between
the spiritual vacancy of the political Zionist will, on the one hand, and the
compromised forms of modern religion (be they cultural Zionist or be they
Orthodox), on the other. This way out of the impasse could not be the next
great synthesis; Strauss rejects such a historicist solution in one of his most
biting texts of the period, a review of Karl Mannheim's *Ideologie und Utopie,*
which Strauss left unpublished.[96] Extracting himself from the ideological con-
troversies of Zionism, Strauss attempts to return from the ever more fancy
words of synthetic philosophical language to the fundamental things themselves, from the demands of the past to the eternal questions, and from a
situation of hybridity and mutual distortions to the only one that afforded an
unobstructed view of the difference between philosophy and religion: that is,
the world as it was "before the biblical consciousness fell upon it."[97] Thus, in
1929, Strauss began his return to the world of Plato.

BEYOND ATHEISM AND ORTHODOXY

Where exactly Strauss was heading was not immediately visible in the late1920s
to early 1930s, nor were the hints he scattered across his publications easily
comprehended for what they were. Even his next monograph, *Philosophy and
Law* (1935), did little to clarify his orientation. Thus, for example, at the end
of the introductory chapter to *Philosophy and Law,*[98] he reiterates his understanding of the modern Jewish impasse by juxtaposing Orthodoxy and (atheistic) political Zionism as inevitable yet equally unacceptable alternatives and
hints at the need to turn backwards to a situation preceding the modern
impasse. This passage met with the same conflicting interpretations that we
saw before.[99] Karl Löwith, for example, understood it as an endorsement of
Orthodoxy, an identification Strauss again denies emphatically: "By the way,
I am *not* an Orthodox Jew!"[100] Gershom Scholem, on the other hand, describes *Philosophy and Law* in a letter to Walter Benjamin as an "unobscured
testimonial to atheism as the most important Jewish solution."[101] In hindsight, both of these interpretations seem as flawed as they were unavoidable.
The atheism described in the introduction to *Philosophy and Law* consists in
the honest and sincere *(redlich)* resistance to all false reconciliations, the resistance to the nineteenth-century obfuscation of the difference between religion and reason. This heroic atheism is explicitly associated with the name of
Martin Heidegger. But Strauss does not simply endorse or identify with the
position of Heidegger. To be sure, as long as this atheism out of *Redlichkeit*
can resist becoming a dogma itself[102] it is the expression of a deeply moral

resistance to all dogmatism. But, as Strauss points out,[103] the modern virtue of intellectual *Redlichkeit* (probity, honesty, sincerity, uprightness) is a far cry from the ancient ideal of the "love of truth" *(Wahrheitsliebe)*. Thus, as Jacob Klein noticed (see below), a wedge is inserted between Heideggerian probity and the classical philosophical attitude.[104]

While it is easy to see how Scholem may have been tempted to mistake Strauss's very attractive description of Heideggerian atheism for an endorsement, it is somewhat more difficult, yet no less possible, to mistake Strauss's suggestion of a return to the medieval enlightenment of Maimonides for an endorsement of Orthodoxy. For in the essays that constitute the bulk of *Philosophy and Law* (and thus follow the introduction in order, but not in date of composition, the introduction having been written early in 1935, whereas the essays reach back to 1931, 1933, and 1934, respectively) Maimonides is still taken as a representative of the tradition of revealed religion then still identified by Strauss with the notion of the insufficiency of reason—that is, he is interpreted in line with the Orthodox Jewish tradition, just as Strauss had represented Maimonides in his book on Spinoza. When Strauss completed the introduction, however, he was just on the cusp of realizing the true implications of his earlier discovery in Avicenna that the medieval tradition regarded Plato's *Laws* (rather than Aristotle's *Politics*) as the source for its philosophical exposition of prophetology.[105] In other words, while Löwith, justifiably basing himself on the entirety of *Philosophy of Law*, took Strauss's endorsement of "the idea of Law" as an endorsement of the Orthodox "idea of Law," what Strauss actually meant to say at the end of his introduction had little to do with what followed in the chapters of the book. The only one who simply accepted what was evident on the page—namely, that the introduction ended in an unresolved tension—and who gave clear expression to this puzzling oddity was Strauss's friend Jacob Klein, whom Strauss called his *perscrutator cordis mei*.[106]

> [B]ut *where* is Maimuni's enlightenment to lead us? It is entirely clear to me that an answer is here not *immediately* possible: it is the situation in which we find ourselves to begin with: to anticipate an answer would no longer mean to-want-to-understand-backward.

Klein continues, anticipating some of the misunderstandings, that "at least one could, *following* your presentation, reach the conclusion: why then not Orthodoxy after all?!" He further reads Strauss's distinction between modern *Redlichkeit* and the ancient ideal of "love of truth" as a critique of the modern virtue, and he correctly fears that the inevitable conclusion for Strauss's

readers to draw was to take this for a further argument in favor of the Orthodox tradition.

> It seems to me that you yourself have said something *very, very* important
> when you do *not* identify "probity" with "love of truth." Hence everything
> remains open. To which I *myself* have no objections. But it is clear that the
> people will raise this objection against you.[107]

From the dissertation on Jacobi to the book on Spinoza, Strauss was guided
by the judgment that the sphere of the intellect is hedged in on both ends of
the spectrum of its activities by irrational first "givens," and that these "givens" are not therefore less real than the human consciousness. On the empirical side, the data of sense perception are themselves prerequisite for all human
knowledge; without their givenness, no intellectual activity could begin. Actions of the understanding or the intellect *(Verstand)* are thus passive and receptive rather than active and generative. This is similarly the case—according to this reasoning—with respect to the highest objects contemplated by
reason, that is, God and the good. Here, too, the assumption is that human
intellect does not generate its objects (e.g., as postulates of practical reason)
but rather receives them from giving *(gebende)* faculties that are more closely
related to the actual realities they perceive than the intellect that merely analyzes and conceptualizes the primary experience. While Jacobi calls the primary perception of reality belief *(Glaube),* he does not identify it with the
dogmas of any revealed religion. Such an identification is a secondary step,
removed from the immediate experience, yet it is necessary because all experience calls for articulation. It must find its form in language. This position is
usually no longer immediately associated with Jacobi, but is nevertheless well
known, as it entered into the nineteenth- and twentieth-century discourse
on religion through Friedrich Schleiermacher and Rudolf Otto.[108]

Strauss transposes this view into the language of Cassirer's interest in "the
problem of knowledge" *(das Erkenntnisproblem).* He uses relatively unsystematic
assertions, scattered throughout Jacobi's writings, to erect a duality of radically opposed attitudes toward the world. One attitude is called "courageously
believing," and the other is called "timidly doubting." As Strauss later pencils
into his copy of the extract from his dissertation, it is ironic that this approach
to Jacobi is so far removed from Jacobi's own approach. It also flies in the face
of Cassirer, whose idealism, as we saw above, he criticizes openly in "On the
Argument with European Science," and who represents just that timidity
and doubting of the Marburg school from which he explicitly exempts
Hermann Cohen.

Strauss was to retain and develop the rhetoric of radical opposites that he applied to Jacobi. But he did not learn it from Jacobi. The assertion that irrational grounds preceded all rationalism was readily delivered to the post-war generation through the writings of Friedrich Nietzsche. Schopenhauer had turned Kant's primacy of practical reason into the all-encompassing power of the will. Nietzsche finally inverted the former's pessimism, heralding the aristocracy of the amoral. Strauss begins with Nietzsche's insight, as culti-vated in the groundbreaking sociological work of Max Weber. The opposite attitudes of the mind described by Strauss are Weberian "types" of attitudes that compete with one another because they are grounded in irreconcilable value judgments. The young Strauss advocates the heroic values that are in line with Nietzsche's rejection of slave morality. In this spirit, he commends the moral radicalism of the arch-anti-Semite Paul de Lagarde to his Zionist readers as a model of "reflectiveness." It only dawns on him very gradually that opposite forms of moral radicalism (such as that of the German inspired by Nietzsche and that of the Zionist writer inspired by entirely different influences; see "Paul de Lagarde") are not only beyond reconciliation, but that no orientation whatsoever can be gained from their decisionist juxtapo-sition.[109]

Equipped with the Nietzschean apparatus, then, Strauss steps into the world of Zionist discourse. Or, as he describes it in an obliquely autobio-graphic reminiscence from 1923 in which he already establishes an ironic distance between himself and his first few publications,

> It frequently happens in the Zionist youth movement that our young stu-dents, writing in one of our journals, immediately apply to our own prob-lems those philosophical, sociological, or historical theories which they have become acquainted with in the universities, somewhat heedless of the pos-sible dubiousness of such applications. While this phenomenon at first ap-pears to be merely amusing, springing as it does from a touching lack of reflectiveness [*Unreflektiertheit*], it nevertheless has a serious background: in the final analysis, it mirrors the spiritual situation of German Judaism as a whole. ("The Holy," p. 75)

Of course now greatly matured, Strauss does not miss the opportunity to extrapolate from his own experience and use it for his diagnosis of the "spiri-tual situation of German Judaism as a whole."

Regardless of the practical use to which Strauss puts his insight into irra-tional first assumptions, his approach is determined by the decisionism that is implied in their juxtaposition. He himself is under the spell of historicism, laboring to determine the Zionist imperative for his time. Yet he diagnoses the conditions under which Zionism is operating with a rare level of clarity, considering the problematic nature of such an imperative. In fact, he is driven by the realization that whatever the driving assumptions of Zionism are, they lack sufficient self-reflection. The acceptance of certain imperatives guiding the Zionist discussions of the time was based on false assumptions. The foremost requirement of the hour was therefore one of critique. It consisted in facing up to the fact that Zionism was not actually a cultural liberation from European presuppositions, since it depended on those very presuppositions. Julius Guttmann was not so far off the mark when he classified the Strauss of the introduction to *Philosophy and Law* as an existentialist, for the stance taken by Strauss can be easily mistaken for an existentialist one. His early writings are permeated by the diagnosis of irreconcilable opposites (e.g., the opposition between Orthodoxy and atheism in the Zionist writings, and the opposition between the assumption of a sufficiency versus an insufficiency of human reason in *Spinoza's Critique of Religion* and even in the chapters of *Philosophy and Law*), or by the diagnosis of dishonest mixtures of irreconcilable opposites (e.g., the mixture of Enlightenment and religion that leads to modern atheist theology). Liberal science-oriented belief in perfectibility is grounded in an irrational rejection of the fear of the gods (the rabbinic trope of *apikorsut*/Epicureanism reverberates through Strauss's essays).[110] Once the extreme opposites are seen as equally grounded in irrational assumptions, and once the reconciliation of such assumptions is excluded, only one alternative seems to remain: the philosopher who articulates this insight gloating in the heroism of the ability to stare back at the Gorgon's head of—absolutely nothing.

Following one of the many veiled autobiographical suggestions that we find scattered throughout his early writings, it seems as if at one point Strauss is looking back on his own effort to arrive at a "standpoint."[111]

> Any standpoint that is at all to be taken seriously is the work of a tremendous effort made by a single person. After having broken through to his standpoint, Kant—who had already scored achievements before that alone would have made him immortal (the Kant-Laplace-theorem), who was not an inexperienced young man still in need of acquiring the necessary knowledge of facts—needed eleven years in order for the *Critique of Pure Reason* not even to be written, but to be thought. ("'Religiöse Lage der Gegenwart,'" in *GS*, 2:382)

If what he writes about Kant can be taken as a reflection of Strauss's own efforts at arriving at a clear notion of what he was really after, it leads us to the exact date at which the essay containing this quotation is written, namely to the year 1930 ("'Religiöse Lage der Gegenwart'").

In the same essay, Strauss turns away from many questions, reducing them to one, the only question that matters, which is a timeless one: Which is the right life? The question has been the same throughout time, but the modern suspicion is that it only seems to have been so. Historical consciousness forestalls the possibility of raising the question naïvely and answering it in an unambiguous manner. Strauss waxes poetic when describing the lures of the present:

> If we pose the question of the right life freely and candidly, convinced that we can answer it if we honestly try and if we mind no detour, then the present blocks our way, clothed in the most luxurious garments and with the raised eyebrows of a person superior in knowledge and high in rank, and calls out to us: Halt! You innocent! Don't you know that, year by year, the inexhaustible earth brings forth new generations, all destined, having barely matured, to march with the whole fire of youth toward the truth, toward *the* truth? This has been going on for millennia. The attempt has been made for millennia, and it has failed again and again. Once upon a time, the later ones were not deterred by the failure of the earlier ones; blinded, they said to themselves: if those ones failed—perhaps they had set out the wrong way; let us simply begin anew; let us begin from scratch. And they began from scratch, and they too failed. The wretched ones did not know—what I, the present, the mighty goddess, know—that they *had* to fail. They had to fail, because they were looking for *the* truth. For *the one eternal* truth does not exist, but every age has *its* truth, and what you, twenty years old, may reasonably pursue, is only your truth, the truth of your age, my, the present's, truth. In full possession of *this* knowledge, that is my highest pride, I may smile at the past: at her naïveté. . . . I grant pardon to the earlier ones because, against their will, they did what I command my children: to be sure, they searched for *the* truth, but they found the truth without time; they failed—measured by *their* standard; measured by *my* standard, they reached the goal. Thus highly enthroned above all past,[112] I call out to you: it is right and proper for thinking beings to *know* what they do and what they can reasonably want: know therefore, and let it get through to you, that you can only find your own truth, the truth of the present, and hence you can reasonably search only for this truth. ("'Religiöse Lage der Gegenwart,'" in *GS*, 2:380f.)

How is this call of the present to be resisted? Having spent almost ten years with analyses of what was then (1930) discarded as the "polyphonous noise of the public," having examined opinions and counteropinions that could not be reconciled in any "synthesis,"[113] Strauss concludes that it is better to "despair in the face of their contradiction than [to argue in support of] a dull and cowardly hodgepodge." But what if "*all* present standpoints" were to "rest on a misunderstanding of basic facts?" Not that he believes it, but whence is such examination of present opinions to be accomplished? Only by stepping out of the present.

> If we want to know the present as it *is*, free of all ruling conceptions that we must first examine, then we must be free of the present. This freedom does not fall right into our lap, but we must conquer it. ("'Religiöse Lage der Gegenwart,'" 384)

In a move that resembles Hermann Cohen's critique of the mythological state of consciousness, Strauss rejects dependence on the presence as a prejudice:

> Just because humanity always has a present, it does not immediately follow that one needs to mind it: our *fate* is *not* our *task*. This is the principal mistake to which the human being of today succumbs again and again: the attempt of determining the task from the fate. ("'Religiöse Lage der Gegenwart,'" 384)

Stepping away from dependence on the opinions of the present means stepping away from opinions altogether. Hence, according to Strauss, we find ourselves in a situation that, in the Western tradition, was first addressed by Socrates.

> This question was posed for the first time by Socrates. Whether, and to what extent he himself gave an answer to it, remains in the dark. In any case, his student Plato answered it: in the *Politeia* [i.e., in Plato's *Republic*]. In this work, in order to illustrate the difficulty of truthful knowing, Plato compares the situation of the human being with the situation of cave dwellers: a cave with a long entrance, extending upwards; the people caught in the cave since childhood, their legs and necks in chains; hence they always remain at the same spot, and they are prevented from turning their heads by the chain around their neck. From above, the glow of a fire shines from afar; a path runs above between the fire and the chained ones, along whose length a low wall has been erected. Passing along this wall, people carry all sorts of instruments, figures, etc. The chained ones can obviously see only the shadows of those instruments that are projected by the effect of the fire onto the opposite wall of the cave; hence, to them the shadows are the true things. If one of them were to be released and able to look up freely toward

the light, something that could only be done by suffering great pain, he would be blinded by the radiance, and hence he would not be able to recognize the things whose shadow he had seen earlier. He would not know where to turn, if he were told that he now saw the things whose shadows he had hitherto seen; moreover, the view of the light itself would hurt him so much that he would turn away and seek to return into the darkness of the cave; and it would need a long habituation and effort, even the use of force, until he was able to recognize the true things, and live in the light of truth. Returned to the cave, he would keep the memory of his life in the light, but for this very reason, he would appear completely incomprehensible and ridiculous to his comrades. —Thus, then, Plato presents the difficulties of doing philosophy, the *natural* difficulties.[114] If they are so extraordinary, no wonder that there are so many contradictory opinions. Mindful of the Platonic parable, we shall not be deterred by the anarchy of opinions, but we will have to try as hard as we can to leave the cave. ("'Religiöse Lage der Gegenwart,'" 385f.)

Yet the difficulties encountered and described by Plato as the "natural" difficulties of doing philosophy do not sufficiently describe those encountered by the moderns. In addition to the natural difficulties of doing philosophy, modernity struggles with the historical religion that placed itself between the ancients and the moderns and added its own set of problems that need to be comprehended before one can successfully return to the level achieved by the ancients. Relative to the ancients, we reside in a "second cave."

To use the classical presentation of the natural difficulties of philosophizing, namely Plato's parable of the cave, one may say that today we find ourselves in a second, much deeper cave than the lucky ignorant ones Socrates dealt with; we need history first of all in order to *ascend* to the cave from which Socrates can lead us to light; we need a propaedeutic, which the Greeks did not need, namely, learning through reading. ("Review of Ebbinghaus," p. 215)

Strauss discovers the analysis of what constitutes the cause for the modern descent into a "second cave" in Maimonides' *Guide of the Perplexed*.

We said: Plato represented the *natural* difficulties of philosophizing. That is, those difficulties that are natural to the human being as such, as a sensual-spiritual being, those difficulties that, according to the Platonic conception, are given through the senses. We say "natural," because there are difficulties that are not "natural," but are effective only under certain preconditions. In the *Guide of the Perplexed*, I:31, RMbM adds to the Greeks' reasons for disagreements in philosophy, and hence for the difficulty of doing philosophy, a fourth reason; in this regard he says literally: "*in our time*, there is a fourth reason that he (*sc.* Alexander of Aphrodisias) did not mention, because it did not exist there, namely *habituation* and *education;* for human beings love by nature what they are habituated to, and they incline toward it; . . . so it goes with the human being in regard to the opinions with which he was raised: he loves them, and he holds on to them, and he avoids deviant opinions. For this additional reason, then, the human being is prevented from knowing the truth. This is what happens to the multitude with regard to the corporeality of God . . . on grounds of their habituation to the *Scriptures* that they firmly believe in and that they are used to, whose literal meaning seems to point to the corporeality of God. . . ." We note: the difficulty of doing philosophy is fundamentally increased, and the *freedom* of doing philosophy is fundamentally reduced, by the fact that a revelation-based tradition has stepped into the world of philosophy. ("'Religiöse Lage der Gegenwart,'" in *GS,* 2:386)

On which Strauss comments further,

In a manner of speaking, the struggle of the entire period of the last three centuries, the struggle of the Enlightenment, is sketched, drawn up, in RMbM's comment: in order to make philosophizing possible in its naturally difficult state, the artificial complication of philosophizing must be removed; one must fight against *prejudices*. Herein lies a fundamental difference between modern and Greek philosophy: whereas the latter only fights against appearance and opinion, modern philosophy begins by fighting against prejudices.[115] Hence, in this respect, the Enlightenment wants to restore Greek freedom. What does it achieve? It achieves the freedom of *answering*, but not the freedom of asking, only the freedom to say no, instead of the traditional yes (mortality as opposed to immortality, accident as opposed to providence, atheism as opposed to theism, passion as opposed to intellect). This liberation from the yes of tradition comes about through an all the more profound entanglement in tradition. Thus, the Enlightenment conducts its fight against tradition in the name of tolerance, i.e., ultimately in the name of the love of the neighbor [*Nächstenliebe*]; thus religion is now made to rest entirely on the love of the neighbor, but in a way that, along with the doubt about the love of the neighbor (in its enlightened understanding), religion as such becomes completely doubtful. Or, to take an example from the later stages of the Enlightenment: when the Enlightenment turns openly atheistic and believes it has found God out as being constituted by the human heart, it does so, of all things, by absorbing into humanity what had hitherto been definitions of the deity: self-redemption of humanity, self-guaranteeing of immortality,[116] taking on of providence.

And when at every stage of the Enlightenment there arise opponents of the Enlightenment, these opponents on their part adopt the achievements of the Enlightenment and reconstruct them in accord with their positions. (E.g.: revelation is understood as human production, as custom and as form, rather than as Law; creation not as the creation of the world, but as the mandate of all humanity, issued before they came into existence.) Since the Enlightenment, it has been *generally* the case that each generation reacted to the preceding generation without calling its foundations into question. ("'Religiöse Lage der Gegenwart,'" 387)

It seems quite possible that, at this point, Strauss is indeed yearning for a retrieval of genuine belief in revelation. Yet the essay also uses language that suggests that he is not speaking of a "back flip into the world of the Shulkhan Arukh," as Rosenzweig once put it. Thus, for example, Strauss says that the answer to the modern conundrum should be sought in a courageous step forward: "We must always look *forward*, straight ahead; reflectiveness will *never* teach us what we need to do" ("'Religiöse Lage der Gegenwart',' " in *GS*, 2:385). In this, he implicitly dismisses one of his earlier maxims ("The Jew is in need of an extraordinary measure of reflectiveness . . ." in "Paul de Lagarde," p. 90). The courageous move forward must not be undertaken without heeding the warnings of the "present," yet the warnings are not to discourage one who wants to leave the present behind.

Strauss feels confident that a new, naïve raising of the question of "How are we to live?" is possible, and it is possible, at least according to "'Religiöse Lage der Gegenwart,'" precisely because we have reached the end of all tradition. We are at the end even of the struggle against tradition. The one credited with accomplishing this end is Nietzsche.

Through Nietzsche, tradition has been shaken to its *roots*. It has completely lost its self-evident truth. We are left in this world without any authority, any direction. Only now has the question πῶς βιωτέον again received its full edge. We *can* pose it again. We have the possibility of posing it fully in earnest. We can no longer read Plato's dialogues superficially only to puzzle over how much old Plato knew about such and such; we can no longer superficially polemicize against him. Similarly with the Bible: we no longer self-evidently agree with the prophets; we ask ourselves seriously whether perhaps the kings were right. We must really begin from the *very* beginning. ("'Religiöse Lage der Gegenwart,'" 389)

But it would hardly be the Strauss of 1930 were he not to turn around on himself, calling into question his own assertion.

> We *can* begin from the very beginning: we are lacking all polemic affect
> toward tradition (having nothing wherefrom to be polemical against it);
> and at the same time, tradition is utterly alien to us, utterly questionable.
> ("'Religiöse Lage der Gegenwart,'" 389)

Hence, in the period with which we end this volume, no definite answer
is given. What remains? Quite a lot, indeed. For Strauss himself concludes
the essay from which we quoted by setting the stage for his entire future
agenda.

> But we cannot immediately answer on our own, for we know that we are
> deeply entangled in a tradition: we are even much lower down than the
> cave dwellers of Plato.[117] We must rise to the *origin* of tradition, to the level
> of *natural ignorance*. ("'Religiöse Lage der Gegenwart,'" 389)

It seems that, after ten years of struggling, Strauss had finally begun to
find his way out of the urban corruption, a way that the Wanderbund Blau-
Weiss had been unable to provide because of the pervasive power of prejudice. Yet this new "return to nature" leads not into the woods but into an
archaeological dig.[118] It is a return to the natural conditions of the city, the
polis. To use a different image (one that Strauss invokes in "Ecclesia militans"),
the situation in which modern man finds himself resembles that of a builder
on top of the Tower of Babel who is so far removed from the foundations
that neither he nor anyone else around him has anything left but opinions
about the static and material conditions of the foundations on top of which,
however, he is required to build further. Strauss decides that the only way of
accomplishing this is to descend to the foundations and reexamine the structure.

THE VIRTUE OF MODESTY

Strauss starts out somewhere in the vicinity of his contemporaries, the dialectic theologians.[119] He himself later points to the preface to Karl Barth's com-
mentary on the Epistle to the Romans as a text that is of interest not only to
theologians;[120] and he sends to Friedrich Gogarten one of the decisive texts of
his phase of reorientation in which he analyzes the "new sophism" of our
age.[121]

Not unlike Rudolf Bultmann's distinction between a *historisch* and a *ge-
schichtlich* approach—one beholden to the fate of the past, the other one a
daring projection into the future—the early Strauss seeks to understand true

religion as that which holds a deeply necessary, deeply rational, and beneficial balm that can heal the modern illness. His early essays tend toward a juxtaposition of the two attitudes he derives from the tradition of Jacobi, Schleiermacher, Kierkegaard, Otto, Barth, and Rosenzweig, the either/or of intellect and faith, which is mediated only through the will. History and politics are constituted by the battle for dominance between ultimately irrational positions that are each and all absolutes and totalities.

As is well known, by 1936 Strauss abandoned the assumption that religion may constitute the great "other" that is juxtaposed to reason.[122] His discovery of the "exoteric" as a stylistic device that is common to all great philosophers makes him realize that the only opposition worth talking about is that between philosophy and nonphilosophy. This is not to say that Strauss abandons the notion of the inherently rational core of revealed religion.[123] What he abandons is the presupposition that religion, as conceived in the context of the writings of the medieval Enlightenment of Maimonides and his Muslim predecessors, rests on the assumption of an insufficiency of human reason. Strauss calls this "Thomistic" stance a detour he had to go through before beginning to understand the exoteric and, by means of it, Maimonides. The concept of the Law is henceforth a political concept. Yet it is interesting that, after the discovery of the political condition of all philosophical writing, Strauss largely abstains from writing about the Torah itself.[124]

As we have said, the virtue at the core of Strauss's early writings is that of courage. He praises "courageously believing" in his dissertation on Jacobi, and recommends it over what then seemed to Strauss characteristic of the Cartesian attitude, that is, "timidly doubting." The early Strauss is a decisionist, and even the late Strauss remains mindful of Nietzsche's critique of morality. Morality, he emphasizes in 1970 in "A Giving of Accounts," is to him *not* the highest value. Yet, beginning in the 1930s, moderation replaces courage as the highest value in the realm of the spirit, as well as in the public sphere. Moderation is the practical ideal of the philosopher who accepts that in the public realm no totalities or absolutes can be realized, nor must such a realization be attempted. With the understanding of the fundamental tension between philosophical reasoning and the political situation, Strauss reaches the "standpoint" from which to argue against the flaws of the modern idealizations of the sphere of human agency. At the end, Strauss's entire work turns into an argument not only on behalf of the freedom to philosophize but also on behalf of the moderate, yet real, liberties of the political being.

The early Straussian agenda could also be described as reaching for a description of the value of the political as distinct from the moral and the religious. This awareness for the political was certainly rooted in the debates among the young German Jewish intellectuals of the renaissance generation on the future of the political Zionism that had been inaugurated by Herzl and that, to Strauss, was most vividly represented by Jabotinsky. But the political Zionism of his day is not what gives Strauss's writings their peculiar edge. What distinguishes his early work from the start is the "dialectical style," the mental agility, and the intellectual subtlety and independence that he absorbed during his earliest philosophical studies on the *Pantheismusstreit* between Jacobi and Mendelssohn concerning Lessing.[125] Thus, when Strauss raises his voice in defense of the political in contrast to the religious and cultural Zionist attempts to create a "third way," a Buberian nationalism "sui generis," he does so as someone who is less interested in practical politics than in a "radicalism of theory."[126] Learning from Spinoza, Strauss separates the political from the question of religious truth, and in keeping with Machiavelli and his Roman tutors he separates the political from moral considerations. Hence when, after years of preoccupation with the problem of the political, Strauss encounters the writings of Carl Schmitt, he not only finds a familiar position but also one that can be brought to greater clarity about itself and its principles.

There is, of course, a deep irony in the alliance of Strauss with Schmitt. What is ironic is that it reveals how unpolitical (in the Schmittian sense of political) Strauss's political philosophy really is. Strauss's alliance with the ultra-conservative Right blooms at a time when this ultraconservative Right sheds its last liberal restraints and begins to act on its anti-Semitic principles. Strauss's agreement on principle with Schmitt's concept of the political does not blind him to the fact that the lines between friend and foe are being completely redrawn. But Strauss, the philosopher, insists on a choice that has nothing to do with Schmitt's concept of the political. In the years 1932-35, Strauss the Jew knows he must leave Germany, but as a political philosopher he cannot deny the right of the German "national uprising," even if it means renewed ghettoization or expulsion of the Jews. To be sure, in 1933 neither Strauss nor most of his conservative German contemporaries were speaking of the possibility of a physical annihilation of the Jews. Strauss's assent on principle to the right of a nation to enact even the most radical conservative national politics must not be mistaken for an assent to the physical eradication of his own people.

In his early writings, Strauss discovered the philosophical problem of the political that arose for him concretely in the context of political Zionism. The political question "How are we to live?" became the tool by which he examined modern philosophies of religion and by which he cut through much of the confusion that characterized the cultural philosophies of the time. It ultimately forced him to turn back to the medieval and ancient sources, where he discovered a kindred type of writing: the exoteric writing of the great philosophical writers of the past. In an interesting parallel to Heidegger's hermeneutic turn, the mature Strauss was someone who had abandoned the attempt to speak the redemptive word for the moment, one who no longer had the desire to participate in a political movement, one to whom the future had nothing to do with the next great synthesis. At the end of the early writings stands a confession of ignorance, one that moves beyond the *docta ignorantia* of Christian Europe that is diagnosed as a regression below, rather than an advance beyond, the Socratic cave. The modern confusion is to be overcome only by way of an unprecedented effort to return to the natural problems originally addressed by Greek philosophy: a return to the roots of Western thought. Ironically, as Strauss points out much later, the act of "returning" that is applied to the Greek strand of Western thought derives from the Hebrew concept of *teshuvah*.[127]

A further irony of Strauss's turn to medieval and ancient sources is its almost total eclipse of biblical and rabbinic sources. As much else in Strauss's oeuvre, this relative eclipse must not be taken as a negative verdict. When, in 1935, Strauss turned his back on religious Orthodoxy as unacceptable to the modern Jew and on political Zionism as ultimately an insufficient solution to the Jewish problem, he did so without issuing a real verdict of condemnation. As a Jew he turned to classical political philosophy, but not without leaving himself open to reengaging Jewish sources and Jewish political reality *after* having worked himself back to the cave of natural ignorance. For *only then* could he envisage himself beginning again to think about the question of what revelation means to natural man, to a man as yet untainted by the many reconciliations, sublations, and mitigations of revelation that have led to the modern ignorance concerning the fundamental difference between religion and philosophy.[128] It may have been this kind of consideration, a consideration of "intellectual probity,"[129] that provided Strauss with the confidence that he was not in fact abandoning Judaism at its darkest hour. If so, it must also be admitted that Strauss was unable to make good on such a promise, perhaps because it was too ambitious for a single lifetime. It may also explain why, today, we see a revival of Straussian thought among conservative and Orthodox Jews. There is a decided feeling of unfinished business that surrounds Strauss's statements about Jews and Judaism, business of a kind that concerns us today. It is therefore hardly for reasons of historical curiosity alone that Strauss's early writings deserve to be put before the English-speaking reader.

NOTES

1. The early years of Strauss are the subject of Eugene R. Sheppard, "Leo Strauss and the Politics of Exile" (Ph.D. diss, UCLA, 2001), written under the supervision of David Myers. While the text of this dissertation was not available to me at the time of the completion of this introduction, Dr. Sheppard was kind enough to read a draft of this volume and offer a number of helpful suggestions.

2. For the following, see Leo Strauss, *Jewish Philosophy and the Crisis of Modernity: Essays and Lectures in Modern Jewish Thought*, ed. Kenneth Hart Green (Albany: SUNY Press, 1997), 3–6; Heinrich Meier, "Vorwort des Herausgebers," in *GS*, 2:ix–xxxiv; and Leo Strauss, "A Giving of Accounts," in *Jewish Philosophy and the Crisis of Modernity*, 457–66.

3. This and the following in Strauss, "A Giving of Accounts," 460.

4. On the following cf. Glenn Richard Sharfman, "The Jewish Youth Movement in Germany, 1900–1936: A Study in Ideology and Organization" (Ph.D. diss., University of North Carolina at Chapel Hill, 1989), and see text and notes to Strauss, "Response to Frankfurt's 'Word of Principle'," below. On the *Wanderbünde* cf. Michael Brenner, *The Renaissance of Jewish Culture in Weimar Germany* (New Haven: Yale University Press, 1996), 230 n. 39; Chanoch Rinott, "Major Trends in Jewish Youth Movements in Germany," in *Leo Baeck Institute Year Book XIX* (London: Secker & Warburg, 1974), 77–95; Walter Laqueur, *A History of Zionism* (New York and San Francisco: Holt, Rinehart and Winston, 1972), 194ff., 484ff.; idem, "The German Jewish Youth Movement and the 'Jewish Question'," in *Leo Baeck Institute Year Book VI* (London: Secker & Warburg, 1961), 193–205; Werner Rosenstock, "The Jewish Youth Movement," in *Leo Baeck Institute Year Book XIX* (London: Secker & Warburg, 1974), 97–102. Cf. also Avraham Barkai, "The Organized Jewish Community," in *German-Jewish History in Modern Times*, ed. Michael A. Meyer with the editorial assistance of Michael Brenner, vol. 4: *Renewal and Destruction, 1918–1945,* ed. Avraham Barkai and Paul Mendes-Flohr (New York: Columbia University Press, 1996), 90–95; and Jehuda Reinharz, *Fatherland or Promised Land: The Dilemma of the German Jew, 1893–1914* (Ann Arbor: University of Michigan Press, 1975), 152f. On the significance of the student corporations for early German Zionism, see also, anecdotally, Richard Lichtheim, *Rückkehr: Lebenserinnerungen aus der Frühzeit des deutschen Zionismus* (Stuttgart: Deutsche Verlagsanstalt, 1970), 79–94.

Blau-Weiss was founded in 1907 in Breslau (the German city with the largest urban Jewish population) and merged with a Berlin chapter in 1912, constituting the Jüdischer Wanderbund Blau-Weiss. The orientation of the Breslau chapter was religious Zionist. The most famous debate on the orientation of Blau Weiss involved *Die blau-weisse Brille*, a set of pamphlets authored by the seventeen-year-old Gershom Scholem and distributed privately between summer 1915 and early 1916, then in *Der Jude* 1, no. 12 (March 1917): 822–25, then in *Blau-Weiss Führerzeitung*, August 1917, 26–30 under the title "Jugendbewegung, Jugendarbeit, und Blau Weiss" (English by Walter Dannhauser in *On Jews and Judaism in Crisis* [New York: Schocken, 1976], 49–53), as well as Scholem's critique of the Prunn covenant of 1922, reluctantly published by Robert Weltsch in *Jüdische Rundschau*, no. 27 (8 December 1922), cited in Rinott, "Major Trends," 89).

5. Reinharz, *Fatherland or Promised Land*, 151, calls Blau-Weiss one of the most active Jewish youth organizations in Germany.

6. On this and the following cf. Laqueur, "The German Jewish Youth Movement," 193ff.

7. Friedrich Ludwig Jahn (1778–1852), better known as *Turnvater* Jahn, pedagogical reformer and politician, promoted physical exercise as part of educational reform and as patriotic preparation for the wars of liberation of Germany from French occupation.

8. Paul de Lagarde (née Bötticher): see below, p. 97n.

9. Julius Langbehn (1851–1907), pan-Germanist, published under the pen name "Der Rembrandtdeutsche"; lyricist of poetic realism.

10. Rinott, "Major Trends," 90. The age of the regular members in the Wandervogel and its counterparts ranged from fifteen to twenty-two (high school and university age).

11. See Laqueur, "The German Jewish Youth Movement," 193.

12. Cf. ibid., 197–98.

13. In contrast to the highly organized Kartell jüdischer Verbindungen with which it merged in 1922 (see below), Blau-Weiss was always considered (from the perspective of the K.J.V.) as more of a youth movement, and the comparison between the majority German youth movement and its minority Jewish counterpart is a firmly established topos in the debates of the 1920s. Cf. "Ein prinzipielles Wort zur Erziehungsfrage," *Jüdische Rundschau* 27, nos. 103/104 (29 December 1922): 675–76, a document coauthored by Erich Fromm, Fritz Goithein, Leo Löwenthal, Ernst Simon, and Erich Michaelis. Here we read that "since one did not find the connection to the non-Jewish youth movement, one took up the Zionist idea . . ." (675), and "The national Jewish youth movement made the very same basic mistake. It proclaimed the autonomy of youth and set this youth (or also the 'Bund') as its highest goal" (676). Also see Herbert Foerder, "Die Aufgaben des K.J.V.," *Der jüdische Student* 2, nos. 4/5 (June/July 1925): 109f. (p. 110: "Unsere Jugendbewegung ist sicherlich nicht knechtisch abhängig, aber verständlicherweise stark beeinflußt von der deutschen Jugendbewegung" [Our youth movement is certainly not slavishly dependent but understandably strongly influenced by the German youth movement]). Cf. Siegfried Kanowitz, "Zum Kartelltag: Erweiterung unserer Grundlagen," *Der jüdische Student* 25, no. 1 (March 1928): 2. These latter two sources are programmatic statements by members of the K.J.V. board of directors, and hence are highly representative of the mainstream of German Zionist students.

14. Cf. Rinott, "Major Trends," 78; and Brenner, *Renaissance of Jewish Culture in Weimar Germany*, 46–49

15. Cf. Kanowitz, "Zum Kartelltag: Erweiterung unserer Grundlagen," 10. The *Altherrenarbeit*, that is, the work of recruiting postgraduates over the age of twenty for involvement with the youth organizations or with other Zionist institutions, was always a major concern of the K.J.V. Cf., e.g., Siegfried Kanowitz, "Zum Kartelltag," *Der jüdische Student* 2, no. 3 (May 1925): 69.

16. Cf. Rinott, "Major Trends," 77, and cf. Fromm et al., "Ein prinzipielles Wort zur Erziehungsfrage."

17. Cf. Sharfman, "Jewish Youth Movement in Germany," 74, 204, 206.

18. Ernst Simon, quoted in Rinott, "Major Trends," 84.

19. On the predominantly middle-class affiliation of Blau-Weiss, cf. Rinott, "Major Trends," 77.

20. Cf. Rosenstock, "The Jewish Youth Movement," 97–102, esp. 99.

21. Cf. the intervention of the seventeen-year-old Gershom Scholem, "Die blau-weiße Brille," 822-25, who criticized Blau-Weiss for its lack of an actual pursuit of immigration to Palestine, for espousing too much desire and too little action, and so on. See Rinott, "Major Trends," 88f. Scholem was not himself a member of Blau-Weiss, but his position was widely debated and even published in the *Blau-Weiss Führerzeitung*, August 1917, 26-30.

22. Cf. Rinott, "Major Trends," 85.

23. Cf. Ibid., 93.

24. Cf. Friedrich Nietzsche, *Jenseits von Gut und Böse*, # 251, in vol. 5 of *Sämtliche Werke: Kritische Studienausgabe in 15 Bänden*, ed. Giorgio Colli and Mazzino Montinari, (München: DTB; Berlin and New York: Walter de Gruyter, 1980, 192f.; and cf. Yirmeyahu Yovel, *Dark Riddle: Hegel, Nietzsche, and the Jews* (University Park: Pennsylvania State University Press, 1998), 119f.

25. Cf. Kenneth Hart Green, *Jew and Philosopher: The Return to Maimonides in the Jewish Thought of Leo Strauss* (Albany: SUNY Press, 1993), 166 n. 119, 178 n. 57.

26. Cf. Strauss, "A Giving of Accounts," 460.

27. Cf. Ernst Cassirer, *Das Erkenntnisproblem in der Philosophie und Wissenschaft der neueren Zeit* (Berlin: Bruno Cassirer, vols. 1-2: 1906-7, vol. 3: 1920, and vol. 4: 1950. English: *The Problem of Knowledge: Philosophy, Science, and History since Hegel*, translated from the manuscript by W. H. Woglom and Charles W. Hendel (New Haven: Yale University Press, 1955–57).

28. Until he met Heidegger, Strauss considered Max Weber "the incarnation of the spirit of science and scholarship." See Strauss, "A Giving of Accounts," 461.

29. On Strauss's conversations with Husserl and his first impressions of Heidegger, see ibid., 460–61.

30. Gadamer et al. were still nominally students of Paul Natorp, after Hermann Cohen the surviving head of the Marburg school of neo-Kantianism. Thus, for example, Gadamer was the editor of the 1924 Festschrift for Natorp. (See *Festschrift für Paul Natorp zum Siebzigsten Geburtstage von Schülern und Freunden gewidmet* [Berlin and Leipzig: Walter de Gruyter, 1924].) But even Natorp's own late philosophy, similar to that of the aging Rickert in Heidelberg, had turned toward the biologism and vitalism of the rhetoric of the youth movement. On the rise and decline of the Marburg school of neo-Kantianism, see Ulrich Sieg, *Aufstieg und Niedergang des Marburger Neukantianismus: Die Geschichte einer philosophischen Schulgemeinschaft* (Würzburg: Königshausen und Neumann, 1994).

31. Cf. also Leo Strauss, *What is Political Philosophy?* (New York: The Free Press, 1959), 246, where he states that Cassirer "had transformed Cohen's philosophic system, the very center of which was ethics, into a philosophy of symbolic forms in which ethics had silently disappeared." I thank Ken Green for pointing me to this source.

32. Strauss was not the only one, but certainly was one of the first ones, to pay

attention to this important difference. Cf. Alfred Jospe, *Die Unterscheidung von Mythos und Religion bei Hermann Cohen und Ernst Cassirer in ihrer Bedeutung für die jüdische Religionsphilosophie* (Oppeln: Reuther und Reichard, 1932).

33. See text of and notes to "On the Argument with European Science." Strauss's radical understanding of Hermann Cohen was unique at the time. It surpassed even the claims made by Rosenzweig in his introduction to Cohen's *Jewish Writings* (1924). While Rosenzweig, in a conscious act of hagiography, argues that Cohen departed from his idealist system when he moved to Berlin in 1912 and went on to write his later work on religion, Strauss asserts that Cohen's entire system rested on religious presuppositions. How he arrived at this conclusion is not clear to me. Perhaps it was, as he recommended to Wobbermin, "nothing less than a reading of the entire work" that persuaded him in this matter. Cohen continued to exert a certain presence also in Strauss's later works. Cf. Strauss, "A Giving of Accounts," 460; idem, the preface to *Spinoza's Critique of Religion*, trans. Elsa Sinclair (New York: Schocken, 1965); and the introductory essay to Hermann Cohen, *Religion of Reason Out of the Sources of Judaism* New York: Frederick Ungar, 1972), reprinted in Strauss, *Jewish Philosophy and the Crisis of Modernity*, 267–82. The essay concludes with the moving statement, "It is a blessing for us that Hermann Cohen lived and wrote" (*Jewish Philosophy and the Crisis of Modernity*, 282). See Green, *Jew and Philosopher*, 185 n. 16, for a variety of views on Strauss's relation to Cohen, none of which can be regarded as having probed the full depth of the matter.

34. In 1920, when Strauss was presumably still zealous, he attempted to convert Jacob Klein to Zionism. He failed in this mission, but Strauss and Klein subsequently became close lifelong friends. Cf. Strauss, "A Giving of Accounts." The entire piece is an homage to this friendship.

35. See Strauss, "Comment on Weinberg's Critique."

36. Cf. Hagit Lavsky, *Before Catastrophe: The Distinctive Path of German Zionism* (Detroit: Wayne State University Press; Jerusalem: The Magnes Press and Leo Baeck Institute, 1996), the first comprehensive study of the institutional and economic aspects of German Zionism from its beginnings until 1933. Dr. Lavsky documents that, in the Weimar years, "Palestinocentrism" displaced the diasporatic orientation of German Zionism. Strauss seems to have remained unaffected by this general trend, or, put differently, Strauss lost touch with (or faith in) the general development of Zionism to the same degree that German Zionism outgrew the preoccupations of the youth movement.

37. See, for example, "Propaganda," *Der jüdische Student* 28, no. 1 (January 1931): 6ff., where Hitler's doctrine of propaganda from *Mein Kampf* is referred to as something from which "we may learn a few things for our own propaganda" (6).

38. Strauss's sympathy for Schmitt may be philosophically rather than politically motivated, but certainly means an affinity with the latter's political philosophy. It may also show the rather German Jewish (and wholly unpolitical) trait of privileging the theoretical over the political, principle over praxis, contradicting the very principle in praxis that is supported in theory. Strauss's critique of (philosophical) pluralism is first presented in "Der Konspektivismus" (1929).

39. Cf. *Der jüdische Student* 18, no. 5 (September–October 1921): 234: "Jabotinsky

machte auch auf die ihm in bestimmten Punkten sachlich nicht Zustimmenden durch die Kraft seiner Persönlichkeit und die Wucht und bildhafte Klarheit seiner Rede einen starken Eindruck" [The strength of his personality and the impact and intuitive clarity of his speech deeply impressed even those who disagreed with him in certain respects]. (From a report by Arthur Stein.)

40. It would be helpful if we knew when Strauss met Jabotinsky, namely, whether these meetings took place in the earliest period (1923–25) or during Strauss's phase of reorientation (1928–), when he was still active in the Zionist movement yet began to be interested in classical modes of political thought. If the meetings took place during the latter period, it might suggest an influence of Jabotinsky and the revisionist movement on Strauss's sympathy for Carl Schmitt and other postliberals. If the meetings took place earlier, such an influence is still not to be ruled out. The wording and tone of the anecdote cited in the following would suggest an earlier rather than a later meeting with Jabotinsky.

41. Strauss, "Why We Remain Jews," in *Jewish Philosophy and the Crisis of Modernity*, 319.

42. Cf. Brenner, *Renaissance of Jewish Culture in Weimar Germany*.

43. As mentioned in n. 13, supra, the declaration of educational principles ("Ein prinzipielles Wort in der Erziehungsfrage"), against which Strauss polemicized in "Response to Frankfurt's 'Word of Principle'" and which appeared in *Die jüdische Rundschau* 27, nos. 103-4 (29 December 1922): 675–76, was signed by Erich Fromm, Fritz Goithein, Ernst Simon, Leo Löwenthal, and Erich Michaelis (Hamburg).

44. Cf. Brenner, *Renaissance of Jewish Culture in Weimar Germany*, 86; and see Gershom Scholem, *Von Berlin nach Jerusalem* (Frankfurt: Bibliothek Suhrkamp, 1977), 190–98. On Fromm, cf. Rainer Funk, *Erich Fromm mit Selbstzeugnissen und Bilddokumenten dargestellt* (Reinbeck bei Hamburg: Rowohlt Taschenbuch Verlag, 1993).

45. See Franz Rosenzweig's letter to Ernst Simon of 6 December 1924, in *Briefe und Tagebücher*, vol. 2: *1918–1929*, ed. Rachel Rosenzweig und Edith Rosenzweig-Scheinmann, unter Mitwirkung von Bernhard Casper (The Hague: Nijhoff, 1979), 1007; and cf. Nahum N. Glatzer, "The Frankfurt Lehrhaus," in *Essays in Jewish Thought* (Tuscaloosa: University of Alabama Press, 1978), 265f., quoted in Green, *Jew and Philosopher*, 199 n. 10. On the Lehrhaus, cf. also Brenner, *Renaissance of Jewish Culture in Weimar Germany*, 86f. At the Lehrhaus, Fromm lectured on Karaism, Löwenthal on marginal figures in Jewish history, and Strauss first on Cohen and later on Spinoza. According to Glatzer, Strauss "led an analytical reading of Hermann Cohen's *Religion of Reason*" in 1923–24 and lectured on Spinoza in 1924–25, that is, at a time when the Lehrhaus had already begun to disintegrate. In the letter to Simon, Rosenzweig associates Strauss with "the really dumb" kind of Zionism, conceding that he, at least, represented it with the "*dehors* of the spirit."

46. *Der Jude*, named by its founder and editor Martin Buber after an earlier journal published by Gabriel Riesser (1832–33), appeared as a monthly from 1916 to 1924. Its orientation was pluralistic.

47. *Die jüdische Rundschau* replaced Herzl's *Die Welt* as the central organ of the World Zionist Organization in the German language. It was published by Robert Weltsch in Berlin. According to Jehuda Reinharz, *Die jüdische Rundschau* was influential far

beyond the circle of its five thousand to seven thousand subscribers. Cf. Reinharz, *Fatherland or Promised Land*, 103.

48. *Der jüdische Student* was founded in 1902 in Breslau by the Bund jüdischer Corporationen (B.J.C.), which, along with the Kartell zionistischer Verbindungen (K.Z.V., the Zionist alternative to the German-Jewish Kartell-Convent der Verbindungen deutscher Studenten jüdischen Glaubens, abbr. K-C), later constituted the Kartell jüdischer Verbindungen, K.J.V. The first *Der jüdische Student* ran for only one year before it went under. It began its regular operations only in 1907, when Kurt Blumenfeld reorganized the structure of the B.J.C. After the merger of B.J.C. and K.Z.V. in 1914, the journal ran first as the *Monatsschrift*, then (from June 1918) as the *Zeitschrift* of the K.J.V. Until 1920, the publication was strictly internal, its content restricted to the membership ("streng vertraulich," "Geheim"). This need for secrecy returned in the early 1930s, when the political situation in Germany began to deteriorate. The journal was discontinued in 1933. Before *Der jüdische Student* dropped its secrecy clause and became a public journal (1920), the Kartell briefly also produced a journal for the general public (*Der jüdische Wille*, 1918–20), which was again revived in 1933 (until 1937). Source: Robert Gidion, "25 Jahre J. St.," *Der jüdische Student* 26, nos. 1/2 (February 1929): 3–5.

49. See *GS*, 2:xxx, and cf. the notes to "Franz Rosenzweig and the Academy for the Science of Judaism," in this volume. Cf. also Scholem, *Von Berlin nach Jerusalem*, 189.

50. In a letter relating to this issue, Franz Rosenzweig once explicitly referred to the possibility that a "Fräulein Doktor" could serve as a fellow.

51. Cf. Franz Rosenzweig, "Zeit ists . . . (Ps. 119, 126): Gedanken über das Bildungsproblem des Augenblicks," reprinted in *Der Mensch und sein Werk: Gesammelte Schriften*, vol. 3: *Zweistromland: Kleinere Schriften zu Glauben und Denken*, ed. Reinhold Mayer and Annemarie Mayer (Dordrecht and Boston: Martinus Nijhoff, 1984), 461–81; and Rosenzweig, "Bildung und kein Ende (Pred. 12,12): Wünsche zum jüdischen Bildungsproblem des Augenblicks, insbesondere zur Volkshochschulfrage," in *Zweistromland*, 491–503.

52. See Franz Rosenzweig, letter to Gustav Bradt, 9 October 1926, in *Briefe und Tagebücher*, 2:1107. Among the other fellows were Fritz Jizchak Baer, Hartwig David Baneth, Selma Stern, and Chanoch Albeck, all "highly gifted scholars" whose "names and achievements," according to Gershom Scholem, "still echo in the Science of Judaism today." See Scholem, *Von Berlin nach Jerusalem*, 189.

53. Franz Rosenzweig himself was highly critical of the direction of the academy that he had helped to initiate. See Rosenzweig, "Bildung und kein Ende (Pred. 12,12)," 491–503.

54. Cf. *GS*, 2:xxxi. In Moses Mendelssohn, *Gesammelte Schriften: Jubiläumsausgabe*, vol. 2: *Schriften zur Philosophie und Ästhetik*, ed. Fritz Bamberger and Leo Strauss (Berlin: Akademieverlag, 1931), Strauss published introductions to "Pope ein Metaphysiker!," "Sendschreiben an den Herrn Magister Lessing in Leipzig," "Kommentar zu den 'Termini der Logik' des Moses ben Maimon," and "Abhandlung über die Evidenz." In Moses Mendelssohn, *Gesammelte Schriften: Jubiläumsausgabe*, vol. 3, pt. 1: *Schriften zur Philosophie und Ästhetik*,. ed. Fritz Bamberger and Leo Strauss (Berlin: Akademieverlag, 1932), Strauss published introductions to "Phädon," "Abhandlung von der Unkörper-

lichkeit der menschlichen Seele," "Über einen schriftlichen Aufsatz des Herrn de Luc," and "Die Seele." An introduction to "Die Sache Gottes oder die gerettete Vorsehung," written in 1936, was to be part of volume 3, pt. 2, but could no longer be published at the time. It first appeared in *Einsichten: Gerhard Krüger zum 60. Geburtstag*, ed. Klaus Oehler and Richard Schaeffler (Frankfurt am Main: Vittorio Klostermann, 1962), 361–75, and was later included also in Moses Mendelssohn, *Gesammelte Schriften: Jubiläumsausgabe*, vol. 3, pt. 2: *Schriften zur Philosophie und Ästhetik*, ed. Leo Strauss (Stuttgart and Bad Cannstatt: Friedrich Frommann Verlag [Günther Holzboog], 1974). In the 1930s, the edition was under the general editorship of Julius Guttmann, whereas its continuation after World War II was steered by Alexander Altmann. Strauss's most significant contribution by far to the Mendelssohn edition was his introduction to "Morgenstunden" and "An die Freunde Lessings," which was first published in 1974. It is not only the most voluminous piece (see *GS*, 2:528–605), but also the most elaborate and, in terms of Strauss's own development, the most interesting one. It was written in 1937, at a time when Strauss felt greatly indebted to Lessing for his own rediscovery of "the distinction between exoteric and esoteric speech and its grounds" ("A Giving of Accounts," 462). After World War II, Strauss planned the publication of an entire monograph built around this and a few other essays that had already been written, and to which he gave the tentative title "Philosophy and the Law: Historical Essays." Cf. *Jewish Philosophy and the Crisis of Modernity*, 467–70; and *GS*, 2:xxxi–xxxiii.

55. Cf. *GS*, 2:xxx–xxxi. The Akademie finally ceased its operations in 1934. Its first director was E. Taeubler, who was succeeded by Julius Guttmann. (Source: *EJ*). On Strauss's relation to the Akademie, see my endnotes to his eulogy entitled "Franz Rosenzweig and the Academy for the Science of Judaism," in this volume.

56. Cf. Strauss, *Jewish Philosophy and the Crisis of Modernity*, 4.

57. Cf. *GS*, 2:12.

58. Cf. Heinrich Meier, *Carl Schmitt and Leo Strauss: The Hidden Dialogue. Including Strauss's Notes on Schmitt's Concept of the Political and Three Letters from Strauss to Schmitt*, trans. J. Harvey Lomax, foreword by Joseph Cropsey (Chicago: University of Chicago Press, 1995), esp. the letter from Paris, 10 July 1933, pp. 127f., and editorial note, p. 129.

59. The volume appeared in 1935, on the occasion of the eight-hundredth birthday of the medieval philosopher. The composition of the essays, and hence their content, as well as the mundane purpose of their combined publication, had nothing to do with the anniversary. Strauss's attempt to receive a call to Hebrew University as a specialist in medieval Jewish philosophy is well documented and provides an important background to the publication of *Philosophie und Gesetz* (1935). Cf. GS, 2:xi–xv, and see below.

60. Cf. Strauss, *Jewish Philosophy and the Crisis of Modernity*, 5.

61. Hilail Gildin, *An Introduction to Political Philosophy: Ten Essays by Leo Strauss* (Detroit: Wayne State University Press, 1989); typographical error ("Liberalixm") corrected. For a full bibliography, see Heinrich Meier, "Leo Strauss, 1899–1973: Eine Bibliographie," in *Die Denkbewegung von Leo Strauss: Die Geschichte der Philosophie und die Intention des Philosophen* (Stuttgart and Weimar: Metzler, 1996), 45–63.

62. See GS, 1:xiii. Not included are writings that remained unpublished during

Strauss's lifetime (see below) and the two more sizable monographs produced during the early period, namely, the full version of the dissertation on Jacobi, first published in *GS*, 2:235–92, and *Die Religionskritik Spinozas als Grundlage seiner Bibelwissenschaft: Untersuchungen zu Spinozas Theologisch Politischem Traktat*, Series: Veröffentlichungen der Akademie für die Wissenschaft des Judentums. Philosophische Sektion, Zweiter Band (Berlin: Akademie Verlag, 1930). The German original of the latter, as well as a first German translation of the preface to the English edition, has recently been published, along with hitherto unpublished handwritten marginalia from Strauss's own copy, in *GS*, 1:1–361. The English translation (1965) is still in print (with the University of Chicago Press), and its preface is also included in *Jewish Philosophy and the Crisis of Modernity*.

Also not included in this volume are a small number of highly significant manuscripts found among the Leo Strauss Papers at the Department of Special Collections, University of Chicago Library, that have only recently been published by Heinrich Meier in *GS*, vol. 2. In order not to delay the publication of the present volume any further, it seemed prudent to limit ourselves to the original scope, that is, to the early published writings. It is hoped that a supplementary publication will soon make these previously unpublished writings available in English. The first of these manuscripts is a review of Karl Mannheim, *Ideologie und Utopie* (1929), entitled "Der Konspektivismus" (= *GS*, 2:365–75). The second text, the draft of a lecture Strauss was to give on December 1930 at the federal camp of the Zionist youth organization Kadimah at a retreat outside of Berlin, builds on ideas first elaborated in "Der Konspektivismus." The third lecture draft that belongs to this group is entitled "Die geistige Lage der Gegenwart" (= *GS*, 2:441–64). The original is a twelve-page lecture manuscript found in an envelope dated 6 February 1932. In these texts, Strauss presents the most scathing critique yet of the modern infatuation with the historical consciousness and undertakes his first steps toward overcoming it. We will refer to some of these texts in this introduction and in the notes to the translations. In stylistic terms, "Der Konspektivismus" and "'Religiöse Lage der Gegenwart'" are replete with irony and playfulness, traits that, with the exception of "Ecclesia militans" (1925), seem rare in the early published writings, at least at first glance. Reading these strongly engaged and less guarded texts allows one to discern more clearly the degree to which Strauss, whose high regard for Heinrich Heine is evident throughout, was himself an ironist, an important thing to keep in mind as one works through his early writings. Finally, among the manuscripts first published by Meier and not included here are drafts for a lecture, entitled "Cohen und Maimuni" (= *GS*, 2:393–436). The actual lecture was given on 4 May 1931 at the Hochschule für die Wissenschaft des Judentums in Berlin. In "Cohen and Maimuni," Strauss first articulates his changing understanding of Maimonides, based on his discovery, in Avicenna, of the passage that, four decades later, he was to use as the motto to his book *The Argument and the Action of Plato's "Laws"* (Chicago: University of Chicago Press, 1975), 1, 3. (Cf. *GS*, 2:xviii, text and note 13.) In this passage, Avicenna claims that the treatment of prophecy and of the divine law was contained in Plato's *Nomoi*. (Cf. also Strauss, "A Giving of Accounts," 462f.) "Cohen and Maimuni" is therefore an important predecessor to "Maimunis Lehre von der Prophetie und ihre Quellen" [= "Die philosophische Begründung des Gesetzes"], which was included in *Philosophie und Gesetz:*

Beiträge zum Verständnis Maimunis und seiner Vorläufer (Berlin: Schocken, 1935), 87–122. The manuscript of the latter essay was completed in July 1931, shortly after "Cohen und Maimuni."

63. Thus in the opening paragraph of "Preface to *Spinoza's Critique of Religion*," reprinted in *Jewish Philosophy and the Crisis of Modernity*, 137.

64. Letter to Alexandre Kojève, 29 May 1962, cited in *GS*, 1:10 n. 2.

65. See the preface to the English translation of the 1965 *Spinoza's Critique of Religion*. The current edition of *Spinoza's Critique of Religion* (University of Chicago Press) retains the reference to this "change of orientation" as having found "its first expression" in an essay added at the end of *Spinoza's Critique of Religion*. This refers to "Anmerkungen zu Carl Schmitt, *Der Begriff des Politischen*" (see the next note), whose English translation had been included in the 1965 edition of *Spinoza's Critique of Religion* but which is no longer part of the reprint by the University of Chicago Press.

66. Carl Schmitt, *Der Begriff des Politischen*, first published in the *Archiv für Sozialwissenschaft und Sozialpolitik* (Tübingen) 58, no. 1 (September 1927): 1–33. This version was reprinted in 1928, without changes. The second edition, *Der Begriff des Politischen: Mit einer Rede über das Zeitalter der Neutralisierungen und Entpolitisierungen* (Munich and Leipzig: Duncker & Humblot, 1932) is the one reviewed by Strauss in "Anmerkungen zu Carl Schmitt, *Der Begriff des Politischen*," *Archiv für Sozialwissenschaft und Sozialpolitik* 67, no. 6 (August–September 1932): 732–49. English (by E. M. Sinclair) in the appendix to *Spinoza's Critique of Religion*, 331–51; and in Carl Schmitt, *The Concept of the Political* (New Brunswick, N.J.: Rutgers University Press, 1976), 81–105. On the details of these publications, see Meier, *Carl Schmitt and Leo Strauss*, 6–7 n. 5, 120.

67. That is, Strauss, "Notes to Carl Schmitt, *The Concept of the Political*," in Meier, *Carl Schmitt and Leo Strauss* (see above, n. 58).

68. Strauss, "A Giving of Accounts," 460.

69. See, for example, Strauss, "How to Study Spinoza's *Theologico-Political Treatise*" (1948), in *Jewish Philosophy and the Crisis of Modernity*, 181–233.

70. "Religiöse Lage der Gegenwart"; see note 62, above.

71. "The Testament of Spinoza" (1932), below.

72. Leo Strauss, *Philosophy and Law*, trans. Eve Adler (Albany: SUNY Press, 1995), 38.

73. If one cares about historical coincidences of this sort: when Strauss wrote his introduction to *Philosophy and Law*, the very laws were being drafted by which Nazi Germany was to put a legal end to the era of emancipation (i.e., the Nuremberg Laws, enacted in September 1935).

74. Thus the tenor of Heinrich Meier, "Vorwort des Herausgebers," in *GS*, 2:ix–xxx.

75. Thus the title and project of Green, *Jew and Philosopher: The Return to Maimonides in the Jewish Thought of Leo Strauss*.

76. For Strauss on Heidegger and Rosenzweig see, among others, Strauss, "A Giving of Accounts," 460f.

77. Quoted in Gershom Scholem, *Walter Benjamin und sein Engel*, ed. Rolf Tiedemann (Frankfurt: Suhrkamp, 1983), 16. Strauss mentions Sussman in "Der Konspektivismus" (1929).

78. See below in "Response to the 'Word of Principle'" (1923).
79. Cf. "Der Konspektivismus" (1929) and "'Die Religiöse Lage der Gegenwart'" (1930), both in *GS*, 2.
80. The most articulate statement of this problem may be found in "'Religiöse Lage der Gegenwart'."
81. Thus in "Sigmund Freud, *The Future of an Illusion*" (1928).
82. Thus in "'Religiöse Lage der Gegenwart'" (1930).
83. Cf. Scholem, *Von Berlin nach Jerusalem*, 192. Here, in 1970, Scholem refers to Blau-Weiss as having turned "semifascist," just as, in 1923, Strauss refers to them as "pagan-fascist" (see below). For Strauss, the term "fascist" was immediately associated with the contemporary Italian movement, whereas Scholem likely presupposes the generalized meaning of the term, which, since the 1960s debates on the historical origins and socioeconomic character of the Nazi dictatorship in Germany, has been serving as a polemical countermodel to an equally politicized concept of totalitarianism. The theory of fascism in the latter sense of the word regards the generalized concept of totalitarianism as an expression of the "neofascism" of the cold war and is thus itself an expression of antifascism. Strauss's usage of the term is, thus, descriptive, while Scholem's involves a negative political judgment. Cf. Karl Dietrich Bracher, *Die Auflösung der Weimarer Republik: Eine Studie zum Problem des Machtverfalls in der Demokratie*, 5th ed. (Düsseldorf: Droste Verlag, 1978), xixf.
84. In this respect, Strauss's stance is not untypical for the German Zionism of his time. As Gershom Scholem recalls in *Von Berlin nach Jerusalem*, "[O]ne may say that if, in the early 1920s, someone made the move [*scil.*, to Palestine] from Germany, it happened only in the rarest of cases out of a political motivation and much more frequently because of a moral decision. It was a decision against a confusion that was perceived as dishonest and against an often undignified game of make-believe. It was a decision for a new beginning that, to us and then, seemed unambiguous, a decision that—whether justified by religious or secular considerations—had more to do with social ethics than with politics, as strange as this may sound today" (191).
85. This opposition is elaborated in "On the Bible Science of Spinoza."
86. Cf. notes to "Comments on Weinberg's Critique" and see "Das Camp in Forchtenberg," *Der jüdische Student* 21, nos. 8/9 (October/November 1924): 196–200.
87. Hans Weinberg, "Zionismus und Religion," *Der jüdische Student* 22, nos. 1/2 (February 1925): 9.
88. Isaac Breuer, *Das jüdische Nationalheim* (Frankfurt am Main: J. Kauffmann Verlag, 1925).
89. Strauss, "Das Camp in Forchtenberg," 198.
90. Cf. ibid.: "Ohne hier endgültige Formulierungen finden zu können, beantwortete er die Frage in mehr negativem Sinne" [Without being able to find definitive formulations in this matter, he answered the question more in a negative sense].
91. See Max Joseph, "Zur atheistischen Ideologie des Zionismus," *Der jüdische Student* 25, nos. 6/7 (October 1928): 8–18.
92. In addition to the immediate critique in the October issue, *Der jüdische Student* published a constructive counterarticle by Max Joseph in its December issue.

93. "'Religiöse Lage der Gegenwart'" is the draft of a lecture Strauss was to give on 21 December 1930 at the federal camp of Kadimah in Brieselang, near Berlin.

94. It should be noted that there is a parallel between the ups and downs of the Zionist movement in general and Strauss's phases of engagement and disengagement. In 1923–25, the phase of Strauss's most dedicated Zionist activities, there flourished immigration to Palestine and building activity. This trend was sharply reversed in 1925, when the Zionist movement encountered a leadership conflict over the question of immigration quotas and when Jabotinsky founded his revisionist organization. While immigration trends and economic factors began to look more favorable in 1929, the same year saw the first wave of large-scale Arab riots against Jewish immigration, as well as a steady deterioration of the social, economic, and political situation of German Jewry. Strauss must have observed these historical trends and may have responded to them in some fashion. However, since there are no direct reference to this effect in his writings, claiming a direct influence of these developments on his thought and decisions remains entirely speculative.

95. Thus explicitly in "Der Konspektivismus" (1929). First published by Heinrich Meier in *GS*, 2:365–75.

96. Ibid.

97. Ibid.

98. Heinrich Meier (*GS*, 2:xxv) calls the introduction to *Philosophie und Gesetz*, written in only a few days, one of Strauss's most brilliant pieces. Kenneth Hart Green (in Strauss, *Jewish Philosophy and the Crisis of Modernity*, 49 n. 4) similarly regards it as "undoubtedly one of the single most important essays of Strauss in the field of modern Jewish thought."

99. Adding yet another possible interpretation to the alternatives described in the following, one may mention Julius Guttmann, who identified Strauss's position with "modern existentialism." See *GS*, 2:xxvif. To be more specific, Guttmann's interpretation chooses to ignore that Strauss does not consider the opposition between Orthodoxy and atheism as a necessarily insurmountable one. All of these misunderstandings really illustrate just how unusual Strauss's way of thinking was at the time.

100. Letter to Löwith, 23 June 1935, in *GS*, 2:xxvi n. 32. See there for a similar statement in a different context about Gershom Scholem.

101. 29 March 1935, cited in *GS*, 2:xxvii.

102. See Strauss, *Philosophie und Gesetz*, 26f. n. 1; English: *Philosophy and Law*, 137f. n. 13.

103. See the previous note.

104. To this one may add, in light of later statements, that Strauss differs from his friend Klein by refusing to attribute to morality a higher status than to the "love of truth." (See Strauss, "A Giving of Accounts.") Generally, Strauss on the hierarchy of virtues is a topic worth exploring in its own right.

105. See *GS*, 2:xiiif.

106. See letter to Gerhard Krüger, 19 August 1932, in *GS*, 2:xxvii n. 34.

107. The passages from the letter by Klein are in *GS*, 2:xxvii.

108. A seminar by Professor Peters of Heidelberg on the history of nineteenth-

century theology, in which I participated, utilized the first date of publication of Schleiermacher's *Reden* (1799) and that of its centennial edition prepared by Otto (1899) to delimit the range of the nineteenth century.

109. Cf. "Der Konspektivismus" (1929) and "'Religiöse Lage der Gegenwart'" (1930).

110. On "Epicureanism," see "On the Bible Science of Spinoza" and "On the Argument with European Science."

111. The following quotations are, for the most part, from my working translation of "'Religiöse Lage der Gegenwart'." It is hoped that a full translation of this and the other relevant pieces from this period made available by Heinrich and Wiebke Meier in *GS*, 2, may soon be published in a full, annotated English edition.

112. Leo Strauss writes "past, even though," followed by a lacuna providing space for the later insertion of the qualification. At the end of the blank, the manuscript continues: "I call out to you." (Source: *GS*, 2:381.)

113. Cf. "Der Konspektivismus" (*GS*, 2:365–75). The word appears eleven times.

114. The parable of the cave is similarly adduced, and interpreted in the same way, in the review essay on Julius Ebbinghaus, namely, as pointing to a fundamental difference between the "natural" difficulty of philosophizing and the one faced by the modern philosopher who first must learn how to retrieve the "natural" difficulty of philosophizing. The difference between the ancient and the modern situation of philosophy is the intervention of biblical revelation. See also the last paragraph of "Der Konspektivismus" (*GS*, 2:373–75).

115. Cf. Strauss, *Spinoza's Critique of Religion*, 181.

116. In the manuscript of this lecture draft, Strauss adds "(museum, etc.)" to illustrate what he means by "self-guaranteeing of immortality," namely, cultural institutions that stand in for earlier religious institutions.

117. This motif of a second, deeper cave is here mentioned for the first time. The first published text where it appears, albeit with almost enigmatic brevity, is the Ebbinghaus review, included in this volume.

118. On Rousseau and the motif of a "returning to" *(Rückgang auf)*, cf. "Die geistige Lage der Gegenwart" (1932) in *GS*, 2:454.

119. Cf. "Biblical History and Science" (1925), where Strauss explicitly refers to the journal *Zwischen den Zeiten*.

120. See Strauss, "A Giving of Accounts," 460.

121. Cf. *GS*, 2:xxix n. 41.

122. Cf. *GS*, 2:xxiiiff.

123. I apologize for being somewhat enigmatic here. There are important aspects of the early work of Strauss that this introduction could not even begin to address. In the early essays, Hermann Cohen appears as one of the last individuals (if not the last; but Strauss's understanding of Rosenzweig is an important unexplored topic in its own right) who were still able to invoke God without embarrassment or hidden atheism. Yet a proper exploration of this topic demands an examination of how Strauss's view of Cohen was affected by Strauss's discovery of the exoteric. In the late thirties, Strauss still believed that Cohen had had the right intuition about Maimonides being influenced by Plato, but he also thinks that the reasoning by which Cohen supported this hunch was

flawed. See *GS*, 2:xxx n. 43, referring to the lecture entitled "Cohen and Maimuni," and much more strongly in October 1935 (when Strauss wrote "Quelques remarques sur la science politique de Maïmonide et de Fârâbî"); cf. *GS*, 2:xxiif. n. 25.

124. This is not to say that Strauss henceforth completely refrained from writing about the Hebrew Bible or that he left us without valuable clues as to how he believed the biblical part of the Western heritage should be approached. Among the notable exceptions to his silence on the question of the Torah and on the Bible are the essays "Jerusalem and Athens: Some Preliminary Reflections," in *Jewish Philosophy and the Crisis of Modernity*, 359–76, and "On the Interpretation of Genesis," in *Jewish Philosophy and the Crisis of Modernity*, 377–405, where Strauss adumbrates what he calls a "postcritical" interpretation of the Bible. Cf. Kenneth Hart Green, preface to Strauss, *Jewish Philosophy and the Crisis of Modernity*, xiv–xv n. 4.

125. Cf. Green, *Jew and Philosopher*, 24–27.

126. Ibid., 24.

127. Cf. Strauss, "Progress or Return?" (1952), in *Jewish Philosophy and the Crisis of Modernity*, 87–136.

128. This is, indeed, the agenda of the few texts adumbrating Strauss's "postcritical" exegesis that we have, such as "Jerusalem and Athens: Some Preliminary Reflections" and "On the Interpretation of Genesis." See n. 34, above.

129. Cf. Green, *Jew and Philosopher*, 166 n. 119, 178 n. 57.

Part II
Leo Strauss: Early Publications
(1921–32)

I

──⟨≳⟩

The Dissertation
(1921)

The full text of Strauss's 1921 dissertation, "Das Erkenntnisproblem in der philosophischen Lehre Friedrich Heinrich Jacobis," was published by Heinrich and Wiebke Meier in *Philosophie und Gesetz: Frühe Schriften* (= *GS*, 2:237–92). The following is a translation of the extract *(Auszug)* from the dissertation published by Strauss himself. The original can also be found in *GS*, 2:293–98. Our translation includes the handwritten marginalia included in Strauss's personal copy, which is among the Strauss papers at the University of Chicago under the auspices of Professor Joseph Cropsey.

The Problem of Knowledge in the Philosophical Doctrine of Friedrich Heinrich Jacobi (1921)

Extract from the Inaugural Dissertation written and presented by Leo Strauss from Kirchhain (Hesse) to the Faculty of Philosophy at Hamburg University for the attainment of doctoral honors.

PRELIMINARY REMARK

This work seeks to limit its consideration exclusively to the intellectual substance [*Gedankengehalt*] elaborated by Jacobi, and to present only the immanent connections of the problems, just as they were seen by Jacobi, without entering more closely either into the historical relations dealt with adequately by others or into the thinker's own development.[1]

A) AN ANTITHESIS OF ATTITUDES AND METHODS

Jacobi distinguishes two types of general attitudes of mind, the essential predicates of which are juxtaposed as "courageously believing" [*mutig-glaubend*] and "timidly doubting" [*furchtsam-zweifelnd*]. This distinction attains purely theoretical significance by virtue of the fact that a duality of methods is unequivocally related to the typological duality of attitudes. To be more precise, the method of "universal doubt" corresponds to the second, devalued type of attitude. This method extends far beyond its most famous representative, Descartes. Jacobi tracks it down everywhere: it is by and large the common method of all his opponents. We have sought to characterize as "descriptive" the method of the affirmed type, which he himself postulates as the "natural" method.

B) THE SUBSTANCE OF JACOBI'S DOCTRINES

1. The Doctrine of Knowledge [Erkenntnislehre]
    a) The Intellect [*Der Verstand*]
On the one hand (following Kant), intellect is the absolute principle of knowledge [*Wissen*], and, on the other hand, it is the faculty of mere reflection, of concepts, and of proof. In both cases it is purely formal; it claims its "matter" ["*Stoff*"] from giving faculties.[2] The objects are beyond the sphere of the intellect. The highest and ultimate certainty of consciousness itself, which is unprovable and yet more certain than all proofs, and the material of knowledge [*Erkenntnis*] that the intellect cannot generate out of itself lead both beyond the sphere of the intellect. Intellectual knowledge [*Verstandeserkenntnis*], the proving of things [*das Beweisen*], continuously refers to [*stetes Ver-weisen*] something other, and from every other to something other again. It always finds its completion only in what is given by other kinds of knowledge [*Erkenntnisarten*]. The relative spontaneity of the intellect, which expresses itself in the conceptualization of the given [*Verbegrifflichung des Gegebenen*], deprives it of knowledge value [*Erkenntniswert*] in the proper sense. For, according to its essence, knowledge [*Erkenntnis*] is receptive (as is implied by the very terms *Wahrnehmung*, and *Vernunft* from *Vernehmen*).[3] Knowledge [*Erkenntnis*] is related to something outside of it which provides it with meaning in the first place, and to which it conforms.

    b) The Giving Kinds of Knowledge [*Erkenntnisarten*]
Our knowledge [*Erkenntnis*] of the sensory world is "forcibly" ["*mit Gewalt*"] determined by the meaning contained in the object. We gain experience of

this meaning primarily through perception [*Wahrnehmung*], and it is from this that we derive all we know of nature. Jacobi pays particular attention to that moment[4] in the act of perception which assures us of the transcendent reality of objects outside ourselves. This moment is "belief." The positive, non-polemical content of Jacobi's doctrine of perception [*Wahrnehmungslehre*] is unfolded in the following theses; they have been compiled on the basis of his utterances, which are unfortunately all too "rhapsodic."

1. Our knowledge [*Wissen*] of reality is an ultimate, and is different in principle from all other kinds of knowledge [*Wissensarten*]. Our "representations" [*Vorstellungen*] of real being are copies of this real being. Thus the way leads from being to pure reductions [*Abschwächungen*] in the representation [*Vorstellung*] and not from representation to being.

2. Perception is the original grasp [*Erfassung*] of reality as such. Only on the basis of this grasp is it possible to distinguish between reality and merely represented being, or rather between perception and representation.

3. An immediate encounter between subject and reality takes place in the act of perception, which is mediated neither by representation nor by inference.

4. In the act of perception, consciousness is equally conscious of both the perception of reality outside itself and of the real in itself. We do not reach consciousness of our own reality before reaching consciousness of the transcendent reality.

5. We ourselves—the knowing subjects [*die erkennenden Subjekte*]—are "included" ["*mitbegriffen*"] in the reality grasped in the act of perception.

6. We obtain our knowledge [*Wissen*] about reality primarily by having a sensation of our body.

Theses 4 through 6 are formulations of what is specific about Jacobi's doctrine of belief that are free of the term "belief." If we insert it in the formulations, then we may say:

"Belief" in natural reality is the immediate certainty of the transcendence of natural reality, which is grounded in the natural-real [*natürlich-real*] connection between knowing subject [*erkennendes Subjekt*] and reality, mediated by the body. Or, stated more generally: "Belief" in a reality is the immediate certainty of the transcendence of reality that bases itself on the (specific) real connection between knowing subject and reality, mediated by its (specific) real structures.

A further attempt is now made to show how this general concept of "belief" holds good in the various spheres of knowledge [*Erkenntnis-Sphären*]. Aside from sense perception, we distinguish the knowledge of reason [*Vernunft-erkenntnis*] and the knowledge of the heart [*Erkenntnis des Herzens*]. To be sure, the two latter kinds are not strictly distinguished by Jacobi. But where, in fact, there are distinctions, the aim of presenting a history of the problem[5] justifies also the use of terminological distinctions. What is common to all three giving faculties of knowledge [*gebende Erkenntnis-Vermögen*] is the fundamental formal structure: that they are located outside, and before, the intellect, that they relate to their object in a receptive manner, and that they grasp a transcendent reality (nature through sense perception, God through reason, the system of ends through the heart).

Just as perception as a kind of knowledge is mediated by the corporeality [*Körperlichkeit*] of the body, so the knowledge of God is mediated by that [part] in us which is not subject to the mechanism of nature, by the free and immortal part of our "essence" [*"Wesen"*], by the divine in us.[6] Hence, corresponding to the *duality of realities* is a *duality of original ways of grasping*, therefore a *duality of "belief,"* and—as is evident from the essence of belief—a duality of "our essence" [*"unseres Wesens"*]. The two parts of our essence, according to their specific structure, are the real mediators in regard to the specific realities, nature and God. The parallelism between these essential parts, in spite of the duality existing between them, is expressed in the doctrine that belief in God is an "instinct" and is as "natural" to the human being "as his upright position." *The meaning of "instinct" is extended in a manner analogous to the extension of the meaning of "belief."* For Jacobi, instinct is no longer limited to the realm of nature. It refers to the whole of human "nature." Thus "human nature," the "essence" [*"Wesen"*] and the fundamental urges of the essence—"natural" and religious instinct—are more comprehensive than nature in the strict sense. They are truly *metaphysical*.

2. The Doctrine of Being [Seinslehre]
   a) Knowledge and Life
The ultimate source of certainty is the feeling of existence. All further evidence is rooted in the feeling of existence. The highest norms of truth harmonize at the core with the existence of *being* [*Wesen*] (instead of with, say, mere consciousness). The principles of the mind [*Geist*] are rooted in the instinct, in the species instinct of humanity that, like every other instinct, relates to "the preservation of the species, toward that which brings it to life and preserves it." Thus the instinct of humanity is most deeply connected with reason. Religion is therefore the truly human instinct. Instinct aims at the substantial; intellect aims at relations. Real refers to real; derived refers to derived. The philosophy of reason limits itself to relations that are immanent in consciousness. It does not seek to found them on grounds beyond consciousness. In leaning toward such a foundation [beyond consciousness], Jacobi

agrees with naturalist philosophy. But his procedure is essentially different from attempts at causal explanation: he ventures upon a metaphysical substructure [*Substruktion*]. Jacobi regards instinct as a metaphysical principle, and can therefore also advocate transnatural modes of consciousness.

The relation of knowledge [*Erkenntnis-Beziehung*] is basically a relation between the substance of the I [*Ich-Substanz*] (essence) and the substance of being [*Seins-Substanz*], which, in turn, must be homogeneous. For the subjects are "included" [*"mitbegriffen"*] in the real.

b) Substance, Time, Causality
In the opinion of Jacobi, the irrational aspects of being are chiefly concentrated in these three principles.

3. On the Philosophy of Religion

In opposition to literalism,[7] Jacobi defends the possibility of an immediate experience of God as well as the possibility, based on this experience, of measuring all historical religions in terms of meaning and of truth itself.[8] In opposition to idealism and rationalism, he upholds the transcendence and the irrationality of God. The necessity for positive religion is based on the fact that no truth can "reach us without form" [*gestaltlos*]. The expression, the "word,"[9] the image, is the necessary vehicle for the hidden, merely expressible, meaning.[10]

CURRICULUM VITAE

I, Leo Strauss, was born on September 20, 1899, in Kirchhain/Hesse. I am of the Jewish faith. After completion of the Volks- und Rektoratsschule of my hometown, I entered the Gymnasium Philippinum in Marburg on Easter 1912 and graduated from there at Easter, 1917. Beginning in the summer semester of 1917, I studied at the universities of Marburg, Frankfurt am Main, Berlin, and Hamburg, except for the time of my service in the army (July 1917 until December 1918). My main areas were philosophy, mathematics, and the sciences. I express my sincere gratitude to all my teachers, and especially to Professor Ernst Cassirer, who kindly advised me during the composition of my thesis.

A HANDWRITTEN ADDITION TO THE EXTRACT

[On p. 7 of a copy of the extract from Strauss's dissertation at the University of Chicago Library there are handwritten additions, apparently by Strauss himself.[11] The following is a translation of these additions.][12]

[First paragraph:]
A non-Jacobian approach to the Jacobian problems.

[Second paragraph:]
Jacobi does not have a proper theory of knowledge [*Erkenntnis-Theorie*]. For this he would need a rigorous concept of "consciousness," which he hates and rejects. Thus in order to extract from Jac[obi] that which is *related* to knowledge, one had to resort to many deflections. Thus, I did not present "Jacobi-in-himself," but rather only insofar as I needed him. Especially his "introspection" [*Innerlichkeit*] came off badly.

[Third paragraph:]
Hegel, "Pref[ace]" to *Phenom[enology of the Mind*], speaks of an "intensity without substance," of the "hollow depth" of the philosophy of perception and of feeling.

NOTES

Source: *Das Erkenntnisproblem in der philosophischen Lehre Fr. H. Jacobis: Auszug aus der Inaugural-Dissertation, verfaßt und zur Erlangung der Doktorwürde der Philosophischen Fakultät der Hamburgischen Universität vorgelegt von Leo Strauss aus Kirchhain (Hessen)* (Hamburg: Julius Schröder, Kirchhain, Bezirk Cassel, 1921). Referee: Ernst Cassirer. Date of oral examination: 17 December 1921.

Friedrich Heinrich Jacobi (1743–1819). First merchant in Düsseldorf and Eutin, then director of the Bavarian Academy of Sciences (1805–12), Jacobi was acquainted with the great figures of the moderate German Enlightenment (Hamann, Herder, Lessing, Mendelssohn) and was a critic of Kant. He developed a philosophical defense of belief as a source of genuine knowledge of reality that, in the version given it by Schleiermacher, became popular in the nineteenth century in form of the notion of a "religious a priori." Jacobi and Mendelssohn exchanged letters on the question of whether Lessing was a Spinozist (a devastating charge at the time). This exchange became famous in the history of philosophy as the debate on pantheism *(Pantheismusstreit)*. Cf. Fritz Mauthner, ed., *Jacobis Spinoza-Büchlein nebst Replik und Duplik* (München: G. Müller, 1912.) Strauss later described Mendelssohn's part in this debate in his introduction to Mendelssohn's "Morgenstunden" and "An die Freunde Lessings" (1937). See *GS*, 2:528–605. Strauss's concern with Jacobi is thus visible at the very beginning as well as at the important juncture of his phase of reorientation, in the mid to late 1930s. The most explicit critique of the notion of a religious a priori, however, appeared in 1924, in the essay "On the Argument with European Science." Similarly, Strauss defended the value of critique, which is here condemned as an expression of the primary attitude of "timidly doubting," in his first Zionist essay, "Response to Frankfurt's 'Word of Principle'" (1923), and again in "On the Argument with European Science." Strauss's interest in Spinoza may also have been stirred by his work on Jacobi, in that it was Jacobi (who rejected Spinoza) who was the first of his generation to argue that the only consistently rational philosophy was that of Spinoza.]

1. Preliminary Remark *(Vorbemerkung):* this paragraph is a summary of the "Preliminary Remark" of the dissertation (see *GS*, 2:241–43). In addition to the disclaimer to which the *Vorbemerkung* is reduced in the extract, the more extensive *Vorbemerkung* offers a few remarks on the overlap and differences between Jacobi's and Kant's respective concepts of reason *(Vernunft)* and on difficulties in Jacobi that arise from inconsistencies in his terminology.

2. In this dichotomous typology of faculties, the term *gebende Vermögen* refers to the necessary precondition of the receptive faculty, namely, an active faculty that provides the material reflected by the receiving faculty, that is, the intellect. The translation of the term as "giving faculties" may not be particularly suggestive, but its meaning should be clear from the context.

3. *Wahrnehmung* refers to the act or process of becoming conscious of something, implying that something that exists in itself is grasped or, literally, "taken." It is the German equivalent of the Latin *percipi* (to perceive). The same relation of dependence on a "given" is implied in the second "name," as Strauss puts it, namely *Vernunft.* Its common English translation, "reason," is derived from the Latin *ratio,* which is based on a different connotation than the German *Vernunft.* The latter, as Strauss points out, derives from *vernehmen,* which, while likewise a derivation of the word for taking *(nehmen),* means "to hear." To the extent that this connotation is present in the noun *Vernunft,* the latter is thus associated with the aural sense. As in the case of *wahrnehmen, Vernunft,* as Strauss claims, appears as receptive rather than spontaneous.

4. Here and elsewhere in his writings, Strauss uses the word *Moment,* whose English equivalent, "moment" (in the sense of factor, element, etc.), is familiar to readers of philosophical texts but may be confusing to others. The connotation of "moment" in this sense is not temporal (as in "one moment, please," or *einen Moment, bitte*) but functional, denoting a single element or factor in a complex process—for example, that of thought or that of perception. In some cases, we try to avoid possible misunderstandings of the term by rendering it as "element" rather than as its relatively unfamiliar English cognate. Wherever confusion is unlikely, however, we render *Moment* as "moment."

5. *Problemgeschichte:* the history of a problem, problem-history, or the problem-historical method *(problemgeschichtliche Methode)* is a method of studying the history of philosophy on the basis of problems that are handed down in its significant texts and in which the reader must participate both in order to understand the historical positions and to continue the history of the problem itself by pursuing the goal of its solution. This method is prominent in the works of the Marburg school of neo-Kantianism (Cohen, Natorp, Cassirer) and beyond (cf., e.g., the work of Richard Hönigswald). In the 1920s, the younger generation of Marburg philosophers (especially Nicolai Hartmann and Hans Georg Gadamer) criticized the problem-historical method. To them, the assumption of immediate access to perennial philosophical problems obscured the fact of the distance between the modern reader and the ancient texts and their assumptions. For the young Gadamer see, for example, Hans-Georg Gadamer, *Festschrift für Paul Natorp zum Siebzigsten Geburtstage von Schülern und Freunden gewidmet* (Berlin and Leipzig:

Walter de Gruyter, 1924), 56f., 74f. In *Truth and Method*, trans. Joel Weinsheimer and Donald G. Marshall, 2d ed. (New York: Crossroad, 1989), 376f., Gadamer continues to dismiss the neo-Kantian history of problems as "a bastard-child of historicism." (I thank Ken Green for the latter reference.) Even the latter derisive characterization contains an indirect recognition of the neo-Kantian effort to overcome the purely historical perspective on philosophy, which prevailed on the Continent before the rise of neo-Kantianism. In the preface to his dissertation Strauss does both: he recognizes the misgivings one may have about the problem-historical approach and justifies its utility. In the case of his study of Jacobi, the focus is on the problem of knowledge, to which Jacobi made certain contributions that he failed to conceptualize in a systematic and coherent manner. Hence the focus is not as much on Jacobi as on "the problems indicated in the title 'Jacobi'," etc. See *GS*, 2:243.

6. Jacobi's position is described here not as postulating human liberty but as somehow "experiencing," and therefore "knowing," human liberty to be a "reality." This is obviously the purpose of identifying all forms or "spheres" of knowledge as "belief." If the certainty of knowledge is but a form of "belief," then any kind of belief is equivalent in certainty to all forms of knowledge. Belief is analogous in certainty to demonstrable truths because even the latter borrow their convincing force from the origin of our certainty, the way we feel our body to be "real." What made this position attractive in the early twentieth century with its various "vitalist" trends was that it reintegrated scientific and intellectual certainty with a larger scheme of knowledge, de-emphasizing what seemed overemphasized in academic philosophy on the basis of an almost pragmatist paradigm of common experience. It seems that Strauss's philosophical contexts influenced him more strongly in this exposition of Jacobi's thought than he cared to admit. (See, however, the later clarification of Strauss's intention in the notes he added by hand in his copy of the text.) In contrast to the possible associations with a vitalist agenda, the dissertation espouses the phrasing and research interest of his teacher Ernst Cassirer both by subjecting Jacobi's doctrine of knowledge to an examination (the later notes point out that this was a rather non-Jacobian way of approaching Jacobi) and by undertaking this examination under the heading of a history of the problem *(Problemgeschichte)*.

7. See Strauss, "Erkenntnislehre" (diss., University of Hamburg, 1921), reprinted in *GS*, 2:289. *Literalismus* is here defined as one of two alternative positions, both of which Jacobi seeks to overcome. More precisely, "literalism" refers to the position that affirms the irrational quality of God, and hence an utter dependence of human reason on positive, revealed religion.

8. Jacobi's theological ideas were perfected and presented in their most influential form by Schleiermacher.

9. Cf. Strauss, "Response to Frankfurt's '*Word* of Principle'" (emphasis added).

10. According to Strauss, the *nur ausdrückbare Sinn*—that is, the meaning that can merely be expressed—corresponds to the positive or historical religions. In this sense it represents Jacobi's compromise between the rationalist insistence on God as an absolute that can never be adequately expressed by any particular religion and the literalist insistence on the irrationality of God that exempts revelation from all critical examination.

Religion expresses the meaning of God, but it merely expresses it, and hence never contains it fully. Cf. "Erkenntnisproblem" (the full text of the dissertation) in *GS,* 2:288f.

11.   The German original was first published in *GS,* 2:297.

12.   It seems to me that the additions were not made all at once. The writing material of the first couple of lines is different from that used in the second and third paragraphs and left no imprint on the facing page. The imprint of the third paragraphs on the facing page is weaker than that made by the second paragraph.

II

Zionist Writings
(1923–25)

The publications from this period represent Leo Strauss as a political Zionist. They coincide with one of the most optimistic phases in the history of Zionism in general, and of the German Zionist movement in particular. (On the following cf. Walter Laqueur, *A History of Zionism* [New York: Schocken Books, 1972], 445, 450–55.) While German Jews no longer experienced the systematic governmental discrimination that had been the rule until the end of the First World War and while its elite had gained access to positions of cultural, political, and economic influence, the Zionist minority perceived signs of a growing anti-Semitic sentiment that confirmed what they had been believing all along, namely, that the future of European Jewry depended on the ability of the Jews to extricate themselves from Europe. With the Balfour Declaration of 1917, in which the British crown recognized its support of the Zionist quest for the establishment of a "Jewish homeland in Palestine," the sought-for extrication from Europe had become a realistic political option, but the process of its realization was still delayed. While the United Kingdom had supported Jewish immigration to Palestine de facto since 1920 (the year of the San Remo conference and of the peace treaty with Turkey) when Herbert Samuel became the first High Commissioner for Palestine, it took until the signing of the 1924 Treaty of Lausanne before Palestine was officially established as a League of Nations mandate, making British control of immigration a de jure reality as well. The German economic crisis ended in 1923, allowing a flow of capital into Zionist projects and settlements, which triggered a veritable building boom in Palestine that provided employment for the new settlers. This development reached its peak in 1925.

While certainly fully aware of these developments, Strauss shows little immediate interest in the practical political side of Zionism. Rather, he raises his voice in the context of the ongoing debates among Zionist youths on the spiritual orientation of Zionism and its relation to European culture. Strauss poses the question of the possibility of a spiritual extrication from Europe, but he finds the cultural Zionist answer to this question deficient. The modernized theology of cultural Zionism that rejects the traditional Jewish religion of exile and its belief in the divine monopoly on redemption appears to Strauss as an unacknowledged atheism, a variant on modern cultural Protestantism with its roots in the Enlightenment critique of religion. While he criticizes cultural Zionism, Strauss maintains with Hermann Cohen that the modern political ideals of liberalism and republicanism are congenial to the ethical monotheism of the biblical prophets. Strauss thus appears to some of his readers as an enthusiastically religious Zionist who opposes the modernism of religion while advocating the political goals of Herzl Zionism. Strauss, however, rejects this interpretation of his position by opening a second front against the religious Zionism of Mizrahi. (See "Comment on Weinberg's Critique" and "Ecclesia militans.") In keeping with the radical intellectual honesty to which he subscribes, Strauss admits that the only acceptable answer to the modern Jewish problem, mere political Zionism, is lacking in spiritual depth. Nevertheless, he advocates political Zionism as the only attitude that renounces all false reliance on either traditional or modern religious sources and thus constitutes a kind of honest atheism. This position, however, pushes Strauss beyond the pale of positions acceptable to the Zionist mainstream. The argument in favor of an atheistic foundation to Zionism (most evident in the 1928 review of Freud's *Future of an Illusion,* here in chapter 4) is rejected as politically and propagandistically detrimental to the centrist Zionist pursuit of a coalition between religious and secular (liberal, assimilated) Jews.

Response to Frankfurt's "Word of Principle" (1923)

PREFATORY REMARK BY THE AUTHOR

I offer the following remarks for the orientation of the reader: At the special convention[1] of the Kartell jüdischer Verbindungen (K.J.V.),[2] held in Berlin at Christmas [of 1922], the fusion between K.J.V. and Blau-Weiss,[3] which was on the agenda, was *opposed* by the Frankfurt faction [of K.J.V.].[4] The main reason for this opposition was the alleged aversion, indeed the spiritual [*seelisch*] incapacity, of Blau-Weiss to entertain the demand for "Jewish content."[5] —The term "Breslau"[6] refers to the German Jewish and power politics-oriented wing of Blau-Weiss, which, in recent months, attained a leading position within Blau-Weiss. The following rejoinder is based on these facts, as well as on the declaration, published in issue 103/104 of the *Jüdische Rundschau,*[7] which is closely related to these facts.

* * *

The following response is governed by a tendency that regards itself in many respects akin to what, until now, has been the tendency of Blau-Weiss. This kinship does not rule out a certain heterogeneity in principle. It especially does not rule out that, on a level concerned entirely with principles, our tendency finds itself opposed to a united front of Blau-Weiss and Frankfurt, namely, because of an affirmation [on our part] of the values of "argumentation" and "formal politicism" that have been denounced by both groups. In this respect, the special convention of the K.J.V. revealed a remarkable unanimity of the most strident opponents and the most energetic friends of the fusion, due to the confident conviction that the time of sovereign science and sovereign politics is at an end. One should not let oneself be deceived by the political demands of Walter Moses.[8] What he calls "political" is political in the ancient sense of the word, rather than in the modern sense that is relevant for us.[9] What is hidden behind this absolute negation of the sphere of the "private" is not a modern Leviathan, but rather the pagan-fascist counterpart of that, which, in the case of the Frankfurt faction, bears a mystical-humanitarian stamp. (To be sure, both of these attitudes are modern, even though they are antimodern, which is precisely what renders them inner-modern.) The same applies to "belief," which both are willing to establish as an ultimate certainty impervious to "argumentation." In this they undoubtedly concur with the tendency of our entire generation. This somehow makes them agreeable to us, but it does not at all prove their legitimacy. For the moment, let us completely set aside the question of whether "science" and "state"— those fruits of the anti-Catholic spirit—are perhaps more closely related to the innermost Jewish tendency than is the decidedly more familiar ideal of our organologists[10]—a "perhaps" at which one may very well arrive if one thinks of the biblical origins of modern science, of the equally *uncanny* character of the biblical world and of the worldview of the seventeenth century, of the role Spinoza plays in the formulation of the modern view of the world and the modern view of the state, as well as of several other things. (The doctrine of the fundamentally utilitarian character of modern science is a sentimental defamation.) Therefore, even if we completely set aside the question of whether the rejection of the modern spirit can be justified at all, it is still self-evident that it is impossible to extricate oneself from modern life without employing modern means. Thus we have no need whatever to enter into a discussion of the usual insults, by now quite hackneyed, hurled at the "bourgeois" attitude.

In the conflict between Breslau and Frankfurt (between Frankfurt and Blau-Weiss), I am compelled—on grounds that obviously lie on a different plane than those just mentioned—to side with Breslau (Blau-Weiss). Despite the external failure of the Frankfurt spirit (as described by Ernst Simon),[11] the convention of the K.J.V. in truth signifies a victory of this spirit. Our inferiority in argument, that is, our emptiness in substance, was brought to light in the most regrettable way. In any case, one thing is certain: we have as yet to find our "word"[12] of principle, nor have we yet matured to an elucidation of ourselves in principle. What posed during the conference as such a word, such an elucidation, was shallow and empty. Unfortunately, it must be said explicitly that this shortcoming is a real shortcoming. We must avoid by all possible means the adolescent sentimentality that, trusting in the inner sincerity of its own tendency, dispenses with the articulation of a "word," a reason, a justification—in our case: a Zionist justification. It was thought that by heaping upon us for years, to the point of nausea, "personal encounters" [*"Erlebnisse"*] and "confessions" [*"Bekenntnisse"*], one could make us forget that there is such a thing as critique.[13] We ourselves were temporarily confused,[14] but now we unambiguously profess the spirit of sobriety as opposed to that of pathetic declamation. "Belief" may still be decisive, yet belief is no oracle but is subject to the control of historical reasoning.

Hence, what matters to us is not to oppose to the Frankfurt theses other theses—be they of Breslau or of Kirchhain[15]—but to subject to critique the theses that were put before us. For these theses claim to be the expression not of the particular will of random Jewish individuals – this sort of thing would not provoke our participation—but of the general and necessary will of the spirit of the Jewish people at the stage of its development that is called "Zionism." Insofar as Zionist reason is alive among the rest of us, we have the opportunity to criticize these demands and to examine the presuppositions of each one of them separately. Even though, at this hour, we are not yet able to articulate our "word," we should ask ourselves even today whether the word of the others is valid.

Even the "Word of Principle" is first of all a word of criticism; it addresses us, that is, it addresses those who are "German Jews" not simply by being such but also by consciously affirming it, in an examining, judging, and convicting manner. The objections to be raised begin with the introductory thesis of the proclamation that asserts that the German Jewish youth movement is characterized by an anarchy of standpoints and positions. This thesis can be easily and conveniently proved if one sticks to the shadowy schematisms of "socialism vs. capitalism," "Buberism vs. irreligiosity," "Pan-Judaism vs. German Jewish particularism," without considering the underlying reality that these names seemed temporarily apt to express in ideological terms. No doubt the unprecedented intellectualism of the youth movement warrants the suspicion that it is pure arbitrariness of subjectivity that governs the changes in the views of Blau-Weiss. However, this is not the case. If we proceed from the general position that is associated with the names of Landauer[16] and Buber[17] and that, right after the war, enjoyed, in a manner of speaking, canonical status in Blau-Weiss, then we notice that a meaningful development leads from this general position to the one prevailing today. Take, for example, Buber's thoroughly immanentist interpretation of religion. If God is "later" than the religious experience [*Erlebnis*] of the individual or of the people (and this is Buber's doctrine), then the trajectory toward absolutizing "the human" is already determined. (It is of lesser concern whether one thinks of the human more in terms of the heroic or of the Hasidic.) *Furthermore*, Landauer's affirmation—oriented towards the German Middle Ages[18]—of an organic community as opposed to a rational society, with [its] characteristic yet completely arbitrary reservations about everything relating to *power*, leads, if one follows the inner dynamic of what is affirmed and not Landauer's wishfulnesses [*Wünschbarkeiten*], to a decisive affirmation of the power principle. It is only the acceptance of the power principle, which is immanently required by his affirmation, that separates Landauer's "socialism" from the politicism of Blau-Weiss as it has been up to now (a politicism that is not in the least "formal"). Now that Jewish nationalism has passed into the contemporary consciousness, one is *finally* allowed to emphasize the specifically German Jewish values, precisely in the interest of Zionism. —A decisive general circumstance helping this development along consists in the fact that just as the German youth has begun to liberate itself from the hysteria of war-weariness, of defeat, and of revolution, so too has the German Jewish youth.

If, instead of latching onto sensational changes of particular individuals, one looks at the development of the whole, then one cannot fail to notice a meaningful, even unambiguous, direction of this development. If, however, one deceives oneself about this immanent tendency of meaning, which in a certain way points toward the future and thereby provides a *genuine* standard for judgment, then and only then is one forced to adopt a so-called objective standard, that is, a standard that is *alien* to the development. It is our opinion that not only is the German Jewish youth movement not lacking a meaningful direction of its own but that this meaningful direction is essentially identical with that of the German Jewish development in general. In order to have a convenient name for this direction, we propose to speak of an *"entering into reality"* [*"Einwirklichung"*],[19] that is, of the tendency to gain access to normal historical "reality" (land and soil, power and arms, peasantry and aristocracy). We see the decisive difference between Zionism and assimilation in that the latter aimed at an entering into reality of individuals only and not of the people. Hence in the final analysis Zionism does not mean a "return to the people"—this is its meaning only in contrast to the "individualism" of assimilation—but rather a return to reality, to normal political existence; and for this reason Zionism *and* assimilation indeed form a *single* front against the *galut*. If one wanted to come back to simple reality, then the world of the *galut*, the world of a "ghost-people" [*"Volksgespenst"*] emptied of reality [*Entwirklichtheit*], had to be forced open from within. This forcing was effected by liberalism through a separation of the religious and the profane, according to which the former was elevated to the distant sphere of the sermon and the divine service—in short, of ceremonies—while the sphere of the latter was flooded by German currents. If we disregard the inner preparedness for one another of both Germans and Jews that existed in the eighteenth century, and if we also disregard the deflection [*Umbiegung*] experienced by the German mind due to the influx of Jewish forces, what remains as the significant element in the German Jewish development is an ever stronger Germanization, especially in the profane realm. When German Judaism was ready to absorb everything connected with the "historical sense," the dynamics of Germanization led to the specific form of German Jewish Zionism (which is something entirely different from the "love of Zion"[20] of past generations). In this development, the Jewish religion had only the negative function of being a steady source of a certain tension and of a feeling of foreignness. The Jewish religion itself did not provide the forces that have been determining our Zionism from within. This is precisely what constitutes our present-day dilemma, namely, that *Germanization was supposed to have just the formal significance of a fortuitous path to the necessary goal of entering into reality, while, in fact, this path has deviated, and has had to deviate, from the content that alone could fill this reality;* for the attitude [*Gesinnung*] that held this content together like an iron ring, the spirit that was alive in them, was the spirit of *galut*.

A further matter is to be considered. Germanization in the profane sphere gave rise to tendencies that transformed from within the entire religiosity of German Judaism. From this religiosity the "content" received an entirely different "conception," that is, the "content" changed completely its character. (Thus, e.g., the conception regnant among the members of the Frankfurt group is identical with that of late romanticism, with characteristic deflections in the spirit of nineteenth-century "messianism," as well as in that of the complex labeled with the name of Dostoevsky.) One simply cannot absorb somewhat deeper German things without absorbing along with them, among other things, a dose of specifically Christian spirit. Further, it should be kept in mind that the internal Jewish reaction to liberalism availed itself, entirely as a matter of course, of the weapons that Christian Europe had forged, during the period of restoration[21] and even prior to it, against the spirit of the Enlightenment. Thus we see ourselves held fast on all sides in the German Jewish world in which we have grown up spiritually—and this is most especially the case if we want to hold on to our Zionism. It must be most willingly conceded to Frankfurt—and we too have thought about this every now and then—that it is imperative to get out of this world *"somehow,"* and that the demand for "Jewish content" has its moral locus in this imperative. However, they seem to believe that the content is just lying ready to be immediately grasped and correctly conceived—or have they no fear of the terrible danger of infusing into the "content" their Scheler[22] or whomever else they happen to be carrying around in their head? A little reflection on this problem is strongly urged.

Thus we maintain that there exists a German Jewish tradition, one that is not at all without merit. Measured by handed-down "content," this tradition may well signify a dilution and castration of such content, but measured by the totality of national needs it has a decidedly positive significance.

This "content" cannot simply be adopted, not only because the content is conditioned by, and supportive of, *galut* and therefore endangers our Zionism but also because inherent in this content as religious content is a definite claim to truth that is not satisfied by the fulfillment of national demands. The distinction we make here between "religious" and "national" undoubtedly contradicts ancient Jewish reality; it is the legacy of the liberal Judaism of the previous century. Nonetheless, it is presently unavoidable. For this ancient Jewish world, which was enclosed in itself, has been destroyed, and the spiritual presuppositions of life in that world have been canceled by the intrusion of modern science. It was thought possible to protect oneself against the danger of science by putting greater emphasis on the earlier efforts to "internalize" religion—indeed, by denying, on the ground of these efforts, religion's every claim to truth. However, if one tries to dissolve the entire *doctrinal* substance into substance susceptible to *interpretation*, then one attacks the innermost essence of religion. A minimal amount of doctrinal substance is completely inseparable from the essence of religion. This minimal amount of doctrinal substance is the existence of God, an existence that is entirely indifferent to human existence and human need. A meaningful observance of the laws, especially of the regulations pertaining to prayer, is possible only on the basis of a literal acknowledgment of this substance that renounces all subtilizing. It goes entirely without saying that no one who does not believe, or who does not at least have the will to believe, can say the prayers "truthfully"; certainly not someone who, as is common practice today, thoroughly undermines the spiritual presuppositions of this belief by seeing in "God" nothing but an expression for needs of the soul (especially for the "sanctification of the human being"). That religion deals *first* with "God" and *not* with the human being, that this conception is the great legacy of precisely the Jewish past—this our ancestors have handed down to us, and this we wish to hold on to honestly and clearly. It is this very precedence that is implied in the proposition that the existence of God is *not "lived,"* but rather that it is *"believed."* In the enclosed world of the past, the separation between "life" and "belief" would have been absurd. A people that, according to its tradition, became a people through God's own hand was unable to separate its life from bearing witness to its origin; this people virtually had no life without knowledge of God. If one's aim is to restore this past life, then one needs this element of knowledge just as much—no more, but also no less—as one needs all the other elements. This means: the belief that *in earlier times* was implicit in every movement of every finger *today* must be explicitly enacted.

Out of the forces supplied by assimilation there grows a will to renewal. It is apparent that neither this, nor even an adoption of the former religious "life," means that the ancient identity of people and belief has been restored. Rather, to repeat, for those who enter this context from the outside, an "explicit" act of faith must take the place of the belief in God, a belief that was self-evident to earlier generations and that was simply invested ("implicit") in their world. This act of faith is necessary even though it may pose the danger of demanding something "non-Jewish," that is, something that would have been absurd in the life of *the earlier times,* but that is unavoidable given the needs of the *contemporary* Jewish situation.

The primordial religious demand is not to believe in *"dogmas"* but to believe in a *being.* We pose the "Gretchen question,"[23] and pose it not just generally with respect to the first principle but with respect to all of the details of which our prayers speak. We contest the right, indeed we declare it a form of counterfeiting when the freedom of dealing with notions of belief that proceeds out of the wealth of *an entire enclosed world* is exploited *from the outside* as ground and legitimization for an arbitrary controlling and an arrogant interpreting of these notions. Let us not even mention the banal nonsense that believes that the national encounter [*Erlebnis*]—the humble and reverent experience of the people forces [*Volkskräfte*] that tower over us—is religion. I simply do not think that even the members of the Frankfurt group are capable of such nonsense. But it is often difficult to draw the line between the two conceptions. It seems to us that what "religion" is must be determined by the biblical sense, rather than by the linguistic usage of certain literati, and that one must say one's yes or one's no to what has been so determined. Any mixing[24] is sacrilege.

What is the use of these objections against a standpoint that, in the age of theological feminism, is so seductive and that will prevail in one way or another, killing off the hidden sting of a severe, manly doubt?[25] All that these objections are meant to do is to emphasize urgently that, concerning things religious, demands based on the needs of national life must mean just as little as demands based on the needs of the sanctification of the human being. These objections are meant to be a protest against the arrogant attempt to impose on us by diktat a definite, mystical attitude, rather than a religious one, while trying to tell us that the affirmation of this attitude requires no "belief." But just so, it unwittingly hits on the truth, for it seems in fact to be an unbelieving attitude.

Finally, let me caution against a misunderstanding: it is not our intention to raise the slightest objection against the concrete demand of the members of the Frankfurt group relating to the study of the Bible and the central position of the Sabbath. It hardly needs saying that these demands follow just as immediately from *our* conception.

NOTES

Source: "Antwort auf das 'Prinzipielle Wort' der Frankfurter," *Jüdische Rundschau* (Berlin) 28, no. 9 (30 January 1923): 45–46. *Jüdische Rundschau*, under the editorship of Robert Weltsch (from 1919 until 1938), was the official journal of the Zionistische Vereinigung für Deutschland (ZVfD).
  1. The occasion for this article was the December 1922 merger between the Zionist students' organization K.J.V. (see note below) and the Zionist youth movement Jüdischer Wanderbund Blau-Weiss, which, at its earlier 1922 Prunn convention, had been reorganized under the leadership of Walter Moses. Cf. "Verschmelzung des *K.J.V.* und des Blau-Weiß," *Jüdische Rundschau* 27, nos. 103–4 (29 December 1922): 676. The new Blau-Weiss was later described by Gershom Scholem as "semifascist." See *Von Berlin nach Jerusalem: Jugenderinnerungen* (Frankfurt: Suhrkamp, 1977), 192.
  2. K.J.V. was the Zionist German Jewish students' confederation. Cf. *EJ*, s.v. "Kartell Jüdischer Verbindungen (K.J.V.)," by Oskar K. Rabinowicz. Main member groups were Bund jüdischer Corporationen (founded in 1900) and Kartell zionistischer Verbindungen (founded in 1906), which amalgamated in 1914 with the intention of "educating its members to strive for the national unity of the Jewish community and its

renewal in Erez Israel." The main alternative to the Zionist students' movement was
the German Jewish Kartell-Convent der Verbindungen deutscher Studenten jüdischen
Glaubens (K-C), which was closely related to the Central-Verein (C-V). On the history
and ideologies of the major German Jewish organizations that were founded in the
second German Reich and dominated the institutional landscape of Jewish life in the
Weimar Republic, see Jehuda Reinharz, *Fatherland or Promised Land: The Dilemma of the
German Jew, 1893–1914* (Ann Arbor: University of Michigan Press, 1975); and cf.
Reinharz, "Three Generations of German Zionism," *Jerusalem Quarterly*, no. 9 (Fall
1978): 95–110.

   3. On Blau-Weiss and the Jewish youth movement in the 1920s, see Glenn Richard Sharfman, "The Jewish Youth Movement in Germany, 1900–1936: A Study in
Ideology and Organization" (Ph.D. diss., University of North Carolina at Chapel Hill,
1989), especially chapters 4 (on the pre–World War One history of Blau-Weiss) and 8
(Blau-Weiss as a "true minority" after the war).

   4. The Frankfurt faction *(die Frankfurter)* referred to in the text consisted of the
five cosigners of a declaration published in *Jüdische Rundschau* 27, nos. 103–4 (29 December 1922): 675–76, namely, Erich Fromm, Fritz Gothein, Leo Löwenthal, and Ernst
Simon, and Ernst Michaelis (Hamburg), who were members of Saronia, a Zionist fraternity associated with the K.J.V. It should be noted that Strauss is later mentioned as a
member of the very same fraternity. See the notes to "Comment on Weinberg's Critique" (1925).

   5. Literally *Inhalte* (contents). So also in the following. On the programmatic
ideals and the style of the Jewish *Wanderbund* see the introduction to this volume. Blau-
Weiss, which tried to maintain its character as a youth movement modeled on the
German Wandervogel, was criticized by representatives of the Zionist students' organization K.J.V. and others because it resisted the adult supervision that K.J.V. sought and
accepted. (K.J.V. was the youth wing of the German Zionist association [Z.V.f.D.],
which was a leading member of the World Zionist Federation.) On the further charge
that Blau-Weiss was lacking in Jewish content, see Sharfman, *Jewish Youth Movement,*
74, 204, 206 (Nahum Goldmann criticizing the "anti-intellectualism" of Blau-Weiss);
223 (Kurt Blumenfeld, 1922), and 226 (Gershom Scholem). In the aftermath of the
breakup of the six-week fusion of K.J.V. and Blau-Weiss, and in response to the same
charges to which Strauss is responding here, some members of Blau-Weiss openly emphasized their rejection of all Jewish tradition, a rejection culminating in a declaration of
the "Bible as worthless." See Sharfman, *Jewish Youth Movement,* 224, who sees this kind
of extreme position as not representative of the majority of Blau-Weiss. Leo Strauss's
religious position within Blau-Weiss seems that of a minority within a minority.

   6. The first chapter of Blau-Weiss constituted itself in Breslau in 1907. In 1912
this and the Berlin chapter merged in the Jüdischer Wanderbund Blau-Weiss. The
Breslau chapter, which remained the strongest group, was under religious Jewish leadership. Cf. Sharfman, *Jewish Youth Movement,* 76f.

   7. Erich Fromm, Fritz Gothein, Leo Löwenthal, Ernst Simon, and Ernst Michaelis, "Ein prinzipielles Wort zur Erziehungsfrage" *Jüdische Rundschau* 27, nos. 103–4 (29
December 1922): 675–76.

   8. Walter Moses was among the leaders who became prominent after the First

World War. He advocated a clearer public stance on Zionist goals and criticized mainstream Zionism for being lukewarm on the issue of emigration to Palestine. While ZVfD argued for a gradual separation of Jews from German culture by strengthening Jewish values, Blau-Weiss under Moses argued for the immediate establishment of a collective settlement in Palestine that was to continue German culture (Wandervogelstyle). A Blau-Weiss settlement was actually established in Palestine but soon collapsed, which led to the dissolution of Blau-Weiss in 1926. Cf. Sharfman, *Jewish Youth Movement*, 200ff. In contrast to Moses' Zionist agenda, the first generation of the leadership of Blau-Weiss (given its character as a youth movement, the members were usually in their late teens, while the leaders had to relinquish their position once they reached the age of thirty) argued for a return to Zion in a rather vague fashion that could be interpreted as referring to a collective "realization" (Buber) of true personhood that could take place somewhere near Karlsruhe just as well as in Palestine. Cf. Gershom Scholem, "Die blau-weiße Brille," *Der Jude* 1, no. 12 (March 1917): 822–25, and elsewhere (English in *On Jews and Judaism in Crisis* [New York: Schocken, 1976], 49–53), and see the introduction to this volume. It is the pre-Moses style of Blau-Weiss that Strauss associates himself loosely with in the first paragraph of the essay.

9. In 1922, Walter Moses authored a manifesto that firmly established the goals and "political" principles of Blau-Weiss; it defined its hierarchical structure as grounded in unquestioning obedience to a *Führer*. Similar to the later Betar ideology, Moses' vision of Blau-Weiss as the spearhead of Jewish emigration was modeled on the structure of an army, an analogy appealing to many youngsters who had not themselves experienced the war and who found the idea of sacrifice to be uplifting and an antidote to the self-deprecating, skeptical, and (during the inflation years) economically threatened culture of the assimilated German middle class. Cf. Sharfman, *Jewish Youth Movement*.

10. Cf. Strauss's emphasis in "The Zionism of Nordau" on Max Nordau's biosophic leanings. Much of the rhetoric of the German and the Jewish youth movements was characterized by an appeal to vitalist ideas that invoked an alternative to the rational, civil, liberal, nihilist, urbanized culture that the youth movements wanted to overcome. Cf., for example, Martin Bandmann (1923): "Our *Bund* is based on a philosophy of vitality and presents itself as a revolt against the dominance of ideology. Its ideal is the real person [*der wirkliche Mensch*] as opposed to the ideological person. Our motto is *Primum vivere deinde philosophari* [*sic*]—first to live, then to philosophize. Real people want life, ideological people want life only with conditions. . . ." Quoted in Sharfman, *Jewish Youth Movement*, 212.

11. Akiba Ernst Simon, who was the same age as Strauss (born 1899), was a reversionist Jew from an assimilated background who belonged to the inner circle around Franz Rosenzweig and Martin Buber. Like Gershom Scholem, Simon moved to Palestine in the 1920s, where he was active in educational reform. See the autobiographical sketch in Hans Jürgen Schultz, *Mein Judentum* (Berlin and Stuttgart: Kreuz Verlag, 1978), 90–102, and cf. Ernst Simon, *Brücken: Gesammelte Aufsätze* (Heidelberg: Lambert Schneider, 1965). In a letter to Simon, Rosenzweig mentions a lecture on the "theory of political Zionism" that Leo Strauss had given at the Frankfurt Lehrhaus, and asks Simon to give a lecture of his own to counterbalance the position taken by Strauss. Rosenzweig regarded the latter as a "really silly Zionism" that was not often heard at

74   Chapter 2

the Lehrhaus. Cf. Franz Rosenzweig, letter to Ernst Simon, 6 December 1924, in vol. 2 of *Briefe und Tagebücher*. ed. Rachel Rosenzweig and Edith Rosenzweig-Scheinmann (with Bernhard Casper) (The Hague: Nijhoff, 1979), 1007. See also Strauss, "Biblical History and Science," below.

12. The pointedly romanticizing usage of the term "word" in the phrase "word of principle" satirizes the Frankfurt group's *prinzipielles Wort* to which Strauss responds in this essay. But cf. also "Erkenntnisproblem," the last sentence.

13. This defense of critique/criticism that Strauss advances more broadly in "On the Argument with European Science" comes as a signal departure from the attack on critique/criticism in the dissertation on Jacobi. On *Kritik* (critique/criticism) cf. below, "The Bible Science of Spinoza, 197 n. 5.

14. This phrase echoes Nietzsche's admission to have been temporarily confused by the sickness of anti-Semitism. See Friedrich Nietzsche, *Jenseits von Gut und Böse,* # 251, in vol. 5 of *Sämtliche Werke: Kritische Studienausgabe in 15 Bänden*, ed. Giorgio Colli and Mazzino Montinari (München: DTB; Berlin and New York: Walter de Gruyter, 1980), 192f.; and cf. Yirmeyahu Yovel, *Dark Riddle: Hegel, Nietzsche, and the Jews* (University Park: Pennsylvania State University Press, 1998), 119f.

15. Kirchhain: Strauss's place of birth.

16. Gustav Landauer (1870–1919), socialist journalist and philosopher.

17. Martin Buber (1878–1965), Zionist journalist, philosopher, and theologian.

18. Among Landauer's writings is a translation of Meister Eckehart into modern German. See Landauer, *Macht und Mächte*, 2d ed. (Köln: Marcan-Block-Verlag, 1923).

19. This and similar terms derived from the word "reality" *(Wirklichkeit)* are somewhat artificial counterterms to Buber's term "realization" *(Verwirklichung)*. Thus, shortly later, Strauss introduces the term *Entwirklichtheit,* which he will use again in "The Zionism of Nordau" and in "Paul de Lagarde." One may call it a diagnostic term, expressing the lack of connection with reality that Strauss associates with *galut* (exile).

20. "Love of Zion": orig. *Zionsliebe,* German for Hebrew *hibbat tsiyon,* which is also the name of the late-nineteenth-century Eastern European Zionist movement that preceded Herzlian political Zionism.

21. *Restaurationsepoche:* period beginning with the Congress of Vienna (1814–; led by the Austrian chancellor Metternich), aiming to restore the powers removed by force in the wake of the Napoleonic Wars, along with a reorganization of the European system of states. Theorists of the restoration (among others, de Bonald, de Maistre, v. Haller, and Stahl) juxtaposed the natural, family-based social order, under the time-honored authority of church and aristocracy, to the "chimera of artificial-bourgeois" order. To the liberal republican forces seeking the establishment of national parliamentary systems (e.g., the Vormärz and Paulskirchenparlament in Germany), the period of restoration represented an age of "reaction" *(Reaktion)*. With the crisis of liberalism around the First World War, views on this period become increasingly differentiated. Source: *RGG.* Western European Jews had generally benefited from the very forces of liberalism that were rolled back after the Congress of Vienna and hence, in Jewish historiography, restoration is associated with "reaction" (outbursts of anti-Jewish sentiments such as the "HEP! HEP!" riots, the rescinding of edicts of emancipation, and the restoration of

ghettos, as in Frankfurt; hence also the vigorous alliance of Jews with the forces of republicanism in the 1848 revolutions). Cf. Simon Dubnow, *Die neueste Geschichte des jüdischen Volkes: Das Zeitalter der ersten Reaktion und der zweiten Emanzipation (1815–1881)*, trans. A. Steinberg (Berlin: Jüdischer Verlag, 1929); and Shmuel Ettinger, *Vom 17. Jahrhundert bis zur Gegenwart: Die Neuzeit*, vol. 3 of *Geschichte des jüdischen Volkes*, ed. H. H. Ben-Sasson (München: Beck, 1980), 103ff.

22. Max Scheler (1874–1928), physician and philosopher. Basing himself on Husserl's phenomenology, Scheler contributed to the turn from psychologism to a renewed affirmation of philosophical metaphysics grounded in a theory of the intuition of values. Strauss acknowledges Scheler in his dissertation. Cf. *GS*, 2:247.

23. *Gretchenfrage:* see, in Goethe's *Faust* I, Gretchen's question to Faust concerning his view on religion: "Heinrich, wie hältst du's mit der Religion?"

24. *Vermischung* (mixing): that is, any mixing of what is God with what is not God. Strauss alludes to a technical term in medieval Islamic philosophy—and, following that, Jewish philosophy (Hebr. *shittuf*)—for belief in a multitude of deities, which was also used critically against the doctrine of the Trinity.

25. "manly severe doubt" (orig. *männlich herber Zweifel*): The "manliness" and "severity" of *this* doubt is emphasized in contrast to Strauss's characterization of doubt in the dissertation on Jacobi, where doubt indicates the despised "nonaristocratic" attitude toward the world. See "Das Erkenntnisproblem in der philosophischen Lehre Fr. H. Jacobis" (*GS*, 2:246), as well as in the extract from the dissertation, translated in this volume.

The Holy (1923)

It frequently happens in the Zionist youth movement that our young students, writing in one of our journals, immediately apply to our own problems those philosophical, sociological, or historical theories which they have become acquainted with in the universities, somewhat heedless of the possible dubiousness of such applications. While this phenomenon appears at first to be merely amusing, springing as it does from a touching lack of reflectiveness [*Unreflektiertheit*],[1] it nevertheless has a serious background: in the final analysis, it mirrors the spiritual situation of German Judaism as a whole. Is this not what all theologians of German Judaism did when they transferred the values and viewpoints dominating the German environment—and thus, by extension, themselves—to the evaluation and consideration of Jewish matters? Whatever, in principle, the fundamental legitimacy of such a transfer[2]—and one may call this question of legitimacy[3] the central problem of our spiritual[4] situation—two cases [of such transfer] seem to be beyond the doubt of even the most skeptical minds.

In the first case, an ideologue of Judaism participated creatively in the formation of the German world of thought, so that Jewish forces entered the German world through him as formative elements. Hence his transfer [*Hineintragen*] of German viewpoints to Jewish matters was preceded by the assimilation[5] of the spirituality of both peoples, realized through his work. Only he who himself has built the bridges can truly judge the condition of the banks, the width and depth of the chasm, and the difficulty of bridging it; he who has merely used the bridge cannot. Regarding this case, the work of Hermann Cohen is for us the most venerable example.

The second case is no less impressive. It obtains when the German spirit, turning toward Jewish tendencies, brings them to life within itself, especially when the efficacy of such tendencies among the Jewish people has been limited or repressed due to its harsh fate. It obtains, for example, in the Protestant scholarship on the Old Testament that elucidated for us the real context from which prophecy derived. It obtains in Nietzsche's critique of culture, which strove to plumb the pre-"Christian" depths of the Jewish as well as of the Hellenic-European spirit. Finally, it also obtains in the theological investigation of Rudolf Otto, on which we will comment briefly.[i]

What is important is the viewpoint that Otto suggests for orienting the history of theology (and thus for classifying his own theological venture) in the history of ideas. We must ask in what way this viewpoint can be applied to Jewish scholarship. The answer would run as follows. The earlier theology—the most essential form of which is, for us, the doctrine of attributes of the Spanish era—had the task of facilitating the victory of the "rational" moments of religion in their struggle against the primitive-irrational ones. Now that this task has been all too completely accomplished, the duty of theology in the present is the reverse. Starting from the realm of the rational, it must advance by means of a conscientious and scientifically irreproachable presentation of the irrational to the construction of a system that is commensurate with its concern. In an earlier day, in a world filled by the irrational moment of religion, it was necessary for theology to achieve recognition for the legitimacy of the rational. Today, in a spiritual reality dominated by *ratio*, it is the office [*Amt*] of theology to bring to life for our era "the irrational in the idea of the Divine" through the medium of the theoretical consciousness. While earlier theology speculated in a religiously closed vault, the new theol-

---

[i] Rudolf Otto, *Das Heilige. Über das Irrationale in der Idee des Göttlichen und sein Verhältnis zum Rationalen* [The holy: On the irrational in the idea of the divine and its relation to the rational], 9th ed., Breslau, 1922.

ogy lives under the open sky, and must itself contribute, according to its ability, to the construction of the vault. Then, the primary fact was God; now, it is world, man, religious experience.

If one sets the task in this way, one arrives at a recognition of both the question that gave rise to the doctrine of attributes as well as of the results it obtained without the need to regard this doctrine as having already been surpassed. Otto operates with categories that permit the integration of the entire doctrine of attributes into the larger context of a new theology. We cannot help but think that the reason the doctrine of attributes has been popularly discredited is not actually the idea of the "attribute" as such, but rather the fact that attributes such as all-powerfulness, all-goodness, and so on, have become hackneyed. Nowadays, one usually invokes the "living fullness of experience," which is contrasted with the emptiness of the "attributes." Otto's investigation shows that in order to comprehend theoretically what is objective in the religious life, it is not necessary to deviate from the straight and direct view of the religious object. The rational and irrational moments are distinguished within the object itself. Within the religious object, the irrational is the "bearer," the *substance* of the rational predicates, of the *"attributes."* The irrationality religion has in mind lies not in the depths of the subject but precisely in the depths of the object. Hence we have no need of the romantic "philosophy of religion." This is where the connection is warranted with our biblical and ritual tradition, on the one hand, and with our theological tradition, on the other. The latter teaches us the general attitude of the Jewish theologian and offers us the results of analyses of the rational "attributes." The former makes available to us the most perfect expression that the substance of the religious object could possibly find "in human language." Hence it is no coincidence that Otto derives his substantial categories not least from the Old Testament and from Jewish liturgy (cf. prayers of *Yom Kippur*, p. 37f., *Melekh Elyon*, translated by Otto, pp. 238ff.).[6]

It should be mentioned, however, that Otto occasionally gives quite vivid emphasis to the opposition between religion and theology, and takes the side of religion against theology. This emphasis is legitimate when it comes to establishing the secondary character of theology, from the point of view of religion. Other than that, it is not binding on us, because Otto (as is evident mainly from his quotations) is in this respect very strongly influenced by Lutheran tendencies that cannot be decisive for us as Jews, for whom the peculiarly Protestant subjectivism must remain farfetched.

It is still possible to approach *The Holy* as a work of "philosophy of religion." However, what sets Otto's analysis apart from the common variety of philosophy of religion is that he immediately turns to the religious consciousness itself, without venturing a naturalist explanation, or even a transcendental "constitution," of this consciousness.

The great significance of Otto's book consists in the fact that it strives to limit the rational element of religion neither primarily nor exclusively by resorting to the irrationality of the "experience" [*Erlebnis*]; rather, it takes as the completely obvious point of departure the transcendence of the religious object. Whatever measure of skepticism may be justified with respect to the notion of a doctrine of attributes, this type of theology is still able to win our sympathy, if only because it makes a fundamental subjectivism impossible by the very formulation of the task. One would have to *demand* a theology in the form of a doctrine of attributes, even though it may be absolutely unfeasible, simply in order to compel from the beginning the retention of the idea of the transcendence of God as a guiding principle. Certainly, the result of Otto's investigation, even if not its intention, is a deeper understanding of the meaning of "transcendence" in the religious context. Transcendence attains the following distinctions:

1. God as being beyond *experience* [*Erlebens-Jenseitigkeit Gottes*], that is, the primacy of God over religion. If God is a being in Himself, independent of His being experienced by man, and if we know about this being from what is revealed in Torah and prophecy, then the theoretical exposition of that which is known is possible in principle, which means theology. To this extent, theology is the expression of simple and unambiguous piety.

2. God as being beyond *life* [*Lebens-Jenseitigkeit Gottes*]. This is experienced in the "creaturely feeling" of the human being, in the feeling of ourselves as "earth, ashes, and non-being," even and especially in that of the *people*, as follows from Isaiah 6.[7] It is identical with the entirely "not naturelike" character of the "wrath of God," and no less so with the character of "holiness" as a "numinous value."

3. God as being beyond the *idea* [*Ideen-Jenseitigkeit Gottes*]. The final determination in the previous paragraph could tempt one into the "idealization" of God. This danger is eliminated by a reference to the characteristic of "energy," that is, to the "vitality" of God.

NOTES

Source: "Das Heilige," *Der Jude: Eine Monatsschrift* (Berlin) 7, no. 4 (April 1923): 240–42, reprinted in *GS*, 2:307–10.
1. *Unreflektiertheit:* cf. *Reflektiertheit* in the essay on Paul de Lagarde.
2. *Hineintrage:* literally "carrying into" from one realm to another.

3. *Rechtsfrage:* German for the philosophical *quaestio iuris.*
4. *geistige Situation:* the German *geistig* (from *Geist*) refers either to the mind or to the spirit.
5. "Assimilation": Strauss uses here a literal German equivalent to assimilation, namely *Anähnlichung,* in order to avoid the negative connotations of the term in a context where he describes the phenomenon of assimilation from a value-neutral perspective.
6. For the relevant passages in *Das Heilige,* see the English translation by John W. Harvey: *The Idea of the Holy: An Inquiry into the Nonrational Factor in the Idea of the Divine and Its Relation to the Rational* (London: Oxford University Press, 1950), 70, 190. This translation, like Strauss's comments, is based on the ninth edition of 1922.
7. Isaiah 6: The theophany at the temple leads the prophet to recognize his own impurity as well as that of the people. The expression *eigene Erde-, Asche-, und Nichtsein* is not a biblical quotation, but is based on Genesis 3:19, Genesis 18:27, Job 34:15, Job 42:6, Ecclesiastes 3:20, and similar passages.

A Note on the Discussion on "Zionism and Anti-Semitism" (1923)

Motto: Joshua 9:7[1]

No fact has been more decisive for the liberation of the Jewish spirit from its *galut*-mentality [*Galuth-Gesinnung*] than that *disruption of Jewish solidarity* which found its most popular expression in Herzl's "Mauschel."[2] It may even be said that the discontinuation of this social condition of our *galut* existence [*Galuth-Dasein*][3] is a symptom of the discontinuation of the very mentality that is supportive of the *galut.* Be that as it may, it is only with the revolutionary change to which we just alluded that the discussion of anti-Semitism has begun—at least with respect to the Western Jews—to become *"decent"* (in Herzl's sense of the word). Yet this condition which concerns the mentality alone is by no means sufficient. It is hardly an exaggeration to say that the level of the anti-Semitic argumentation of a man such as Paul de Lagarde[4]— he too, of course, entangles himself every now and then in expressions of malice—has not even been reached in Zionism. To be sure, the problems that arise here are of no use to the practice of apologetics, which is rather satisfied with simpler and coarser things, preferably with figures and charts. The best influence that anti-Semitism could exercise on our national life is, of course, lost as a result of this limitation.

We therefore refrain from entering into the problem of the inner justification of the existence-as-citizens [*Staatsbürger-Dasein*] of the German Jews. It would be quite difficult to provide such a justification, at least for someone

who does not really believe in the ideals of 1789—the ideals that, as is well
known, largely gave rise to emancipation; but it suffices that this existence-
as-citizens rests on current law, and that the circle of rights and duties determined by it has been drawn in an essentially unambiguous way. To put it as
a formula:[i] existence-as-citizen demands loyalty to the German state as well
as (although this may sound high-flown and impolitic) love of the German
people. Without the latter it is simply inconceivable: love and love alone can
bridge the national gap in such a way as to make political action possible.
Even if German Jewry possessed sufficient means of power, and had attain-
able irredentist goals in mind, it is not a minority in the sense of constitutional
law, nor a national minority in the political sense, and so cannot insist on
national minority rights at the expense of the state and the nation [*Staatsvolk*].

The rights that German Jewry possesses in Germany are the rights of
individuals possessing German citizenship, as well as the rights carried over, in
part, under the title of a *"confession"* [*"Konfession"*] into the administrative
practice of the new state from the old Christian state.

By conferring on us the rights of citizens, the German people has demonstrated its confidence in us. We are able to safeguard our political and
economic interests as individuals, and to look after our group interests (which,
to be sure, are essentially limited to concerns of education) as a matter of
religious (even though private) freedom, and thereby to exert influence on
the direction of German politics in a way that is commensurate with our
strength. It would be disloyal and contrary to the behests of conscience if one
were to believe that one may influence and exploit German politics for the
sake of Jewish interests. We German Jews received the rights of citizens only
on the basis of repeated express assurances given by the protagonists of our
emancipation that we maintain no national connection other than to the
German nation. And even though we regard the denial of the Jewish national
connection as unjustified and illicit, surely we must also further draw the
*practical conclusions from this denial, which was the conditio sine qua non for our civic
emancipation*. This means, however: in our political activity as German citizens, we must not allow ourselves to be diverted from the line of German
politics by any national Jewish interests (with the exception of those understood and granted under the title of a "confession").

As for our collective rights (as a "confession"), these concern areas of our
national interest in which the Germans have declared their disinterest. Of

---

[i] Everything that is said here of the German Jew relates, of course—as the title
states—only to the Jew whose orientation is nationally Jewish. (The Author).

course, we are free to elaborate them in a national direction, inwardly liberated from confessional narrowness, as long as our elbow room is not enlarged at the expense of the host people. Here we are our own masters as we have always been, and as we will continue to be as long as Bolshevism does not overrun the West.

All this makes it abundantly clear that an infinitely high measure of reflection is required of the national Jew who wants to participate in the political life of Germany. Any naïve politicizing on his part drives him easily to confuse the Jewish with the German interest, as well as the Jewish— specifically[5] the *galut*-Jewish—idea of political life with the corresponding German one. (Consider, among other things, marriage laws, the death penalty, prohibition, etc.). Specifically, it drives him to fight those political circles that had taken a skeptical stance toward the emancipation of the Jews even when it comes to political decisions that are entirely unrelated to this issue. May I remind you of the storm against the "war psychosis," which a great many Germans call the "spirit of August 1914," and which unfortunately found its way even into the editorials of national Jewish papers.

The advocacy of Jewish national interests on the basis of our constitutional rights as German citizens is legally unjustified. To advocate these interests "surreptitiously," by means of parties and organizations, is contrary to the nature of the Zionism that derives from Herzl. Anyone to whom this solution seems unworthy should consider whether it is not more worthy to relinquish a claim openly and honestly if one lacks the factual, legal, and moral presuppositions for its verification, rather than to maintain it for reasons of prestige or even out of fear. Anyone to whom this solution seems narrow and imperfect should be reminded of the saying of Ahad Ha'am[6] to the effect that the perfect solution to this question, as to all questions of the *galut*, has to be sought beyond the limits of the *galut*.

NOTES

Source: "Anmerkung zur Diskussion über 'Zionismus und Antisemitismus'," *Jüdische Rundschau* 28, nos. 83/84 (28 September 1923): 501. Now also in *GS*, 2:311–13. In the original, an editorial paragraph is added by the editors of *Jüdische Rundschau* expressing a disagreement with Strauss:

We publish the following essay, which does not aspire to more than being a "remark on the *discussion*" of the topic. It should be noted, however, that in our view the demands that the German *people* (not just the state) have been making on us and that any serious national-Jewish politician has to deal with should be derived not just from an abstractly construed "promise" made at the time of emancipation, but from reality.]

1. Joshua 9:7 (JPS version): "And the men of Israel said unto the Hivites: 'Peradventure ye dwell among us; and how shall we make a covenant with you?'" And cf. Deuteronomy 7:2, "and when the Lord thy God shall deliver them up before thee, and thou shalt smite them [i.e., the Hivites among them]; then thou shalt utterly destroy them; thou shalt make no covenant with them, nor show mercy unto them."

2. Under this title, Theodor Herzl (1860–1904), published a vitriolic essay in the newspaper of the World Zionist Organization, *Die Welt* (vol. 20, 15 October 1897), attacking the clientele of wealthy Jews who refused to back him financially. *Mauschel* (derived from the Western Ashkenazic pronunciation of the name Moses, *Mauscheh*) was a derogatory term for Jews and their German Jewish idiom *(Judendeutsch)*, and, in colloquial German, today still refers to indistinct speech (to mumble), to dishonesty in business (to cheat), or to a specific card game. By using this anti-Semitic term, and by bringing this internal Jewish fight into the public arena, Herzl broke two major taboos of what Strauss calls the mentality of the exile *(galut)*. Strauss may be implying here that, by breaking these taboos and by thus establishing an internal Jewish division between friend and foe, Herzl inadvertently achieved a new level of politicization of Jewish affairs. On Herzl's "Mauschel" see Theodor Herzl, *Zionist Writings: Essays and Addresses,* ed. and trans. Harry Zohn (New York: Herzl Press, 1973), 1:163–65; and cf. Ernst Pawel, *The Labyrinth of Exile: A Life of Theodor Herzl* (New York: Farrar, Straus, Giroux, 1989), 345–46, and Jacques Kornberg, *Theodor Herzl: From Assimilation to Zionism* (Bloomington: Indiana University Press, 1993), 164, 219 n. 35. (I thank Ken Green for these references.) In the jargon of the German Zionist students, *Mauschel* referred to the anti-Zionist faction among the German Jews, that is, to those represented in the Central-Verein. So, for example, in Paul Hirsch, "Fehldiagnose, weil Ferndiagnose," *Der jüdische Student* 18, no. 5 (September–October 1921): 242.

3. Parallel to this construction is the expression *Staatsbürger-Dasein*, forming two distinct forms of Jewish existence, namely, that of existing in exile and existing as the (emancipated) citizen of a state. In the view of the Zionist, neither one is ultimately legitimate or even sustainable. The point of the "Remark" is to emphasize the importance of recognizing the unsustainability of illegitimate strategies of Zionist agitation that are rooted in a *galut* mentality, a fact that, if only one were able to read it properly (as Strauss understands it), is revealed in anti-Semitic polemic.

4. See the essay on Paul de Lagarde in this volume. It must have been fairly shocking to the readers of Strauss, then a novice author, when he praised the anti-Semite Lagarde as well as Herzl at his worst.

5. In the original publication, the word *Militarismus* appears between *speziell* and *galuth-jüdische*. With Meier (*GS,* 2:313, 2: 618), we regard the word *Militarismus* in this sentence as out of place.

6. Ahad Ha'am, originally: Asher Hirsch Ginsberg, 1856–1927, Hebrew essayist, leader of the Hibbat Tsiyyon movement and main voice of "cultural Zionism."

The Zionism of Nordau (1923)

It is the view of political Zionism that the plight of the Jews [*Judennot*] can only be alleviated by the establishment of a Jewish state, by the consolidation of the power of Jewish individuals into the power of the Jewish people. In pursuit of this end, Herzl played off the power of the moneyed Jews (not at all a Jewish power as such) against the political powers, and, on the other hand, he played off the political legitimization of his project by the Great Powers, who in matters of political significance were the only decisive element, against the Jews. Neither of these factors was really under his control. But as he played them off against one another, the politically amorphous power of Jewish individuals solidified into a political will, into the political significance of the Jewish people.

While thoroughly approving of this goal, Nordau rejects Herzl's means as "underhanded" [*"hinterhältig"*]. He wants the power, but he rejects intrigue as a means of obtaining power. He wants the power, but he calls for the admission that, at this time, we have no control over any power. *Thus he brings about the transition from political to spiritual Zionism,*[1] which makes a principle of the Jewish people's powerlessness—indeed, of its aversion to power.

The motive for this falling away from Herzl is itself already a spiritual one: "honesty." We know that the Zionism of Herzl was itself essentially determined by impulses of decency and loyalty. But Herzl knew all too well that, in politics, to speak of truth or untruth is ambiguous. Politics must create realities, and under certain circumstances the most effective and most likely means to succeed in creating realities is to pass off preconditions as having already been fulfilled, and thus to evoke the necessary efforts. This is particularly true in the case of preconditions of a moral nature that are brought about only by great efforts that the dull masses are reluctant to make. Today's untruth, perhaps precisely by being passed off as truth today, may actually become tomorrow's truth. The sky blue of the Zionist optimism of Herzl was, in good part, conditioned by the considerations of an agitator. Nordau put into circulation the fairy tale of Herzl's enthusiastic trust in his people, a fairy tale in which he himself did not believe, so that in this quite drastic way he could substantiate the betrayal by the Jewish people of its leader: in other words, he did so for political reasons.

We learn something about Nordau's judgment of Herzl from Herzl's comments in his diaries, in a form unrefracted by the purposes of agitation. "Nordau finds me insincere and underhanded in my dealings with princes and with the Jewish people. I think that one day he will make public this reproach of his, and thereby disgrace himself, me, and all of us" (III 63). The diaries show that this "underhandedness" constitutes the essence of Herzlian politics. Nordau recognizes this tendency; he condemns it, and calls for a politics of trust. Thus, for example, instead of the *negotiorum gestio* of the dictator Herzl, Nordau calls for a democratic authorization and supervision of the leader (*Tagebücher* II, p. 251f.). He does not merely call for these politics, he enacts them to the detriment of Zionism and to the great vexation of Herzl. On the occasion of a speech by Nordau, Herzl notes:[i] "He made entirely unjustified advances to socialism, exposed all of our weaknesses, reported on our helplessness, etc." (*Tagebücher* II, p. 258). The sympathy for socialism as well as the antipathy for secret diplomacy have the same root, and lead in the direction of dissolving the major contours of Herzlian politics, which has a tendency that is conservative and thoroughly "conducive to the maintenance of the political order" [*"staatserhaltend"*].

In the statements about Herzl in Nordau's *Zionist Writings* no trace can be found of the reproach that must have been uttered more than once in person. On the contrary! "My heart aches, when I trace his nine-year-long path of suffering, to see him grope with wounded hands through the thorns and thistles of reality, *confused as in a fog by his beautiful trust in the Jews*" (*Zionistische Schriften*, p. 160). Perhaps Nordau wrote this sentence—which, incidentally, is typical of his flowery, or rather weedy, style—for poetic reasons, and that may account for the tastelessness of the expression. Or he may have written it for reasons of agitation, as an appeal to the Jewish heart, which is always susceptible to an appeal to innocent suffering and disappointed idealism. Otherwise, this sentence is as incomprehensible as it is, in any case, absurd. Much the same can be said about Nordau's claim that Herzl was dominated by the image of "twelve million noblemen standing behind him," or about the utterance made under the immediate impression of Herzl's death: Herzl's "exquisite sensitivity made him the originator and leader of Zionism." If today Herzl appears to many as a long-suffering visionary in Israel (cf. the recent apotheosis by Emil Cohn),[2] it is largely Nordau who is to blame for it. While posing as an admirer, he diminished Herzl. He contributed much to the frustration of Herzl's original impulses by explaining the greatness of Herzl to himself and to the Jewish people in sentimental categories. This was all the more deplorable because, in terms of its ideology and hence

---

[i] As proofs for the correctness of Herzl's judgment see especially Nordau's address to the Eighth Congress (*Zionistische Schriften*, pp. 174–87) and his speech in Amsterdam (op. cit., pp. 288–311).

also in other respects, Zionism failed from the outset to reach the level intended by Herzl. It is with full intention that Herzl limited himself to an argumentation that was both more accessible and more immediately effective. Nordau remained on this lower level and, compared to Herzl, managed to move on it with no less skill and zeal, and with greater subtlety.

"Zionism, like any historical movement, emerged from a strongly felt and clearly recognized need, the need for a normal existence under natural conditions" (*Zionistische Schriften*, p. 178). *For Nordau, Zionism is a product of the newly acquired sense of reality, which had been lacking in the previous eras of galut and assimilation.*

In the *galut*, the Jewish people lived as a *Luftvolk*[3]—it lacks the ground beneath its feet in both the literal and the figurative senses, and it depends on all of the contingencies of the behavior of other peoples. In this condition life is sustained by a strong will to existence. All ideas and all forms of Judaism are unconsciously in the service of preserving the national existence as well as heightening the will to existence. The ideas of Chosenness and of the Messiah uphold under all circumstances the faith in the possibility and necessity of holding out the faith in a national future. On the other hand, by aiming at what is miraculous, at what is unattainable by human effort, these same ideas prevent that faith from leading to action. All Jewish customs and ways serve the purpose of segregation from the peoples, hence they are in the service of preserving the national existence; on the other hand, by keeping [the people] away from the conditions of normal life of a people, they prevent this very life. The absence of a political center has the same effect: the Jewish people cannot be annihilated at any one spot—and, on the other hand, just for that reason all comprehensive political action is impossible. This, therefore, is *the essence of galut: it provides the Jewish people with a maximal possibility of existence by means of a minimum of normality.* In the long run, the lack of natural conditions of existence was bound to ruin our people. Persecutions could have such terrible effects only because the people, lacking natural conditions of existence, also lacked the possibilities for a real recovery and a real uplift. In the *galut*, Zionism and messianism coincide, inasmuch as the return to Palestine is expected to be the work of the Messiah, something miraculous and to-be-prayed-for, something not to be prepared for rationally. This coupling with messianism, which empties Zionism of its reality [*entwirklichend*],[4] was removed only by assimilation. Nordau does not feel grateful. Assimilation separated the two ideas from one another in order to facilitate the easy death of the Jewish people in Europe by abandoning Zionism and watering down messianism into missionism.[5] *Assimilation has basically no other motive than the egoism of Western Jewish individuals. It worsens the illusionism of the galut,* expressed in the belief in the "mystical" redemption by the Messiah, *by secularizing the ideas of the galut* that, for all their mysticism, had a very sober vital function. Assimilation takes away from the Jews the self-assurance of ghetto life, and gives them instead the illusionary surrogate of trust in the humanity of civilization. Its politics, not unlike that of the *galut*, is limited to the needs of the moment. But it is less useful inasmuch as it completely deludes itself about the attitude of the host nations, believing that the Jewish question can be resolved once and for all by shutting one's eyes to it. It is nothing but a "sacrifice of fidelity, of dignity, of historical consciousness."

This was the sacrifice Western Judaism brought to its emancipation. The basis of this emancipation was the doctrinairism of the French Revolution, which deduced the necessity for the emancipation of the Jews from a syllogism. However, precisely as a result of the French Revolution and the strengthening of the civilizing tendencies that derived from it, national antagonisms showed themselves all the more sharply—quite the opposite of the good-natured hopes of liberal Judaism.

The emancipation emerged from a change that took place solely in the non-Jewish world. This change was a move in the direction of absolute ideas (humanity, de-confessionalized religiosity), which were intelligible to all human beings, and hence also to the Jews. This secularization of Christian ideas is, to Nordau, as self-evident and rationally necessary as the secularization of Jewish ideas in missionism is "foolish and presumptuous." Apparently the idea of chosenness, even in a castrated state, possesses a significantly lesser degree of rationality than the idea of universalism in the sense of the Christian enlightenment.

Zionism retains the separation, effected by assimilation, between Zionism and messianism, between national, worldly ends and spiritual means—but it abandons messianism. In opposition to assimilation's will to perish, it goes back to the *galut's* will to live. Nordau rebukes assimilation for its abandonment of Zionism,[ii] but he does not acknowledge that, in a deeper sense, this previously mentioned separation prepared the ground for Zionism. Indeed, just as he viewed the assimilatory-emancipatory development as conditioned only by the non-Jewish world, so he is forced to regard Zionism as the product of the non-Jewish phenomena of nationalism and anti-Semitism. For this reason, he fails to achieve an understanding of the internal legitimacy, the Jewish

---

[ii] The term "Zionism" is used by Nordau in two different senses that are impossible to confuse with one another.

necessity, of a Jewish development that is influenced by and learns from European nationalism and anti-Semitism.

At this point, we should consider two things. *First*, we see how Zionism continues and heightens the de-Judaizing tendency of assimilation; it does so, more precisely, for the sake of its struggle against the illusionism, the lack of grounding in reality [*Entwirklichtheit*][6] of the *galut*, which it recognizes in the missionism of the assimilation. *Second*, Nordau's critique of emancipation displays something typical of current Zionism, namely, the coexistence of a naïve Enlightenment faith in the ideals of 1789 and a realistic skepticism concerning their actual significance for the Jewish question. In Nordau, just as much as in Herzl, the sober kernel of Zionism emerges once the shell of the lofty ideals of the French Revolution, which are self-evident to both assimilation and Zionism, is peeled away.

Zionism is a child of the nineteenth century. Instead of the "volcanic" conception of Jewish history, which orients itself by the great national catastrophes, Nordau demands a "Neptunian," less melodramatic conception, which sees in the accumulation of minor political and economic facts[7] the cause of large revolutionary changes. Both the plight of the Jews and its alleviation lose all semblance of the miraculous. We are not dealing any more with the coming of the Messiah but with "a long, difficult, common effort" of the Jewish people. In Zionist matters, theology has no say; Zionism is purely political. The most general philosophical foundations are supplied by a biologically grounded ethics. The question of whether it is legitimate to apply this standpoint to the Jewish question does not arise: This is the voice of a science that is free of presuppositions [*voraussetzungslose Wissenschaft*]! If we disregard the question of legitimacy, it is true that, once one has replaced teleology with causalism in regard to the organic, one is also predisposed to replace missionism with the demands of national needs. What we are dealing with is yet another example of the general rule that change in the motives of German Jewish (generally: Western Jewish) intellectual life is a function of change in the motives of European intellectual life.

The close relation to biology characterizes the Zionism of Nordau just as much as the enthusiasm for technology characterizes the Zionism of Herzl. To put it bluntly, Herzl has the attitude of the northern German engineer—"With our technological achievements, we'll get the job done"—whereas Nordau has the attitude of Homais the apothecary,[8] who puts his famous scientific knowledge in the service of the public by engaging in the improvement of cider making, while constantly emphasizing his virtue.

Assimilation denied the existence of the Jewish question while Zionism acknowledges it. One might surmise that this acknowledgment belongs to that series of endeavors of the nineteenth century that addressed all "questions" resulting from the problematization of self-evident facts of life (i.e., the death penalty question, the school question, the religious question, the sexual question, etc.). This nuance in the treatment of the Jewish question is also present in Nordau, which should come as no surprise in a student of Lombroso,[9] and in the author of a book entitled *The Conventional Lies of Civilized Humanity*.[10] However, he goes further. He has the contemporary sympathy for the helots and the corresponding indignation at the Spartans. But it is self-evident for him that one must replace the helotry of assimilation with the Spartan spirit of Zionism. This, however, is none other than the consequence that follows for ethics, and hence also for Jewish politics, from the displacement of teleologism by the more manly causalism.

NOTES

Source: "Der Zionismus bei Nordau," *Der Jude: Eine Monatsschrift* (Berlin) 7, nos. 10–11 (October–November 1923): 657–60, reprinted in *GS*, 2:315–21. As Strauss indicates in a footnote, this relates to Max Nordau, *Zionistische Schriften*, 2d enl. ed. (Berlin: Jüdischer Verlag, 1923).

Max Nordau (originally: Simon Maximilian Südfeld), 1849–1923, physician, journalist, and critical essayist. He met his Hungarian compatriot Theodor Herzl in Paris in 1892, and eventually assumed the responsibility of vice president of the Zionist congresses. After Herzl's death in 1904, Nordau broke with the "practical Zionists" who took over the organization and whose goal it was to settle in Palestine even without first obtaining the political guarantees of the Great Powers. After 1911, Nordau, whose oratory on the Jewish question had fired up the earliest congresses, no longer participated in these meetings. The occasion for Strauss's essay was Nordau's death on 23 January 1923, in Paris. Cf. Michael Stanislawski, *Zionism and the Fin de siècle: Cosmopolitanism and Nationalism from Nordau to Jabotinsky* (Berkeley: University of California Press, 2001).

1. *geistiger Zionismus: geistig* means "mental" (where *Geist* refers to "mind"), "intellectual" (where it refers to the activity of the mind), or "spiritual" (where *Geist* refers to the "spirit"). To avoid the possible religious connotations of the latter, one might prefer "intellectual Zionism" to "spiritual Zionism." Yet the reference to "honesty" in the following shows that Strauss sees Nordau's intellectual home in the context of "cultural Zionism," which is not so much an intellectual movement as it is a hybrid of cultural/intellectual and religious traditions. One of Strauss's intellectual projects (fueled by an intellectual honesty all his own)— that is, the project to distinguish between the intellectual/cultural and the religious—has its origin right here: in their hybridization in the concrete case of Zionism. Herzl's revolutionary achievement (at least as it is understood in the school of Vladimir Jabotinsky to which the early Strauss belonged) consisted in the politicization of the Jews, a cause that Strauss sees here as betrayed by

Nordau. Strauss generalizes this insight when he insists that the political constitutes a sphere in its own right to which religious or intellectual motifs/motivations attach only secondarily. In method, his work, here as elsewhere, is "archaeological" in that it identifies "secondary uses" of (intellectual and spiritual) materials and, based on such identification, reconstructs their original locus.

    2. Emil Cohn, *Judentum: Ein Aufruf an die Zeit* (München: Verlag Georg Müller, 1923. In the same issue of *Der Jude* (vol. 7, April 1923), Franz Rosenzweig published a review, entitled "Ein Rabbinerbuch," of Emil Cohn's book. See Rosenzweig, *Zweistromland: Kleinere Schriften zu Glauben und Denken*, ed. Reinhold Mayer and Annemarie Mayer (Dordrecht and Boston: Martinus Nijhoff, 1984), 671–76, 858.

    3. *Luftvolk:* literally, a "people living on/in the air." Derived from the more common expression *Luftmensch*, that is, someone living on air.

    4. The term Strauss uses here is *entwirklichend*. Cf. similarly *Entwirklichtheit* in "Response to Frankfurt's 'Word of Principle'" and in "Paul de Lagarde."

    5. "Missionism" refers to a common ideological tenet of nineteenth-century Jewish theology, especially of Reform Judaism—namely, to the idea that it is the "mission" of Israel to disseminate ethical monotheism. Cf. Michael A. Meyer, *Response to Modernity: A History of the Reform Movement in Judaism* (New York and Oxford: Oxford University Press, 1988), 137f.

    6. *Entwirklichtheit:* see four paragraphs earlier: "entwirklichende Verkopplung des Zionismus mit dem Messianismus," and cf. in the essay on Paul de Lagarde, where Strauss introduces the noun *Entwirklichtheit* as "an almost impossible" coinage of his own, whereas here (in an earlier publication) he uses it without apology.

    7. In *Der Jude* 7 (1923): 660: "summierenden und politischen wirtschaftichen" (*sic*). We follow Meier's emendation in *GS*, 2:320: "summierenden politischen und wirtschaftlichen." The major nineteenth-century source for a conception of history that emphasized the significance of the *petits faits significatifs* was Hippolyte Taine.

    8. Homais: a character in Flaubert's *Madame Bovary*. I thank Ken Green for pointing me to this source.

    9. Cesare Lombroso (1835–1909), Italian. Beginning with *L'uomo delinquente* (1876), Lombroso interpreted data of craniology, physiognomy, and other now largely discredited forms of phrenology in evolutionary terms and determined the nature of criminal behavior as a biologically conditioned atavism. Because of their direct impact on the nature of crime, prevention, and punishment, his studies were widely influential at his time among criminologists and jurists and helped to inaugurate the field of criminal anthropology. Nordau and Lombroso exchanged signed presentation copies of their works and enjoyed a close rapport. Nordau's main work, *Die konventionellen Lügen der Kulturmenschheit* (Leipzig: Elischer, 1883), is dedicated to Lombroso, while the latter dedicated *Le Crime: Causes et Remedés* (Paris: F. Alcan, 1907) to Nordau with the words: "que vous dédie, comme le frère le plus aimé et le plus puissant." The friendship also extended to Lombroso's daughters, Paola and Gina.

    10. *The Conventional Lies of Civilized Humanity* is a translation of *Die konventionellen Lügen der Kulturmenschheit* (1883). The published English translation renders the title somewhat inaccurately as *The Conventional Lies of Our Civilization*.

Paul de Lagarde (1924)

The Jew is in need of an extraordinary measure of reflectiveness [*Reflektiertheit*]; while for the peoples of the world[1] a distance is given from the start, he must first attain it by a great effort. This reflectiveness is especially characteristic of the Zionist. Our "renaissance" is not a blossoming of naïve forces, but the effort and achievement of the Jewish mind [*Geist*] in rendering itself problematic.[2] It has its origin in the will; it is a morally conditioned phenomenon. If justice is the capacity to be able to see oneself, if need be, through the eyes of the other, then the Zionist's concern with the ways and means by which the Jewish essence [*das jüdische Wesen*] is mirrored in the mind of other peoples is an act of national justice that is likely to be more than its own reward. We shall look at Paul de Lagarde's position on the affairs of the Jewish nation from this point of view.

The intellectual context in which Lagarde consciously positions himself is that of the struggle for a "Greater Germany" against Prussia,[3] of the historical school against the Hegelians.[4] But Lagarde is far from being a romantic.

In order to avoid such stale expressions as "rationalism" or "mechanism," which now no longer convey anything intelligible, we would like to start from the decisive characterization of the nineteenth century as one of probity[5] and somberness [*redlich-düster*]. This character becomes apparent in the struggle against so-called epigonism [*Epigonentum*] that preoccupies the entire middle of the century. This struggle brought together in contention two camps that are separated by a great psychological distance. The members of one come by their somberness and probity *naturally*, out of a powerful tradition, while the members of the other group, yearning for the "Great Life" [*"Großes Leben"*], come by their somberness and probity *out of resignation* in the face of the bourgeois-proletarian-Cossack future of Europe. The former, essentially a group of "enlighteners," in an advanced stage of de-romanticization, appear as the "romantics" only because their work preserves a romantic heritage. Lagarde belongs to the second group.

In Lagarde, the ideas of "life," "development," "individuality," "formation" [*"Gestaltung"*], and "peoplehood" [*"Volkheit"*] appear in a moralistic coloring. Life has its origin, its center of gravity, in the *task* of life [*Lebensaufgabe*]. This life, this unfolding of individual forces of life, is a *duty*, not at all in the sense of a duty to the "Great Life," but in the sense of a duty distinguished by "hard work," by humility and devotion to the cause: the life of the scholar, the officer, the peasant. This is a Hohenzollern concept of life, not a Medici-Bourbon-Hapsburg one. "We [Germans] are not equipped for hero worship." In spite of his leaning toward the Germanic-Christian Middle Ages, Lagarde is a modern. He contrasts the *monasticism* of Catholicism with *work* as the evangelical stance: this is more important than all the romanticizing sympathy with celibacy and the mass, with the worship of the Virgin Mary and of the saints. Modern science destroyed the foundations of the medieval world, to which belong such things as the Ptolemaic system, and it was right to do this because these foundations did not stand up under *scientific examination*. It is *truthfulness* that demands the abandonment of the Orthodox doctrine about the way in which the biblical books came into being. In short, probity, the will to work, and frugality are the virtues that Lagarde praises most highly and most frequently.

The background for this ideal of life is an ascetic, spiritual religion. "Religion is never related to nature; it arises and develops within the human community." Natural religion is a secondary integration of nature into the human context, the only context of religious relevance: no man cometh unto the Father, but by the Son. The deep-seated union between this asceticism with the strongest emphasis on, and affirmation of, the spiritual-corporeal [*geist-leiblich*] character of everything human is surely typical of the epoch of Protestantism that preceded cultural Protestantism [*Kulturprotestantismus*].[6]

For Lagarde, religion is the belief in the tendency toward the better that is inherent in human life, allied with the humble and serious endeavor to better oneself. This tendency is not just identical with "morality": it is the will to mastery of the innermost life, of the individual center of meaning, of the "spirit" over the facts of the "flesh."

A coherent version of this doctrine turns up for the first time in the gospel. The content of Jesus' preaching is "the exposition of the laws of spiritual life." It contains nothing that could not also have been gathered from life by means of induction. Dogmatics has the task of presenting systematically the laws that were found "by means of the religious genius" by the author of Christianity.

Compared with Jesus' teaching, the church is something essentially new, something essentially *more*. The person of Jesus is the most perfect fulfillment of the demands of his teaching. The historical impression of the life and death of Jesus, of the lives of the apostles, martyrs, and saints enters into the church as a real factor. Thus history has a place alongside dogmatics, and revealed religion has a place alongside the religion of reason. In the language of the eighteenth century, the truths of revelation are not added to the truths of reason, but rather the truths of reason reach their full meaning only in actual religion. The truths of reason are in need of a completion, not by other truths of another value, but rather by the context whose abbreviation and reflection they are.

A history that has as its subject the Christian life must be critical history. If the Christian life were the immediate and direct continuation and unfolding of the teaching and life of Jesus, and thus if the gospel were the center of meaning for the entire development of the church, in the sense that all spiritual property would, so to speak, acquire its evangelical place immediately upon its reception, then the question of whether or not this spiritual property previously belonged to a heterogeneous context, and whether or not it lost its original meaning by virtue of its evangelization, would remain peripheral. This question would, at most, be of antiquarian interest, but definitely not of religious interest. Given, however, that diverting and disturbing influences impeded the unfolding of the evangelical truth in the Christian life, it is necessary, in order to know the pure teaching of the gospel, that these influences be separated from the original: critical history is needed. *Theology as a historical discipline becomes a desideratum of religion.*

The Protestant character of the argument is unmistakable precisely by reason of its turning primarily against Protestantism. For what was it that Luther did? Originally he was solely concerned with remedying certain abuses of the Catholic Church, within the framework and in the service of this church.[7] The merely ad hoc formulations were soon generalized in almost absurd ways and, when it came to the break with Rome, the hardly touched structure of Catholic dogma was provisionally patched up with the Reformational loci.[8] Thus, from the very beginning, the Protestant Church was not viable. Protestant Germany owes its religious life not to the existence of the Protestant Church, but to the removal of certain impediments of the Catholic Church. For the return to the gospel, to which Luther saw himself compelled, remained a half-measure because the gospel was identified with the New Testament. The New Testament was itself a product of the church; hence it was itself, in part, determined by all those defects and lapses in understanding of the actual meaning of the gospel that were already characteristic of the early period of the church. Thus, it too must be analyzed critically. In this process, one hits on a whole series of such fundamental lapses in understanding.

First of all, there is the dogmatic hardening of the "poetry" of the gospel: the hardening of the divine sonship of all human beings into the dogma of the only begotten Son, and then the hardening of the superiority of the spirit over death into the dogma of the resurrection of the Lord.

The most far-reaching consequences resulted from Paulinism: in the person of Paul, Judaism—of which, as a matter of principle and pronouncement, the gospel is the antithesis (because Judaism is essentially Pharisaism)—gained mastery over the gospel. It is Jewish "to regard as the object of religious feelings what happened once instead of what always happens anew, what is past instead of present."[9] What the fulfillment of the Law from Sinai, immutable and given once and for all times, is to Judaism, the belief in the unique event of the Crucifixion and in the unique event of the Resurrection of Jesus Christ is to Pauline Christianity. In both cases religion is the attitude toward something finished, rigid, and objective, which is the exact opposite of evangelical piety and Germanic inwardness [*Innerlichkeit*].

This should suffice to clarify the motives and the perspective by which Lagarde would have been led to concern himself with Judaism even if there were no "Jewish question" in Germany.

What is essential in the Old Testament is not monotheism, but rather "the great acquisitions of the pious soul, which have found their expression in words such as holy, righteous, humble, and the like." The value of Judaism consists neither in the veneration of the "Eternal One, that idol of papier-mâché that serves as a room decoration,"[10] nor in the ostensible representation of the principles of humanity, but rather in "that the Jews wanted to fulfill God's commandments under all circumstances, therein consisted their strength"; not in the ostensibly lofty social ethics, but in "the poetry of the Jewish cult."[11]

The prophets apply to the life of the people the standard of the task God set for them. Thus they come into conflict with the national-liberal patriots and statesmen who, instead of worrying about the harm done to Joseph, are driven by their vanity into world politics. The national arrogance of Israel and Judah brings about the loss of the state: the people had rejected its God and chosen idols. From now on, it is eliminated from historical development.

The will to life of the people preserves it after its political destruction. From the heterogeneous remnants of the previous era, Ezra constructs the building of postexilic Judaism. The turbid mass out of which he brews his theocratic system acquires its external form through its exclusiveness, and achieves its internal firmness through the defense against the assault of Antiochus Epiphanes. But the people purchases its continued existence only at the price of the renunciation of great values. What it can no longer do itself, the deeply despised Gentiles must do for it: the Law makes life possible only as a result of the "ever available Gentile complement." Lagarde judges no differently than his contemporaries Nietzsche, Mommsen, and Wellhausen.[12] "[T]he priests of the Temple in Jerusalem, concerned with establishing YHWH's kingdom on earth, were burdened with none of the difficult and serious responsibilities of a self-sufficient community" (Mommsen).

Ever since, Judaism has been essentially pharisaic, eliciting "mockery and disgust from all who came into contact with it." Ancient Israel never had to suffer from such hatred. And why not? Because it was naïve. The "fanatic aversion" for Judaism is directed against its artificiality, its homunculus-like existence. The peoples of the world had to perceive it as scandalous when "the impudent people," relieved as they were of all real tasks by the alien state, "nevertheless acted as if they had no need of it" (Nietzsche).

The characteristic features of Judaism are its being devoid of reality [*Entwirklichtheit*][13] and its "materialism." What Lagarde understands as Jewish materialism is the putting of the law before the spirit, of the finished matter before the process, and of culturedness [*Gebildetheit*] before the acquisition of culture [*Bildung*]. In the community that is materialistic and devoid of reality, and as its antithesis, there arises in the line of the prophets Jesus; he contrasts the election of Israel with the divine sonship of all human beings, the synagogue-state with the kingdom of God, descent from Abraham with spiritual rebirth. There is no reconciliation between Judaism and Christianity; Judaism is the anti-Christian principle pure and simple.

How was it possible for the Jews to become emancipated in Germany? The Jews owe their admission to the circumstance that the Jewish spirit has gained mastery over Germany; for liberalism is nothing but secularized Judaism. It too is characterized by a superstitious belief in the rigid, objective, unique, and isolated fact. Only thus have the Jews been able to gain influence over the Germans, without rebirth in the German spirit. Germanism [*Deutschtum*] on the basis of the Jewish religion: this is a contradiction in terms.

Indeed! Thus, and only thus, may one put the question: how could the so-called assimilation[14] take place in spite of the inner alienness of Germanism and Judaism? And the answer to this question cannot but take the general form given to it by Lagarde: only through a kind of "Jewification" [*"Verjudung"*] of the German spirit was this assimilation possible. We do not deem it necessary to specify to what extent Lagarde ignored essentials when he contented himself with pointing to the spirit of culturedness. But most certainly this spirit was an important moment in nineteenth-century German Judaism: *Gumpelino!*[15]

Assimilation poses a threat to the German essence [*deutsches Wesen*] because, despite certain diminutions, it continues in the main the traditional exclusiveness of Judaism with respect to the outside world. As long as Jews hold on to the religious Law, they cannot become Germans. For the meaning of this Law is the prevention of intimate contact between Jews and non-Jews. It alienates the Jews from the "fullness of life" by, for example, making farming and ranching impossible through its prohibition against the gelding of animals. And if, in addition, the religious Law permits the otherwise prohibited vital measures to be carried out by non-Jews, it thereby shows distinctly that it is not commanded "for the sake of humanity," as its apologists claim, since "it is immoral to cause the Gentile to do something that one regards as prohibited to oneself, yet which one cannot and does not want to do without."[16]

Exclusiveness is the meaning of the Law; consequently, as long as the Law is in effect, no amalgamation with the host people is possible. And what if the host people cannot tolerate an alien people in its midst?

The Jews are alien: one sees it in the style of their synagogues, and one sees it in the incomprehension and hatred with which they look on the highest German traditions, that is, the Middle Ages, and on the deepest feelings of the Germans, that is, the appreciation of rank, which they chide as "common slavishness of mind"! (Here Lagarde is thinking of Geiger and Graetz.) And then there is the attitude of these people toward their own history: what they do not like, they deny. "Modern Judaism always sails under false colors." They have but one tendency, which is the political-apologetic tendency. Liberal Judaism praises as the virtues of Judaism: 1. monotheism—but that has as little to do with religion as knowing the number of German residents has to do with patriotism; and it is by no means specifically Jewish; 2. absence of dogmas—but it is no virtue to have no consistent view of God and divine matters; it is a downright moral deficiency; 3. tolerance—but that is a sign of a lack of seriousness; every religion is exclusive.

After this evaluation of Judaism, it is easy to guess at the *Jewish policy* advocated by Lagarde. In order to understand it fully, we need to glance at his general attitude toward political matters.

Life is real only in individuals, and its value is measured solely according to the power it has in the individual and on the individual. For Lagarde, the individual is the particular soul created immediately by God. To be sure, the souls do not exist in isolation but stand in a national context. The nation is a character rather than an ideal of the souls, namely, a character that, as it were, colors the ideal of the souls, that is, God. The state resides in a much more superficial stratum. What the entirety [*Allheit*][17] of the monads of a specific nation cannot achieve monadically, it delegates to the state. However, since everything connected with the innermost life must be acquired by each monad itself, it follows that the state can only assume technical tasks.

If the innermost value of the nation is independent of the state, then the state, in contrast, is necessarily national. The state is only a means of national existence, and yet a means necessarily of national character. The garment must fit the body of the nation. Furthermore, if it is formally sovereign, it must rule in order to be able to serve. The deeper concerns of the nation come under its authority only with respect to their technical side, "regarding their manifestations." However, in the legitimate sphere of the state, it suffers no power beside itself. There is no "right" by which the individual could justify a rebellion against measures that belong to the domain of tasks of the state and are adverse to the individual.[18]

There is no criterion for the value of a state other than its usefulness for satisfying the needs of the nation. An essential national necessity is the security of the nation vis-à-vis other nations. If need be, the state provides this security by means of war. War, as the form of the highest reality of the state, is not in the service of ideas: wars need not be dressed up as crusades [*Missionskriege*].

One sees here the absence of all ideological presuppositions for the emancipation of the Jews. Since the state is a function of the nation, in that the nation transfers, within certain limits, powers over the individuals to the state, one cannot really speak of human rights as rights of individuals. And the equality of all nations? Lagarde resolutely denies it. A chauvinistic Jew could no more resolutely rule out the equating of Yugoslavs or Magyars with Jews than could Lagarde the equating of Yugoslavs or Magyars with Germans.

The state is a national state, which means: 1. in its territory, the needs of its constitutive people [*Staatsvolk*] have priority over all others; if necessary, the state has the power and the duty to put before the aliens the choice between either complete assimilation or emigration; 2. if necessary, it must enlarge its territory in the interest of the nation and put before the subjugated peoples the choice between either assimilation or expulsion. "This politics is somewhat Assyrian, but there is no alternative to it," says Lagarde.

The above explain the following conception of the Jewish policy of the German Reich insisted on by Lagarde. Since it is poorly consolidated nationally, the German people cannot tolerate an alien people in its midst, least of all one that is as nationally coherent and as spiritually dangerous as the Jewish people. The state must, therefore, either assimilate the Jews (or, rather, prepare the ground for assimilation, which, itself, actually lies beyond the possibilities of the state), or expel them. "But, for God's sake, get them either entirely in or entirely out."[19] Should the founding of a Central Europe be achieved, with the Germans as its constitutive people [*Staatsvolk*] as the result, say, of a war on two fronts against France and Russia, then the second possibility is the only suitable one, especially with regard to the Eastern Jews. In such an eventuality, Lagarde leaves it open whether they will have to be deported to Palestine or to Madagascar.

But this is, so to speak, only Lagarde's ideal. What he discusses concretely is the following.

1. Restriction of the Jewish influence on Germans through legal measures: (a) monopoly control of the stock exchanges; (b) banishment from the country in cases of either profiteering, or buying and selling by job lot; (c) laws regulating the press. Lagarde finds that legislation of this kind would save the Jews from themselves.

2. Calling a halt to Jewish internationalism: "No religious officials who received their education abroad are allowed to be employed in Germany."

In reviewing these demands, one does well to be clear about the fact that they are supported by a radical moralism—by the same moralism that prompted Lagarde's rejection of Paulinism. No sooner do they almost touch than they move apart—the radical moralism of the German hailing from Fichte, and the radical moralism of the Zionist writers and politicians who stand under entirely different influences.

NOTES

Source: "Paul de Lagarde," *Der Jude: Eine Monatsschrift* (Berlin) 8, no. 1 (January 1924): 8–15. The figure Strauss chooses as a point of orientation for his ruminations on Zionist "reflectiveness," Paul de Lagarde (1827–91), was one of the most significant sources of—as Lagarde himself called it—"radical conservatism," namely, of the reactionary type of modernism that was eventually absorbed, via the German youth movement, into the program of national socialism. Some of the major features of the later program of the NSDAP—unification of a Greater Germany, colonization of the East, and the transfer of the Eastern European Jewish masses to Palestine or Madagascar—are fully developed and advocated as the necessary vocation of Germany even in the earliest of the lectures included by Lagarde in his vastly popular *Deutsche Schriften* [German writings]. See Paul de Lagarde, *Deutsche Schriften: Gesammtausgabe letzter Hand*, 5th ed. (Göttingen: Dieterich'sche Buchhandlung, 1920). A first such collection of, as Lagarde called them, "theological-political treatises" was published in 1878, to which a second volume was added in 1881. In 1886, both volumes were combined into one and new material was added (popular, i.e., less expensive, edition: 1891). Other editions followed. Also see Lagarde, *Ausgewählte Schriften*, ed. Paul Fischer, 2d enl. ed. (Munich: Lehmanns, 1934).

As a student of Semitic languages at the University of Berlin, Lagarde (originally: Bötticher) had been a protégé of Jacob Grimm (1785–1863), the author of the *German Mythology*, and a close friend of the poet and Orientalist Friedrich Rückert (1788–1866). After spending a fellowship year traveling and studying in Paris and London, Lagarde returned to Halle, where he had been teaching oriental languages, to give his first political lecture, "Ueber die gegenwärtigen Aufgaben der deutschen Politik"

(November 1853). This lecture was later published in several editions, most notably among the *German Writings*. It was this text, among others, that Strauss drew on as a source for his essay "Paul de Lagarde."

Lagarde's scholarly reputation was based mostly on his studies on the history of the text of the Hebrew Bible. His critical stance toward conventional religion, however, put him at odds with all major theological trends, from Protestant orthodoxy to the liberal school of Ritschl. Unfavorable reviews of his works prevented him from receiving calls to universities, until in 1869, supported by the Prussian king Frederick Wilhelm IV, he took a position in Göttingen that previously had been held by Heinrich Ewald, whose forced retirement was due to political reasons. Lagarde continued to remain isolated, and his extreme political views, along with his biting public diatribes on the Protestant culture of his time, did little to improve his reputation among his colleagues. Toward the end of his life, Lagarde achieved additional notoriety by lending his still considerable scholarly prestige to the cause of the defense of the Marburg teacher and anti-Semitic politician Ferdinand Fenner, who, in 1888, was brought to court for making libelous statements about the ethics of the Talmud. The expert witness on the plaintiff's side was Hermann Cohen. (Cf. Ulrich Sieg, "'Der Wissenschaft und dem Leben tut dasselbe not: Ehrfurcht vor der Wahrheit': Hermann Cohens Gutachten im Marburger Antisemitismusprozeß 1888," in *Philosophisches Denken: Politisches Wirken: Hermann-Cohen-Kolloquium Marburg 1992*, ed. Reinhardt Brandt and Franz Orlik (Hildesheim, Zürich, and New York: Olms, 1993), 222–49; and cf. Lagarde, *Deutsche Schriften*, 246–49.) It speaks to the ideological broadness of the editorial policy of *Der Jude* that an essay on Hermann Cohen by Robert Arnold Fritzsche had appeared in the same column as Strauss's essay on Lagarde. See *Der Jude* 7, nos. 7/8 (July–August 1923).

Strauss credits the prominent nineteenth-century anti-Semite with having set the highest standard in honesty and seriousness in the political arena, a standard he commends for emulation by the Zionists. The essay "Paul de Lagarde" develops further what, in "A Note on the Discussion on 'Zionism and Antisemitism'," had been simply a jarring statement, namely, that "it is hardly an exaggeration to say that the level of the anti-Semitic argumentation of a man such as Paul de Lagarde . . . has not even been reached in Zionism."

Wherein lies the affinity between Strauss and Lagarde, between the "German hailing from Fichte, and the . . . Zionist writers and politicians who stand under entirely different influences"? According to Strauss, the affinity lies in the "radical moralism" that is present in both, an attitude that reaches beyond the conventions of liberal or religious discourse and that is rooted in moral or, more precisely, in political convictions. Something else reverberates as the point at which the mind of Strauss "almost touch[es]" the mind of Lagarde. The latter was not a racialist, but a religious thinker and a thinker about religion. To Lagarde, religion was the decisive factor in establishing political differences between nations. This idea clearly appealed to Strauss, and it is certainly not accidental that both Lagarde and Strauss (across the distance of almost a century) speak of their concern as a "theological-political" one. Cf. Lagarde, introduction to *Deutsche Schriften*, 3, and Strauss, "Preface to *Spinoza's Critique of Religion*" (1965), reprinted in *Jewish Philosophy and the Crisis of Modernity: Essays and Lectures in Modern Jewish Thought*, ed. and trans. Kenneth Hart Green (Albany: SUNY Press, 1997), 137.

Of course, the "Zionist writer and politician" Strauss also knows of the fundamental difference between his own radical moralism and that of the German hailing from Fichte: "no sooner do they almost touch than they move apart." Or, could the Jews find a more radical enemy than the one who wrote, "Mit Trichinen und Bazillen wird nicht verhandelt, Trichinen und Bazillen werden auch nicht erzogen, sie werden so rasch und so gründlich wie möglich vernichtet" (Lagarde, *Ausgewählte Schriften*, 239)?

Most importantly, in order to understand what Strauss is up to in this essay one must keep in mind that the association he belonged to (Blau-Weiss) was in many respects the spitting image of the German Wandervogel (see text and notes to "Response to Frankfurt's 'Word of Principle'," as well as the introduction to this volume), which counted Lagarde's *German Writings* as one of its sources of inspiration. The political doctrine that finds its expression here is to Strauss not essentially anti-Semitic, but merely incidentally so, based on a political stance that is in itself consistent, and that is similar to the one embraced by Blau-Weiss. Strauss wishes to legitimize the Zionist struggle not on the basis of liberal values but on the basis of the competition between values that is the law of political existence to which, according to the young Strauss, Zionism is to return the Jews.

1. *Völker der Welt*, and also, further down, *d(ie) Völker*, is German for the rabbinic Hebrew expression *umot ha'olam*. Strauss uses this expression as the correlate to the notion of the chosen people that, to his mind, even Zionism does not necessarily deny or, at least, must confront as an aspect of traditional religious Jewish self-understanding that poses a challenge to the "self-critical Zionist." Cf. "Ecclesia militans" in this volume, and passim for similar expressions. As consistently as possible, I translate *Volk* as "people," *Völker* as "peoples," and *Nation/en* as "nation/s."

2. Cf. "Ecclesia militans" (1925): "Not 'a people like all other peoples' is the program of self-critical Zionism, but being the chosen people does not necessarily mean: to be a people of merchants and lawyers."

3. "Greater Germany" *(Großdeutschen)* refers to the opposition to the "minor German solution" *(kleindeutsche Lösung)* of the German question, promoted by Prussia since 1866 and realized under Chancellor Bismarck, when Germany was unified under the Protestant Hohenzollern, excluding the states of the Austro-Hungarian Empire then ruled by the Catholic house of Hapsburg.

4. The historical school included Burke's critique of revolutionary rationalism, Savigny's historical doctrine of law, and Ranke's critique of general political theory. Usually associated with romanticism, it took issue with Hegel's apriorism in the construction of history and emphasized the need to take into account the irrational, the particular, moral freedom, and the constellations of forces and fate. Source: *RGG*.

5. On *redlich* and *Redlichkeit* (probity), cf. the introduction to *Philosophie und Gesetz* (Berlin: Schocken, 1935), 26f., and see the introduction to the present volume.

6. *Kulturprotestantismus:* a term denoting the phenomenon of a broad mutual affirmation of the Protestant empire and Protestant academic theology that characterized German Protestantism in the late nineteenth century and until the First World War.

7. For Lagarde's views of the Protestant Reformation, cf. "Ueber das Verhältnis des deutschen Staates zu Theologie, Kirche, und Religion," in *Deutsche Schriften*, 42ff.

8. *loci:* Scholastic technical term for dogmatic formulations of the faith. The most

100   Chapter 2

important Lutheran author of such loci was Philipp Melanchthon. See his *Loci theologici* (1521) as well as his role in the drafting of the *Confessio Augustana* of 1530. Cf. *Die Bekenntnisschriften der evangelisch-lutherischen Kirche,* hg. vom Deutschen Evangelischen Kirchenausschuß im Gedenkjahr der Augsburgischen Konfession 1930 (Göttingen: Vandenhoeck & Ruprecht, 1930), xvi–xxi.

    9. Lagarde, *Deutsche Schriften,* 67.

    10. Lagarde, "Ueber die gegenwärtigen Aufgaben der deutschen Politik," in ibid., 25.

    11. Ibid.

    12. Nietzsche, Mommsen, and Wellhausen: Friedrich Nietzsche (1844–1900), Theodor Mommsen (1817–1903), and Julius Wellhausen (1844–1918) were known to be anti-anti-Semitic, but in their respective historiographic views on Judaism in antiquity they largely agreed with Lagarde. In his *Römische Geschichte,* 2d ed. (Berlin: Weidmann, 1856), 3:550, Mommsen had called Judaism "an active ingredient of cosmopolitanism and of national decomposition," a sentence Heinrich v. Treitschke hurled back at Mommsen during the great debate on anti-Semitism in 1880, after Mommsen had signed a declaration distancing himself from Treitschke's views. Cf. Walter Boehlich, *Der Berliner Antisemitismusstreit* (Frankfurt: Insel, 1965), 209f. Similarly, Wellhausen regarded the Jewish theocracy established by Ezra the Scribe after the Babylonian exile as a phenomenon of degeneration, a step down from the life-affirming religion of ancient Israel, and a proto-Catholic Church. See his *Prolegomena zur Geschichte Israels,* 5th ed. (Berlin, 1899); and cf. Lothar Perlitt, *Vatke und Wellhausen: Geschichtsphilosophische Voraussetzungen und historiographische Motive für die Darstellung der Religion und Geschichte Israels* (Berlin: Töpelmann, 1965); and Rolf Rendtorff, "The Image of Postexilic Israel in German Bible Scholarship from Wellhausen to von Rad," *Sha'arei Talmon: Studies in the Bible, Qumran, and the Ancient Near East,* ed. M. Fishbane and Emanuel Tov (Winona Lake, Ind.: Eisenbrauns, 1992), 165–73. On Nietzsche and Judaism, see Yirmiyahu Yovel, *Dark Riddle: Hegel, Nietzsche, and the Jews* (University Park: Pennsylvania State University Press, 1998). By putting Lagarde into this context of ostensibly legitimate historiography, Strauss does not exculpate Lagarde but points to the fact that anti-Judaism is endemic to the entire enterprise of Protestant scholarship on "late Judaism" *(Spätjudentumsforschung).* Yet, in contrast to the named liberal opponents of anti-Semitism, the anti-Semite is at least ready to act upon his beliefs; that is, his views are of one cloth, honest, up-front, and radically moral, rather than softened by appeals to weak humanistic imperatives. While this may appear distasteful to us, Strauss proved clairvoyant in that, when German liberals were put to the test not much later, their resolve failed them, whereas the anti-Semites acted upon their radical political beliefs.

    13. Literally: *Entwirklichtheit.* Strauss used this word in several variations on two earlier occasions, namely, in "Response to Frankfurt's 'Word of Principle'" and in "The Zionism of Nordau." Although the word is not in the dictionary, its meaning is quite clear, yet a precise equivalent can not be formed in English without creating an awkwardness that is absent in the German ("de-realizedhood," "de-realitization," etc.). Whereas in the present essay Strauss accompanies the word with an apology for "an almost impossible word formation," in "The Zionism of Nordau" he introduces it as a matter of course. The apology is omitted in this translation because the English expres-

sion used instead of the above-mentioned mongrel terms is perfectly reasonable: "devoid of reality." In fact, there is nothing very odd about the German expression *entwirklicht*, which simply means the opposite of *verwirklicht*. The somewhat more clumsy neologism *Entwirklichtheit* evidently refers to the result of a process by which one has lost one's reality, or, as one might say today, the result of a process of disembodiment. More precisely, Strauss uses the term in order to provide a vivid expression for the status of *galut* (exile), which he sees as a condition caused by the loss of the ancient Jewish state, or, more generally, as the case of a loss of the trappings of a genuine political existence (cf. also the more common expressions *Luftmenschen, Luftvolk, Volksgespenst,* etc.). Strauss's terminology has a polemic edge in that it constitutes a counterterminology to Martin Buber's popular motto of *Verwirklichung*.

14. "Assimilation": cf. also in "On the Argument with European Science."

15. "Gumpelino": a character in Heinrich Heine's "Bäder von Lucca," depicting in a most biting satire the stereotype of a rich Jewish upstart and social climber. Christian Gumpel, who unsuccessfully tries to transform himself into the Italian noble Marchese Christoforo di Gumpelino, represents a figure of artificial and soulless "culturedness," involving even the adoption of pious Catholic habits, without—to again use the language of Strauss's essay—either experiencing a genuine spiritual rebirth or without even knowing the difference between religious form and genuine religious substance. My thanks to Ken Green for identifying the source of this reference.

16. Lagarde, "Ueber die gegenwärtigen Aufgaben," 37.

17. *Allheit:* see Hermann Cohen, *Logik der reinen Erkenntnis,* 4th ed. (Hildesheim and New York: Olms, 1977), index, p. 683.

18. "There is no 'right'," etc.: cf. *Der Jude* 8, no. 1 (January 1924): 14: "Es gibt kein 'Recht', mit dem der Einzelne gegen eine Auflehnung die in den Aufgabenbereich des Staates fallen und dem Einzelnen widrig sind, Maßnahmen rechtfertigen könnte." The words *gegen* and *Maßnahmen* are out of order. Heinrich Meier corrects this in *GS,* 2:330: "Es gibt kein 'Recht', mit dem der Einzelne eine Auflehnung gegen Maßnahmen, die in den Aufgabenbereich des Staates fallen und dem Einzelnen widrig sind, rechtfertigen könnte." Cf. *GS,* 2:618f.

19. Lagarde, "Ueber die gegenwärtigen Aufgaben," 37.

Sociological Historiography? (1924)

Every author is measured first of all by the standard that he expressly acknowledges in his own work. The best way to dispose of an author is therefore to prove that he fails to achieve what he strives for.

The ideal of knowledge striven for in Dubnow's[1] historical research is that of "objectivity."[2] Now, objectivity can be understood in very different ways. Let us assume that what it means is refraining from passion-driven judgments; a calm weighing of both sides of every issue (and hence also of Jewish history in the period from 1881 to 1914); avoidance of all doctrinairism in assessing historical facts; a critical, possibly skeptical, assessment of even those facts which the party politics of the author's position could, for tactical reasons, bid him take seriously in good faith. This arbitrary and not well organized list of criteria of "objectivity" conforms with the most blatant forms of "subjectivity" that characterize the historical work of Dubnow.

I begin with the point mentioned last. For example, in the enthusiastic account of the English protest movement against the Russian pogroms I miss the blunt recognition of the geopolitical background of this movement. Specifically, while genuinely convinced of the purely moral origin of their struggle on behalf of minorities, the English do not engage in the least political action if it is not in their political interest to do so. This being so, the historian, whose function it is to represent realities, should, I think, call attention to this reality with some emphasis. Of course, a politician who wished to make use of the fact under discussion in order to exert pressure on the Russian government did not at all have to know about the conditional nature of this fact; its serviceable massiveness was sufficient for him, no matter what its motivation.

As an example from internal politics, consider the following. No one will doubt that it is an expedient political trick to speak of negotiations "between the descendant of the Hasmoneans and the descendant of the Crusaders" in order to fight against Herzl's political efforts directed at the German kaiser. This is perhaps as expedient as, in German politics, discrediting a Russophile foreign policy by making frequent use of such names as Apfelbaum and Braunstein. However, this is obviously not a conscientious historical characterization, and perhaps not even an entirely fair politics.

Dubnow is indignant at the Russian government's struggle against the Jewish state within the state, but he hails enthusiastically the struggle of the French radicals against the clerical congregations as a struggle against "a state within the state—a hotbed of clerical fanaticism and hatred of democracy." According to the same reasoning, a government at war should be permitted to root out the Jewish state within the state as a "hotbed of defeatism," at least if our author is correct in translating the Sixth Commandment as "Do not kill." What is the point of such meaningless quotations of biblical passages, anyway? I have often wondered why, in discussions about the essence of Jewish politics, people always adduce the same passages from the prophetic writings (taken out of context), which could obviously be countered by just as many other passages saying precisely the opposite. Naturally, Dubnow too is convinced that the Jewish spirit can be reduced to the formula of a struggle of justice [*Gerechtigkeit*] against force [*Gewalt*]. In his case, however, this formula receives an original and shrewd, rather than moral, interpretation, in which the representation of Jewish interests is identified with "justice" ["*Gerechtigkeit*"], and the struggle against Jewish interests is identified with "force" [*"Gewalt"*]. I prefer to stick with the entirely unambiguous passage in Joshua 9:7, which can be easily applied to our situation in the *galut*.[3] But we digress.

What is before us now is Dubnow's "subjectivity." He characterizes the war of 1870/71[4] as a "senseless brawl"; Germany before the war was a "barracks state" [*Kasernenstaat*], where the blind worship of the fatherland and the army suppressed and depersonalized everything"; there is a "holy right of man's freedom of movement," and so on. One could regard such things as mere silliness, too trivial to make a great fuss about, were they not so thoroughly characteristic of the entire attitude of the work.

The ideal of "objectivity" is supposed to be realized by means of the method of "sociology."[5] Now, according to Dubnow, a sociological approach is one that draws equally on economic, political, and cultural facts.[6] We do not wish to enter into the fundamental difficulty that attaches to the demand for drawing *equally* on economic, political, and cultural facts. It is readily conceivable that nothing is less "objective," and nothing fits the object less, than such coordination; this would be the case if *one* group of facts were unmistakably *predominant* in the object to be dealt with. Be that as it may, "objectivity" in the sense of doing justice to the facts could in any case have been achieved by Dubnow by means of sociology, especially by means of sociology of the economic variety. After all, there is in Jewish history a series of facts traceable to economic factors. Thus it can be easily explained why, for example, the guilds were more hostile to the Jews than the absolute monarchy; this would imply that the Jewish problem is unaffected by democracy. Or it can thus be explained why nineteenth- and twentieth-century Poland is more hostile to the Jews than the Poland of the fourteenth century; from this it would be possible to learn that the Jewish problem is unaffected by civilization, and so on. By comprehending that many historical facts are caused by amoral circumstances, such as economic competition, one is able to avoid cheap moralizing, whining, and scolding.

If one thinks that this is what one may rightly expect from a sociological investigation, then one will be disappointed in Dubnow. Dubnow belongs to those historians that Nietzsche, with Treitschke and Sybel in mind, referred to as historians with "heavily bandaged heads."[7] It does not even occur to Dubnow to see in anti-Semitism anything but hatred, either groundless or grounded in the lowest urges. Brutal absurdity [*brutale Sinnlosigkeit*]—the Franco-Prussian War—brings about a heightening of the will to brutal absurdity

(German militarism) and hence to anti-Semitism as a special form of brutal absurdity. Dubnow has a predilection for entering into the embarrassing (or, as they say, "personal") motives of the leaders of anti-Semitism. It should be obvious that an examination of this sort cannot understand anti-Semitism. How would it propose to deal with a man as thoroughly honest as Lagarde?[8] The same holds true for Dubnow's judgment of German-Jewish relations. Of course this is not to say that the historian must be lukewarm about, or dispense with, evaluations. Pinsker[9] understands anti-Semitism ten times more thoroughly than Dubnow, and it is for this very reason that he expresses his hatred much more deeply and much more effectively.

Aside from this fundamental flaw, Dubnow's work is absolutely indispensable as the only comprehensive presentation of Jewish history of the recent past that treats all the accessible material. However, it is *not* what it claims to be: a "synthesis" of the material.[10] It is often nothing more than a convenient compilation of news reports and editorial opinion pieces. It is devoid of any idea that would construe the historical facts from their inner law; the author's political ideals are somewhat mindlessly juxtaposed with the historical facts.

There is, however, one viewpoint that justifies the structure of Dubnow's work, a linear enumeration of mostly very sad encounters of the Jewish people. The detailed portrayal, inspired by strong feelings, of the suffering of the Russian, Polish, and Rumanian Jews has an intrinsic value: as *martyrology*. No one should contest its importance. This is so because, first, it has the vital function of keeping alive in us the deep hatred that facilitates our existence in this world of hatred, and that takes for us the place of an army and of fortresses; and because, second, it is the cognitive preservation of an essential form of the life of our people, namely, suffering as such. For this is by no means a merely passive experience of force, but rather it is prepared from within, almost willed, before this experience of force could have been much of an issue. The conception of the peoples of the world as none other than the cruel tormentors of the defenseless is as absurd from a sociological viewpoint as it is meaningful and unavoidable here, where the peoples of the world are considered as the *mere* correlate of the suffering of the Jewish people, that is, as those who cause that suffering. In this context, the notion that is opposite to force [*Gewalt*] is not "right" [*"Recht"*], but the *experience* of force. Any appeal to a league of nations or to democracy, any assertion of a *claim* not to be tormented, is here invalidated as embarrassing. All that remains is *selicha* [forgiveness]. It hardly needs saying that Dubnow misses this aspect as well. It is completely shut out from his view by his vigorous faith in national-cultural autonomy.[11]

NOTES

Source: "Soziologische Geschichtsschreibung?" *Der Jude: Eine Monatsschrift* (Berlin) 8, no. 3 (March 1924): 190–92, reprinted in *GS,* 2:333–37.

1. Note by the editor of *Der Jude,* Ernst Simon: "S. M. Dubnow, *Die neueste Geschichte des jüdischen Volkes,* vol. III, Berlin, 1923. After the more favorable review by Josef Meisl (issue no. 10/11, 1923) we publish also this harsh critique without any intention of concluding a discussion that is of methodological importance. Rather, we certainly encourage new, alternative statements." Josef (or: Joseph) Meisl, a regular contributor to *Der Jude* whose more favorable review is mentioned here as an alternative to Strauss's "harsh critique," went on to become a contributor first to the German *Encyclopaedia Judaica,* then to the English *EJ* (begun under Cecil Roth for Keter, Jerusalem), and was the director of the Central Archives for the History of the Jewish People, Jerusalem. He was also the author of the first part of the *EJ* entry on Simon Dubnow (second part: H. H. Ben Sasson).

2. Simon Dubnow (1860-1941), Russian autodidact, Jewish historian, and journalist, whose political vision of Jewish political autonomy and the hegemony of cultural centers was at odds with both assimilation and Zionism. His *Neueste Geschichte des jüdischen Volkes* (3 vols., 1920–23) appeared simultaneously in Russian, German, and Hebrew. The well-known ten-volume *Weltgeschichte des jüdischen Volkes* (Berlin: Jüdischer Verlag, 1925–29) reproduces the content of *Neueste Geschichte* in an edited form in volumes 8 (corresponding to vol. 2 in the modified edition of *Neueste Geschichte,* 1928) and 9 (without reference to the previous edition, published in 1929). On Dubnow's principles of historiography, see *Weltgeschichte,* 1:v–vi, xiii–xxxi, and again in 9:5–7.

3. Joshua 9:7: "And the men of Israel said unto the Hivites, Peradventure ye dwell among us; and how shall we make a league with you?" This passage, representing an ideal conquest of the Land of Canaan based on deuteronomic law, provides the background for the specific story that exemplifies that the conquering Israelites are loath to transgress the injunction against making a covenant with the aliens who dwell among them (i.e., the original inhabitants of the land). By the same token, Strauss implies, one must concede to the non-Jewish powers holding sway over the Jews in exile the right to refuse to enter into protective arrangements with the Jews if they feel so compelled. What is right for the conquering Israelites must be right for others as well, even if and when the Jews are on the receiving end.

4. The war of 1870/71: the Franco-Prussian War, leading to the Versailles proclamation of the Second German Reich.

5. Cf. Dubnow, *Weltgeschichte,* 1:xv: "Es ist nun eine Errungenschaft der letzten Zeit, daß man endlich zu einer umfassenderen, rein wissenschaftlichen Auffassung der jüdischen Geschichte, die man als die *soziologische* bezeichnen kann, vorgeschritten ist" [Only recently have we, at last, progressed to a more comprehensive, purely scholarly conception of Jewish history, a conception that may be called a sociological one]. But cf. p. xx: "Diese Auffassung weist unserer Geschichtschreibung [*sic*] den Weg aus dem Labyrinth der theologischen und metaphysischen Theorien und stellt sie auch eine feste *bio-soziologische* Grundlage" [This conception leads our historiography out of the labyrinth of theological and metaphysical theories and establishes it on a solidly *bio-sociological*

foundation]. In a final note to his introduction to *Weltgeschichte*, Dubnow remarks that the description of his method as sociological had given rise to a "scientific controversy." Hence, in order to avoid further "misunderstandings and futile polemics," he distinguished his method from that which Max Weber had shortly before applied to the study of ancient Judaism (*Das antike Judentum*, 1923). Dubnow, who from early on was influenced by Comte and Mill, uses "sociological" or "bio-sociological" to describe a sphere of historical relevance that is neither identical with the nation-state nor with religion. Thus he aims to strengthen his argument for a sound political existence of the Jews in autonomous hegemonic centers of political, economic, and cultural life that, in order to function properly, is neither necessarily in need of a state nor to be reduced to the beliefs, rituals, and the literature of Judaism as a religion.

　　6. Cf. Dubnow, *Weltgeschichte*, 1:xxi.

　　7. Friedrich Nietzsche, *Jenseits von Gut und Böse*, "Achtes Hauptstück: Völker und Vaterländer," no. 251, in vol. 5 of *Sämtliche Werke: Kritische Studienausgabe* (München: DTB; Berlin and New York: Walter de Gruyter, 1980), 192.

　　8. See "Paul de Lagarde."

　　9. Leon Pinsker (1821–91), Odessa physician and leader of the Hibbat Zion movement. As the anonymous author of *"Autoemancipation": Mahnruf an seine Stammesgenossen von einem russischen Juden* (Berlin, 1882), Pinsker analyzed the roots of anti-Semitism and was one of the first, and most widely read, to advocate the establishment of a Jewish national center as the only viable answer to anti-Semitism.

　　10. Cf. Dubnow, *Weltgeschichte*, 1:xiii: "Wie in der Weltgeschichte der Menschheit, so muß auch in der Weltgeschichte des Judentums die *synthetische Methode* die vorherrschende sein" [Just as the *synthetic method* must dominate the universal history of mankind, so it must dominate the universal history of the Jews]. And on p. xxii: "Auf der Suche nach einer umfassenden Synthese der jüdischen Geschichte, einer Synthese, der ich vom ersten Tage meiner wissenschaftlichen Forschung an unausgesetzt nachging . . ." [In the pursuit of a comprehensive synthesis of Jewish history, a synthesis I have pursued from the first day of my scientific research . . .].

　　11. For Dubnow's views on religion—critical in his youth, and more appreciative later on as the expression of the spirit of the people (along the lines of Renan, Tolstoy, and Ahad Ha'am)—see *EJ*, s.v. "Dubnow, Simon," by H. H. Ben Sasson.

Review of Albert Levkowitz, *Contemporary Religious Thinkers* (1924)

In *Contemporary Religious Thinkers: On Changes in the Modern Views of Life*, which is a detailed review of the literature, *Albert Levkowitz*[1] wants to acquaint with contemporary philosophy those Jewish readers who, because of their other pursuits, have not had the leisure to learn about it from the sources, or from the usual reports in the daily newspapers. As a result, a certain crudeness in the argumentation and a certain repetition of things well known are unavoidable. Standing on the solid ground of the religion of Judaism, the author can easily pass judgment on particular philosophers. He strives for a "serious and deep argument with the spiritual forces of the world around us." This argument results in the identification of the ancient Jewish worldview with a synthesis of Bergsonian creative evolution with the ideals of Cohen's ethics of humanity and with the holy according to Otto. It is not without doggedness that the author is able to emphasize the ideal over against the philosophers of life, and to emphasize life over against the idealists.

Aside from the previously mentioned, unstated aim of the work, there is also an aim that is expressly emphasized by the author: namely, that of taking on, in give-and-take, the (!) Jewish role in the religious search of our time. To be sure, according to the author, this wrestling [*Ringen*]² for participation in modern culture derives from the classical universalism of Judaism.

NOTES

Source: "Bücherschau: A. Levkowitz, *Religiöse Denker der Gegenwart,*" *Der Jude: Eine Monatsschrift*, (Berlin) 8, no. 7 (July 1924): 432. The full title of the book under review is Albert Levkowitz, *Religiöse Denker der Gegenwart: Vom Wandel der modernen Lebensanschauung* (Berlin: Philo Verlag, 1923).

1. Albert Levkowitz (usually: Lewkowitz) (1883-1954), rabbi and scholar, received his theological education from the Jewish Theological Seminary in Breslau, where he later also briefly lectured on the philosophy of religion and on pedagogy (1914). His first philosophical teacher was Hermann Cohen, an influence he attests to in his contribution to the *Festschrift Judaica* (Berlin: Bruno Cassirer, 1912), 167–76. His main work is *Das Judentum und die geistigen Strömungen des 19. Jahrhunderts* (1935). Cf. *EJ*, s.v. "Lewkowitz, Albert."

2. For *Ringen*, cf. "Der Konspektivismus" (*GS*, 2:367), where this term is even more strongly ironized.

On the Argument with European Science (1924)

Now and in future, this journal will report on works on the science of religion that, for the most part, are not animated by any specifically Jewish interest. What right do we have to do this? What right do we have to endanger our so fragile Jewish cohesion even further by troubling a Jewish public with comments on works that belong entirely to the European context (even though some of their authors may happen accidentally to be Jewish)? For it should be self-evident that a Jewish reviewer's private relation to some European matter does not yet establish any relation between the Jewish context and that very matter. Moreover, if some European fact is of European significance, it does not yet follow that it concerns us in any way as Jews, unless, of course, one shares the view of "Jewish universalism" held by a certain liberalism. What has Europe to do with us as Jews!

What has Europe to do with us? Quite a lot, it seems. But what things European are of concern to us, what concrete European facts are of concern to us, can only be ascertained on the basis of a concrete examination. Our center of gravity lies in the Jewish context. And if as Jews we presume to busy ourselves with something non-Jewish, then the place that this non-Jewish matter is meant to occupy in the Jewish context must be shown with some conceptual precision [*Bestimmtheit*]. This can and must be a matter of *concrete* conceptual analyses [*Bestimmungen*] alone, and not of blather about Jewish rhythmics and the like, blather that makes it possible to requisition virtually anything as a legitimate Jewish possession.

There is a European endeavor that as such has an immediate relation to the Jewish context, and this endeavor is the entire complex of the modern science of religion. For when Europe criticized itself, that is, its Christianity, it eo ipso criticized Judaism. That this critique *made an impact on* the Jewish context is illustrated historically by the fact that the Jewish tradition, insofar as it was not able to reconstruct itself with regard to this critique, succumbed to Europe's attack. Herein lies the decisive cause of what is known as assimilation, which therefore is Jewishly legitimate also from this perspective. To pass off some idiotic "enticements" of Europe, or "pagan" motives, as the essential cause of the defection from tradition is to be guilty of defamation. The Orthodox side should finally stop using a polemic that was meaningful in the case of Alexandria and Rome. What happened in the nineteenth century was anything but *apikorsut*, "Epicureanism" in the literal sense.

In any case, the result of the critique in question is the limitation it puts on the claim to validity of tradition. In the present day, even on the Orthodox side, one no longer argues, proceeding from the Bible, against the propositions of natural science. We expect that this camp will also come to terms with biblical criticism in like manner, that is, likewise by means of a Jesuit-pragmatist interpretation, or rather by means of a transcendental-idealist one. However, a tradition that, because of a critique launched against it, has relinquished certain claims (claims that presumably arose from it not without inner necessity), indeed, a tradition that has reconstructed itself so that it is no longer even *able* to make those claims—such a tradition, if it is honest, will have to admit that it is no longer the old, unbroken tradition. If the renunciation of the claim to scientific validity is such a self-evident matter, as is today often asserted even from pulpits, how is it that such significant minds as all positive religions count among their orthodox theologians defended their tradition against science with almost unprecedented tenacity? Obviously the blow struck by science did not miss. That Moses wrote the Torah was regarded as true not just in the traditional context and "inwardly," but true, pure and simple; and whoever thought otherwise was a radical denier of the faith. There was a time, not so long ago, when the two powers, tradition and science, did not coexist peacefully on parallel planes, with no points of contact, but engaged in a life-and-death struggle for hegemony on the *single* plane of the "truth."

Religion was saved not by its own defense, but rather by the self-critique of the critique. Kant "needed to deny knowledge in order to make room for faith." In the context of this self-critique, religion was saved at the price of an idealist, romantic reinterpretation. However, the more the science of religion (now no longer in need of *criticizing* religion) devoted itself to the concrete actuality of religion, the clearer it became that the claim to transcendence, which, if not relinquished, was still endangered by romanticism and which is the ultimate root of the specific claim to truth of religion, is also the vital principle of religion. Accordingly, while an idealistically reinterpreted religion may perhaps be the most amusing thing in the world, it can in any case no longer be religion. The phenomenon of the knowledge of transcendence presented itself in the context of the spirit, which provided the undisputed basis for the argumentation of post-Kantian science of religion. Once religion was comprehended scientifically by means of the category of the "religious a priori," it no longer stood opposed as brutally factual revelation to the domain of science, of knowledge open to inspection[1] and control, as it did in the arguments of the age of Enlightenment. In a fundamentally different intellectual situation, the problem of theology had to be posed anew, as one that could be dealt with scientifically.

Whoever wishes to get to know the most important stages of this way should turn for a first look (if only that) to the "compendium of sources" entitled "Philosophy of Religion" edited by *Wobbermin*.[2] To be sure, what one misses most among the newest sources are those that prepared a new theology; above all, one misses Hermann Cohen himself.

It is possible for the science of religion to liberate itself completely from an Enlightenment approach of the *critique* of religion and to concern itself solely with a pure understanding of the historical actuality of religion.[3] This possibility becomes a matter of course when the dogmatic elements of religion are conceived as secondary as compared with "religious experience," perhaps only as its "expression." However, if one believes that one must take the dogmatic seriously, as it is and as it presents itself to us, then one will not view the argument between science and religion—Cohen calls this determining the "concept of religion in the system of philosophy"[4]—as a "violation" of religion. Not the least reason for the fruitfulness of Cohen's theology is that, while it "rationalizes" the dogmas of the Jewish tradition and thus develops them further, it leaves them on their own plane.

In his introduction to the previously mentioned "compendium of sources," *Wobbermin* deals with the "concept, task, and method of the philosophy of religion." Here he polemicizes against viewing religion from the vantage point of "the context of a philosophic system that has been devised without paying heed to religion." Whether and where something of this sort actually exists is of no interest to us at this point. But if it is Hermann Cohen against whom the Protestant theologian turns in the passage in question, then he forgets that the entire context of Cohen's philosophic system rests on religious presuppositions.[5] To be sure, a reflection on more than its title, *The Concept of Religion in the System of Philosophy*,[6] and indeed, nothing less than a reading of the entire work, would have shown that this is the case: system and science are decisively *prepared* by religion. In the final analysis, scientific critique of religion is an *immanent* critique.[i] It exists already where the term "science" cannot yet be spoken of in the Scholastic sense. The theologians only continue what the prophets had begun. There can be no doubt that with such theses Cohen interpreted and judged his own system correctly—although this is to speak generally, for when it comes to the details, he occasionally claims too much.

If we are compelled to defend ourselves so expressly against the reproach that to start from critique[7]—and, from our perspective, the philosophic system is none other than the context in which the critique is rooted—signifies a "violation" of religion, then, on the other hand, we are equally compelled to let pass the positive moment[8] in Wobbermin's philosophy of religion, that is, the transcendental constitution of religion from "religious experience." Indeed, as Wobbermin himself has often emphasized, this moment is conditioned by specifically Protestant presuppositions. Here, as Jews, we must disqualify ourselves.

In the previously mentioned work, *R. Winkler* (on pp. 16 through 27) provides a catalog of names and subjects (with the sole flaw of not being alphabetized) that he entitles "Survey of Work in the Philosophy of Religion from Kant to the Present" and that, according to his own judgment, "elaborates

---

[i] This is not to say that the entire range of critique exists historically in Judaism or that, in this sense, critique is permanently Jewish.

the most fundamental trends in the context of ideas in the philosophy of religion of the nineteenth century." Concerning Winkler, suffice it to quote his categorical judgment on Kierkegaard. "As a result of his unmethodical, strongly journalistic method and of his pathological inclination toward exaggeration and paradox, Kierkegaard was unable to exercise a decisive influence on the movement of the philosophy of religion" (p. 23). Also worth reading is the reference to the historical case of a "markdown" [*"Ermässigung"*] on Hegel's panlogism (p. 24), which opens up surprising possibilities for financial conduct in theology.

On a previous occasion,[9] we drew attention to the significance, in this context of the history of theology, of Rudolf Otto's investigations into "the holy."[ii] Otto operates with categories that are useful for the reconstruction of traditional theology in a situation created by the critique of tradition. This scholar primarily tries to determine the moments of the religious *object*. His analyses can almost be characterized as a theory of attributes. In this connection, it makes good sense to dispense with an exposition of the ways and means by which religion and its object are "constituted" in the context of human existence. Theology is needed as an autonomous science, insofar as it makes sense to speak of God's being-in-Himself [*An-Sich-Sein Gottes*], and insofar as there is knowledge of this being-in-Himself [*An-Sich-Seiendes*]. On this basis, it is possible to regain recognition for those moments that had been lost in the concatenation of Enlightenment critique and romantic reinterpretation. Put in terms of a formula: the transcendence of God is determined as (1) beyond *experience* [*Erlebens-Jenseitigkeit*], (2) beyond *life* [*Lebens-Jenseitigkeit*], and (3) beyond *ideas* [*Ideen-Jenseitigkeit*].[10]

However theologically legitimate it may be to renounce an exposition of the human contexts from which religion arises, such renunciation leads to difficulties on a matter of principle when it comes to understanding the *history* of religion. Undoubtedly, this also involves a Jewish interest of the greatest contemporary relevance. The argument between Orthodoxy and Liberalism, and even more so the argument of both of these parties with Zionism, cannot dispense with reliance on the Bible. Time and again, Jewish journalism of the recent decades has circled around, albeit mostly in a dilettantish way, the problem of the relation between prophecy and monarchy, a problem that can be dealt with only by Bible science. Now, the principle of the history of

---

[ii] Rudolf Otto, *Das Heilige. Über das Irrationale in der Idee des Göttlichen und sein Verhältnis zum Rationalen,* 7th edition, Breslau, 1922. Idem, *Aufsätze, as Numinose betreffend,* Stuttgart/Gotha, 1923.

religion, proposed by Otto, is here entirely inadequate. This is not to diminish the contribution that Otto makes whenever he provides concrete historical analyses. In this connection, special mention should be given to the essay "Prophetic Experience of God,"[iii] in which a decisive step is taken toward a renewed understanding of eschatology, which for a long time had been buried beneath prejudices of Christology, Enlightenment, and especially romanticism. But we have misgivings about the way in which myth is passed off as a preliminary stage of religion. "The *daimonion* becomes the *theion*. Dread becomes devotion. Disjointed feelings flaring up in confusion become *religio*. . . . The *numen* becomes God and Godhead" (*Das Heilige*, p.132). This development, as Otto claims, is not identical with the "rationalization" of the numinous, that is, with the other moment in the history of religion. In contrast to the process of rationalization, it unfolds "purely in the sphere of the irrational itself." However, it must be asked whether these two developments are as "coordinated" [*"nebengeordnet"*] as Otto thinks, and whether the numinous actually "attracts" those independently existing "rational" ideas after the fact. In a polemic against Xenophanes, Otto remarks: "However, in the actual history of religion, things happened in an entirely different way. Here the development proceeded not from the known, the familiar, and the canny [*das Heimliche*],[11] but rather from the uncanny [*das Unheimliche*]" (*Das Numinose*, p. 17). Religion is the experience of the wholly other, of the "opposite to everything human." Precisely for this reason, however, it is very doubtful that the historical development *proceeds* from the uncanny. What Otto says is, at the very least, misleading. It may be valid for some stretches in the history of religion, say, for the development from Amos and Isaiah to the Rambam and to Cohen. Concerning the situation in which biblical prophecy finds itself, it is characterized by the fact that pre-prophetic[12] "religion" is passionately rejected not for being "uncanny" but precisely for being canny, for being all too canny. And the result of this *rejection* of the canny is the "rationalism" of the prophets. One can easily make this clear, for example, by quoting Amos 9:7: "O Sons of Israel, are you not to me like the Ethiopians, declares YHWH? Have I not brought up Israel from the land of Mizraim, and the Philistines from Caphtor, and the Arameans from Kir?" This shudderingly harsh tearing away of the national God from His nation—which is, indeed, something like a "rationalization"—can be viewed as a step forward [*Weiterschritt*][13] from the uncanny to the canny only if one thinks in terms of the recent, in fact very canny, pamphlet literature on the universalist

---

[iii] Rudolf Otto, "Prophetische Gotteserfahrung" in: *Das Numinose,* no. 17.

monotheism of the prophets. What appeared to their contemporaries as the height of danger and of the uncanny vanishes in contrast with the level of the uncanny meant by the prophets. The way from myth to religion is a way from the canny to the uncanny. What is the meaning of the struggle of the prophets against "human" customs (historically concrete, these customs consisted in the contents of pre-prophetic "religion"), and what is the meaning of their (as one says) "ironic" use of popular ideas and hopes, if not the branding of the canny as an abomination?[14] And "rationalization" asserts itself not only *simultaneously* with this cutting oneself off from the canny [*Abstich vom Heimlichen*], not only *beside* it, but as *identical* with it. The identity of these two moments governs the work of Hermann Cohen from the beginning, even and especially his *Logic of Pure Cognition*, which was "designed irrespective of religion."[15] Here the term is: "*Cutting off from the given*" ["*Abstich vom Gegebenen*"].[16] And, proceeding from this particular "systematic" approach, Cohen summarizes the peculiar quality of the prophetic development in the formula: struggle against myth as that which remains within the "given," within the human, seeking in *it* security against the uncanny.[17]

On a first reading of the most recent works of *Ernst Cassirer*,[iv] one might think of him as a successor of Hermann Cohen.[18] On the basis of materials gathered from the special sciences and of the attendant discussions, Cassirer reaches the conclusion that the peculiar form of mythic thought consists in a concentration of givens [*Gegebenheiten*] around the psychosomatic unity [*geistig-leibliche Einheit*] of the human being. Things are classified either in accord with the character assigned to them by the primitive affect or in accord with an analogy to the parts of the human body, and so on. Thus it is true that myth forms the givens [*Gegebenheiten*], but "it soon recedes again, along with its own product, into the form of the given [*Gegebenheit*]" (*Festschrift für Paul Natorp*, p. 51). It is true that myth, like all other forms of the mind, creates a realm of "meanings"; in this respect it too idealizes the world of things. But, to myth, "the moments of thing and meaning indiscriminately" flow into one another. For instance, it regards the names of things as real *material* properties or powers. Now, to a certain degree, the mythic concept formation is the fundamental layer that certainly does not vanish in the more mature consciousness of humanity, which has overcome it in principle. If one asks, however, what

---

[iv] Ernst Cassirer, *Die Begriffsform im mythischen Denken* [Studien der Bibliothek Warburg, vol. I], Leipzig: Teubner, 1922. Idem, "Philosophie der Mythologie" in Gadamer, Hans-Georg (ed.), *Festschrift für Paul Natorp zum Siebzigsten Geburtstage von Schülern und Freunden gewidmet,* Berlin/Leipzig: Walter de Gruyter, 1924.

motive brings about the overcoming [*Überwindung*] of myth, or rather its "sublation" [*Aufhebung*], Cassirer answers in a typically idealistic manner that the overcoming is brought about by virtue of the fact that the mind reads the world of myth as its own product, that the mind recognizes itself in the world of myth—and thereby this world loses its "compulsory"[19] character for human beings. "The sequence of stages of the intellectual forms of expression" leads from myth to language to art, in which the mind attains its highest freedom.

Naturally, this theory cannot be applied to the biblical development. To be sure, when the formations of pre-prophetic "religion" are seen as "the work of man," this also means the negation of their compulsory character. However, the *work* of man that compels human beings is now replaced not by the autonomous human spirit, but rather by a different, stronger compulsion, the "one and only" compulsion [*der "einzige" Zwang*].[20] The products of myth are rejected not because they *compel* human beings but rather because, in view of their human origin, they *cannot* compel them. It is characteristic of the difference existing *from the beginning* between Cohen and the Marburg school that *Cohen's* polemic against myth—aiming, as it does, not at its "sublation" ["*Aufhebung*"] but at its elimination [*Beseitigung*]—is guided precisely *not* by idealist motives. Cohen teaches that the *ethical* motive, that is, the interest in the question "to what end?" [*das Wozu*], *supersedes* (not: sublates) the mythical motive, that is, the interest in the question "whence?" [*das Woher*]. What does this mean? In the concrete context of human existence, the transcendence of the Ought in relation to Being demands by its very nature, as Cohen stated over and over again, that ethics be further developed into religion.[21] In Cohen, the ethical motive of transcendence contains within it, from the outset and in latent form, the power and depth of the religious motive of transcendence. In this respect it is essential that, when eventually in his theology he takes up the prophetic polemics against the worship of images—a polemics, to say it again, that constitutes a passionate rejection rather than a "sublation"—he does so by proceeding from the *religious* notion of transcendence. Here, the inner connection between Cohen's entire philosophical system and Judaism[22] is revealed, a system that in every respect *fulfills* itself in his theology, and here a real, systematic understanding of the rise of prophecy has been achieved. It seems to me that it is no accident that Cassirer, in his attempt to sketch the relations between the mythic and the religious formation of concepts, refers to Vedic religion, to Parsiism, to Calvinism, and to Jansenism, but *not* to Judaism. This fact is a symptomatic indication that Cassirer's theory of mythology is not a congruent expansion of the Cohenian system but its dismantling, a fact barely hidden behind the occasional agreement regarding idealism.

NOTES

Source: "Religionsphilosophie: Zur Auseinandersetzung mit der europäischen Wissenschaft," *Der Jude: Eine Monatsschrift* (Berlin) 8, no. 10 (October 1924): 613–17.

1. *einsichtig:* Strauss uses the adjective *einsichtig* in an unusual way, as if it meant something that is open to inspection, examination, etc. Usually *einsichtig* denotes the attitude of someone showing *Einsicht* (insight, discernment), that is, it refers to a person, rather than to a thing, a person who is reasonable, sensible, and so forth. I assume that Strauss means to speak of knowledge that is based on observation and thus *einsehbar* rather than *einsichtig*, and hence I translate the word as "open to inspection."

2. Georg Wobbermin (1869–1943), Protestant systematic theologian. Influenced by Troeltsch (history-of-religion school) and the newly emerging school of the psychology of religion (W. James), Wobbermin renewed Schleiermacher's approach to religion. Strauss refers to Wobbermin's *Religionsphilosophie*, Series: Quellen-Handbücher der Philosophie, 5. Band (Berlin: Pan-Verlag Rolf Heise, 1924).

3. Literally: "with historically actual religion." Cf. similarly two paragraphs earlier: "the concrete actuality of religion."

4. Cf. Hermann Cohen, *Der Begriff der Religion im System der Philosophie* (Gießen: Töpelmann, 1915).

5. This claim is unique to Strauss. In comparison, Rosenzweig's depiction of Cohen's move from Marburg to Berlin in 1912 as implying an abandonment of idealist philosophy in favor of a return to genuine religiosity (a depiction that raised the hackles of the surviving members of the Marburg school and incensed the widow, Martha Cohen) does not assert that the entire systematic philosophy of Cohen rested on religious presuppositions. (Cf. Rosenzweig, "Einleitung," in *JS*, and see the many passages in Rosenzweig's letters from the period in which he admits to bending the facts in order for them to fit into a hagiographic scheme.) It is even more outrageous when Strauss insinuates, as he does here, that Wobbermin should be mindful of a view on Cohen that no one (except for Cohen himself and mostly in not-so-well-publicized places) had ever suggested before. Given this and what follows in the text, Strauss's appreciation of Cohen seems to be growing rather than diminishing. For this reason alone it is false to assume that the essay "Cohen's Analysis of Spinoza's Bible Science"—written and published before "On the Argument with European Science"—indicated a growing distance from Cohen. Cf. Kenneth Green, *Jew and Philosopher* (Albany: SUNY Press, 1993), 52. Strauss asserts on several occasions that "when it comes to details" Cohen "occasionally claims too much," but in the main he is deeply impressed and inspired by Cohen's intuitions. This is particularly so with respect to Cohen's interpretation of Maimonides. Cf., for instance, in the letter to Krüger, 7 May 1931 (*GS*, 2:xxx n. 43) and in the letter to Scholem, 2 October 1935 (*GS*, 2:xxiii n. 25).

6. See note above.

7. This defense of critique elaborates a view first expressed in "Response" (1923), where we find a strong indication that Strauss had turned away from the position that he had endorsed in his dissertation, which was critical of "criticism."

8. "moment": The German *Moment* that is used rather frequently in this essay and

that occurs frequently in the philosophical literature of the time (especially in the works of Hermann Cohen, under whose stylistic influence Leo Strauss seems to be operating), could be translated by "element," a much more common word in English. Yet moment, a perfectly common English word as well, preserves the aspect of motion that is intended here and that is lacking in the word "element." I therefore translate *Moment* as consistently as possible as "moment." This seems all the more appropriate because Strauss also uses the word *Element.*

9. Cf. "The Holy," supra pp. 75–79.

10. The triplet of "beyonds" indicates as a strength of Otto's approach its ability to avoid the most common reductions of transcendence—namely, the psychological reduction (grounding the object of religion in human experience), the vitalistic reduction (grounding the object of religion in the vital urges of human physiology), and the idealist reduction (grounding the object of religion in the spontaneity of the human mind).

11. "the canny": in German, *das Heimliche* (hidden, secret) should actually be *das Heimelige* (the homely, cozy). Since *g* can in some cases (and in some local dialects such as the Hessian) be pronounced like the soft *ch, heimlich* and *heim(e)lig* can sound identical. Based on this, Otto uses *heimlich* (meaning *heimelig*) as the opposite to *unheimlich.* Strauss builds on this pun in the following argument: The prophets reject the simplistic, yet natural, notion of an unseverable tie between God and nation (a mythological, not *unheimlich,* and even *heimelig* notion); prophetic monotheism has a far more uncanny/unhomely idea of God than its pre-prophetic, mythological predecessors.

12. In the original publication, as well as in *GS,* 2, we find here "prophetic" instead of "pre-prophetic." Without our emendation, however, the text makes no sense. My thanks to Ken Green who, after long discussions back and forth, finally resolved this problem very much to my satisfaction.

13. *Weiterschritt:* a pun on *Fortschritt* (progress).

14. "Branding the canny an abomination." In the original: *Perhorreszierung des Heimlichen.*

15. Hermann Cohen, *System der Philosophie, Erster Teil: Logik der reinen Erkenntnis* (Berlin: Bruno Cassirer, 1902); 2d ed.: 1914; 3d ed.: 1922. A fourth edition has been published as vol. 6 of Hermann Cohen, *Werke,* Hermann-Cohen-Archiv at Philosophisches Seminar of Zurich University, directed by Helmut Holzhey (Hildesheim, Zürich, and New York: Georg Olms Verlag, 1977).

16. Strauss misquotes Cohen in a meaningful way. Firstly, the unusual term *Abstich* (translated here as "cutting off") is indeed used by Cohen, namely (as Hartwig Wiedebach kindly pointed out to me) on p. 93 (fourth edition), where it refers to an act of thought, more precisely to one of the "moments of thought in the judgment of origin" *(Moment des Denkens im Ursprungsurteil)* . What is negated in this act of thought is, however, not "the given" *(das Gegebene),* as Strauss has it, but a "relative naught" that is not the opposite of ought but merely a "springboard" by means of which thought achieves "separation" *(Sonderung),* which, along with "unification" *(Einigung),* constitutes the moments of thought. The aim of Cohen's phenomenological description of the acts of thought is to establish what it means to say that objects of cognition are constituted by thought rather than "given" to sense experience. Strauss is therefore correct when he

generalizes as he does. One may simplify Cohen's intention without falsifying it too much by saying that the methodological reflection of philosophical thought à la Cohen proceeds by negating (i.e., an act of *Abstich*) the givenness of what seems to be given to sense experience. The problem of the constitution of the object in contrast to the assumption of something given to sense experience *(das Gegebene)* is, hence, a major problem that *Logik der reinen Erkenntnis*, and Cohen's thought in general, tries to solve. See, e.g., *Logik der reinen Erkenntnis* (4th ed.), 27f., 81f., 91f., 192f., 587.

17. See, e.g., H. Cohen, "Die Errichtung von Lehrstühlen" (1904), in *JS*, 2:118. "Es gibt nur Eine Religion, welche von allen Zaubern der Mythologie sich grundsätzlich frei macht, das ist die Religion der Propheten, das ist die Religion des Judentums" [There is only One religion that liberates itself fundamentally of all enchantments of mythology, namely, the religion of the prophets, which is the religion of Judaism]. Cohen's preoccupation with the problem of mythic thought reaches back to his earliest publications. See, for example, "Mythologische Vorstellungen von Gott und Seele, psychologisch entwickelt" (1868/69), in *Schriften zur Philosophie und Zeitgeschichte*, ed. A. Görland and E. Cassirer (Berlin: Akademieverlag, 1928), 1:88–140. And cf. Michael Zank, *The Idea of Atonement in the Philosophy of Hermann Cohen* (Providence, R.I.: Brown Judaic Studies, 2000), 31.

18. On Cohen's concept of myth in comparison with Cassirer's, see the dissertation of Alfred Jospe, "Die Unterscheidung von Mythos und Religion bei Hermann Cohen und Ernst Cassirer in ihrer Bedeutung für die jüdische Religionsphilosophie," published in 1932 in Oppeln by Reuther und Reichard.

19. "'compulsory' character." In the original: "*Zwangs*"-*Charakter*, that is, the character of that which is diametrically opposed to the freedom attained through the course of cultural development. The word *Zwang* is the common German translation for the Greek ἀνάγκη.

20. Since Strauss explicitly reads Cassirer against the backdrop of Cohen, the use of the word *einzig* refers back to Cohen's emphasis on God's "uniqueness" *(die Einzigkeit Gottes)*. See Cohen, *Religion der Vernunft*, chap. 1.

21. What Strauss claims here as having been stated by Cohen "over and over again," namely, "that ethics be further developed into religion," stands in curious opposition to what is usually asserted to have been Cohen's program: the resolution of religion into ethics.

22. Cf. Cohen's dictum, "im Zusammenhang meiner wissenschaftlichen Einsichten steht mein Judentum," in a letter, dated 11 December 1904, and published as "Antwort auf ein Glückwunschschreiben der Frankfurtloge," *Bericht der Großloge für Deutschland U.O.B.B*, no. 2 (February 1905), reprinted in the notes to Franz Rosenzweig's introduction to *JS*. In context: "You are quite right when you point out that it was the duty of truthfulness that demanded the recognition of Judaism in my systematic ethics. My enthusiasm for Judaism is rooted in the conviction that our idea of God is of ethical value; *in the context of my scientific insights stands my Judaism*. For this reason I consider myself fortunate to have been able to demonstrate its significance in the context of a philosophical system before publishing more extensive works on the idea of Judaism" (*JS*, 1:333, emphasis added).

Comment on Weinberg's Critique (1925)

What I presented at camp[1] was the very preliminary result of my long-stand-ing preoccupation with the problem of Zionism. Since I never had the op-portunity, either inside or outside the Kartell,[2] for a real debate with the Zionist public, there was no reason to anticipate that I would immediately make contact with my *Bundesbrüder*[3] assembled at Forchtenberg.[4] I would like to emphasize that this was due not to the ostensibly "philosophical" character of my ideas, but merely to the fact that I made the effort to see things as they are, unprejudiced by vulgar Zionist "ideologies," which are distinguished by a thoughtless application of European categories to Jewish, that is, non-European, matters (and, concomitantly, by a blathering pompos-ity). What seemed "abstract" was in truth the rigorous formulation of our real inner state of affairs.

In order to make my intention as clear as possible I shall proceed from its practical-political effect. I believe that the grouping of German Jewry into parties no longer corresponds to the spiritual situation of our generation. The alliance of Zionism and Orthodoxy will have to be replaced by the alliance of Zionism and liberalism. Today, the enemy is on the Right![5] The more we are concerned with doing concrete "cultural" work [*"Kultur"-Arbeit*] the clearer it will become that the Zionism that I would like to characterize as primarily political Zionism is liberal, that is, it rejects the absolute submission to the Law and instead makes individual acceptance of traditional contents depen-dent on one's own deliberation. This, however, is what matters at the present moment. It should not be said that I am absolutizing what is merely relative to a "cultural" view: it is sufficient to mention the name of "Mizrahi"[6] in order to make clear even to the most ignorant what eminently practical mat-ters of financial politics depend directly on this "cultural" decision.

I am pleased to be able to state that this conception is in no way merely my private *meshugas* [craziness]. I know that it is shared by political leaders, for example, by Blumenfeld[7] and Landsberg.[8] Above all, however, it was my experience in recruitment [*Keilerfahrung*],[9] most recently again in Cologne, that showed me that it is not difficult to establish contact even with ex-tremely liberal Jews, just so long as we start honestly from the real situation of German Jewry and not from some other, "abstract," false nationalisms.[10]

At camp, I began with the formulation of the question as sketched in the neo-Orthodoxy of Ernst Simon.[11] In our context, it is of no concern to us whether one takes the individual representatives of this neo-Orthodoxy es-pecially seriously. I thoroughly understand the skepticism of most of our *Bundesbrüder* and am today inclined to share it. What matters is the demand for an acceptance of tradition, a demand that is justified by the well-known ideology of "return." An expression used in this context is "Jewish legitimacy." I raise this expression because it forces one to take seriously the debate with tradition, and because it makes impossible one's continuing with the comfortable jog trot.

Now, in all members of the K.J.V. there is a certain "I know not what" that objects to this demand. And this "I know not what" varies according to the being and essence of each individual; seen from the standpoint of the Kartell, it is a "private matter"! I attempted to determine whether this avowed distance from tradition, which is alive in all of us, does not possess a certain objectivity within the Kartell. I therefore asked myself, what is actually the minimum that we presuppose in each *Bundesbruder?* I said—and this is not contested by anyone—[that this minimum consists in] political Zionism. Now I raised the question whether this "indispensable" minimum does not already justify the distance toward tradition. This question had to be answered in the affirmative, since tradition, according to its meaning, excludes politics, that is, "politics" understood as a will sustained by the consciousness of responsibility for the existence and dignity of a people, whereby such existence is seen as depending on purely "natural" conditions, whether human or extrahuman. For the sake of brevity, I shall not discuss the proofs that I adduced in support of my argument from traditional writings as well as from contemporary Orthodox literature.

Hence, politics as opposed to tradition. To be sure, the question arises whether this opposition does not admit of being overcome from within. From this perspective, I examined the only two attempts that have been made in this direction, namely, *first* the attempt to reach that synthesis of politics and religion by way of the "political" elements in the biblical world (Judges and Kings in Wellhausen's conception),[12] and *second* the attempt of *cultural Zionism* to bridge the opposition by reducing religion to altruistic ethics (Ahad Ha'am),[13] or to the socialism of a "community" (early Buber)[14]— in short, to a merely interhuman phenomenon, and by perverting into a politics of the "spirit" the realpolitik devised by Herzl.[15] I believe that I have demonstrated that these attempts do *not* accomplish what we need. I closed my presentation with the statement that I knew of no way leading out of this crisis; at the same time, I objected on principle to any attempt to deprive this crisis of its seriousness through cheap simplifications or through even cheaper hopes (in the style of: "In Palestine this synthesis is sure to come about organically").

My critic asserts that I said: "The dualism [of nationalism and religion] consists in the following: nationalism is political, while religion is apolitical."[16]

What I contrasted was not religion and nationalism, but religion and political Zionism. This is quite simply a real antagonism, rather than a "logical antagonism" or even less so—unless we are bobbysoxers [*Backfische*]—an "emotional" antagonism. To speak in the terminology of Weinberg, I must leave it to some philosophers to determine how this reality relates to logic, or to emotion.

It would not occur to me to deny that "handicrafts, oil painting, and beekeeping are also apolitical" and yet are not in opposition to politics, just as little as it would occur to me to deny that there are black, crooked dogs (dachshunds),[17] just because "crooked" is not a color, and especially not black. May I, too, draw on "logic": one learns from this discipline that there are several kinds of negation. "Apolitical" may mean: lying on a different plane than politics, and it may also mean: excluding politics. Of course I only had the second meaning in mind when speaking of the apolitical character of the Jewish tradition.

I do not know how Weinberg comes to impute to me a decision in favor of Orthodoxy, and to impute it to me, outrageously, as a decision "from honest enthusiasm."[18] I trust that the *Bundesbrüder* who heard my Forchtenberg presentation will agree with me when I conclude that there was no trace of "enthusiasm" to be found in it. As concerns my "decision for Orthodoxy,"[19] this anticritique will not leave any remaining doubt and thus may serve as an example [of my true position].[20] However, if what I am being reproached for is my understanding that there are things in the Jewish tradition that are essential and obligatory for us, then I am being reproached for not being a perfect horse.

I now turn to Weinberg's positive positions. It will not surprise him if I accept his conclusion—or rather if I acknowledge it as my own (with the necessary grain of salt, of course)—that it is impossible for us to accept the Law. However, I cannot make my own his justification. This is so for the simple reason that Weinberg has at his disposal a worldview [*Weltanschauung*]. This worldview has been picked up from the alleys of Europe, or, at best, from its brochures, and I do not understand how it is supposed to be justified as obligatory for Zionists. When we Zionists speak ex cathedra, that is, as Zionists, we may only rely on things that are justified by the situation of Jewry, in our case by the situation of German Jewry. What is justified by this situation is the will to the Jewish state, to Jewish external politics. Correctly understood, that is, understood in the Zionist sense, "freedom" and "individualism" are "private matters." What is not private, however, but of an objective Zionist character, is the fact that the Jewish tradition was devastated in the nineteenth century by so-called assimilation, which, according to its legitimate sense, is nothing but a critique of tradition. In *this* sense, therefore, we are "assimilated," "liberals," or whatever other expression one prefers. And if there is something like "individualism" in *this*, then, for God's sake, we are even "individualists." But not because individualism and freedom are so beautiful, oh so beautiful.

Undoubtedly, we all endorse Weinberg's critique of Mizrahi. What I see as the greatest danger, however, is its "organic" interpretation of Orthodoxy. This neo-Orthodoxy is a softening of the traditional context, whose greatness consists in its "rigidity."

Finally, I did not say that "nationalism" is unable to fulfill a man,[21] but that the political will is unable to do so. This is, I believe, somewhat more precise.

NOTES

Source: "Bemerkung zu der Weinbergschen Kritik," *Der jüdische Student* 22 (1925): 15–18. In the heading of the essay, Leo Strauss is identified as a member of the Frankfurt chapter of Saronia, which, in the early 1920s, included the famous Frankfurt rabbi Nehemia Nobel as an *Alter Herr h.c.* Leo Löwenthal and Erich Fromm—members of the "Frankfurt" group against whose "prinzipielles Wort zur Erziehungsfrage" Strauss argues in his "Response to Frankfurt's 'Word of Principle'"—were also members of this group. Cf. also anecdotal observations by Gershom Scholem in *Von Berlin nach Jerusalem* (Frankfurt: Suhrkamp, 1977), 193–98.

In this essay, Leo Strauss responds to Hans Weinberg's "Zionismus und Religion," which was published on pages 8–15 of the same issue of *Der jüdische Student* (vol. 22, 1925). Here Weinberg, a member of the Ruder Verein jüdischer Studenten in Berlin, criticized a lecture given by Strauss at the 1924 retreat of the K.J.V. Strauss's lecture had been solicited by the board of the K.J.V., and the same board, which also edited *Der jüdische Student*, introduced Weinberg's response to Strauss as a polemical ("stark subjektiv gefärbt") statement on the relation between Zionism and religion, which they called "one of the most burning problems of Zionism," and invited others to contribute to this debate.

The K.J.V. retreat had taken place 29 July–1 August 1924 in the village of Forchtenberg (near Heilbronn in Württemberg-Hohenlohe). The main points of Strauss's lecture are briefly summarized in "Das Camp von Forchtenberg," *Der jüdische Student* 21, nos. 8/9 (October–November 1924): 197f.

Two further lectures of Strauss at Zionist retreats are known, namely, "Religiöse Lage der Gegenwart" (1930), first published in *GS*, 2:377–91, a "lecture, to be held on Dec. 21, 1930 at the federal camp of *Kadimah* in Brieselang, near Berlin" and "Die geistige Lage der Gegenwart," a twelve-page lecture manuscript dated 6 February 1932, first published in *GS*, 2:441–64.

1. Here and below, Strauss uses the word *Kamp*, the Germanized spelling of an Anglicism then fashionable.

2. That is, the Kartell jüdischer Verbindungen (K.J.V.), an association of two major confederations of Zionist students' fraternities (see note above).

Chapter 2

3. *Bundesbrüder:* The literal translation, "confederates," conveys distracting secondary meanings in English that are far from the neutral and technical German term. Translating the word as "comrades" would convey similarly unintended connotations and may invoke confusion with one of the early Jewish *Wanderbünde* by the name of Kameraden. Since the term is part of the jargon of student fraternities that is evident nowhere else in Strauss's writings, I leave this term untranslated. This allows some of the unusually insiderish flavor of the essay to be preserved in translation.

4. Cf. "Das Camp in Forchtenberg," 196–200, a detailed report on the retreat held 29 July–1 August 1924, at Forchtenberg, where Leo Strauss had been invited by the board of directors *(Präsidium)* of the K.J.V. to present a lecture entitled "The Problem of Jewish Culture in the Context of Our Program of Education" ("Das jüdische Kulturproblem in unserem Erziehungsprogramm").

5. Cf. "Ecclesia militans" (1925).

6. Literally "Easterner," name of the religious Zionist movement, derived from the term *MerkaZ RuHanI* (spiritual center). Founded in Vilna in 1902, its motto was "The Land of Israel for the People of Israel according to the Torah of Israel." Mizrahi aimed to keep political Zionism limited to working toward the attainment of the political goal of statehood, opposing the growing popularity of *Kulturarbeit*, that is, the agenda of cultural Zionism. After the First World War, its center was at first in Frankfurt am Main. It was during its "Frankfurt period" that Mizrahi began to develop its educational network. Subsequently it established numerous schools and institutions of teacher training in Palestine and abroad, as well as a university (Bar Ilan in Ramat Gan). After the founding of the State of Israel, Mizrahi united with the Ha-Po'el ha-Mizrahi and established the National Religious Party (Mafdal).

7. Kurt Blumenfeld (1884–1963), president of the German Zionist Federation from 1924 to 1933, later member of the directorate of Keren Hayesod in Palestine. Blumenfeld, born to an assimilated family in East Prussia, joined the Zionist movement as a law student at the universities of Berlin, Freiburg, and Königsberg, and became an influential younger member of the Zionistische Vereinigung für Deutschland (ZVfD), which, between 1905 and 1920, had its center in Berlin. Jehuda Reinharz credits Blumenfeld with a decisive "radicalization" of German Zionism: "Insofar as historical change can be attributed to a single personality, one can say that Blumenfeld altered the ideological course of the German Zionist organization between 1910 and 1914" *(Fatherland or Promised Land: The Dilemma of the German Jew, 1893–1914* [Ann Arbor: University of Michigan Press, 1975], 152). The shift in ideological orientation accomplished by Blumenfeld consisted in a change from a "political-philanthropic" to a "practical" orientation for Zionism, involving settlement, immediate action, and other values reflecting the concerns of the Zionist youth movement. Cf. *Fatherland or Promised Land,* 154–58. Cf. also Avraham Barkai, "Die Organisation der jüdischen Gemeinschaft," in *Deutsch-jüdische Geschichte in der Neuzeit,* vol. 4: *Aufbruch und Zerstörung, 1918–1945* (München: Beck, 1997), 91–95 ("Die Zionisten"), English translation by William Templer on pages 90–95 of *Renewal and Destruction, 1918–1945,* ed. A. Barkai and Paul Mendes-Flohr, vol. 4 of *German Jewish History in Modern Times,* ed. Michael Meyer and Michael Brenner (New York: Columbia University Press, 1996).

8. Like Blumenfeld, Alfred Landsberg was a representative of the younger gen-

eration of German Zionist leaders, similarly hailing from an assimilated background. He preceded Blumenfeld as the chairman of the Zionistische Vereinigung für Deutschland from 1923 to 1924. Cf. Reinharz, *Fatherland or Promised Land,* 103.

9. *Keilerfahrung:* a term from the vocabulary of student fraternities, meaning recruitment.

10. Strauss's reference to his *Keilerfahrung* in Cologne shows that he was active in the ongoing effort of recruiting new members (*Keilfüxe* or *Keilfüchse*) to the Zionist students' organization. The results of the recruiting efforts were periodically published in *Der jüdische Student.* See, for instance, "Keilbericht für das Sommersemester 1921," *Der jüdische Student* 18, no. 5 (September–October 1921): 228–31. The author of this report, Arthur Stein, insists that "die Frage der Keilarbeit eine Existenzfrage nicht nur für das *K.J.V.,* sondern für die ganze zionistische Bewegung bedeutet" [the question of recruitment work is a question of existence not just for the K.J.V. but for the entire Zionist movement" (230). Cf. also the critical remarks on the shortcomings of these recruitment practices by a new Kartell member, Martin Flesch, in the same issue of *Der jüdische Student.*

11. In the early essays, Strauss repeatedly takes as his point of departure positions formulated by Simon or by the Frankfurt group to which Simon belonged. As someone advocating a "primarily political" Zionism, Strauss shows great concern with the opinions of cultural Zionists. His predominant interest in religion could even be said to be somewhat at odds in the context of a "primarily political" Zionism. Simon is also addressed in "Response to Frankfurt's 'Word of Principle'" (1923) and in "Biblical History and Science" (1925).

12. Julius Wellhausen (1844–1918), Protestant Old Testament scholar, gave the documentary hypothesis of the sources of the Hexateuch its definitive formulation in his *Prolegomena zur Geschichte Israels,* 5th ed. (Berlin, 1899). Cf. the reference to Wellhausen in the essay "Paul de Lagarde" (1924). The political reading of the biblical sources, posed as a problem in the *Theological-Political Treatise* of Spinoza, was first addressed by Strauss in his essay "Cohen's Analysis of Spinoza's Bible Science" (1924). A close parallel to the political interpretation of the biblical Judges and Kings referred to above is found in Strauss's essay on Simon Dubnow, "Biblical History and Science" (1925).

13. Ahad Ha'am, pen name of Asher Hirsch Ginsberg (1856–1927), the main voice of "cultural Zionism." See notes to "A Note on the Discussion on 'Zionism and Anti-Semitism'" (1923).

14. As a sociological term, *Gemeinschaft* was coined by Ferdinand Tönnies in opposition to *Gesellschaft.* Buber adopts this distinction in his early work, influenced by the social philosophy of Georg Simmel. Cf. Paul Mendes-Flohr, *From Mysticism to Dialogue: Martin Buber's Transformation of German Social Thought* (Detroit: Wayne State University Press, 1989). Strauss's critique of Buber here is consistent with that in his 1923 "Response to Frankfurt's 'Word of Principle'."

15. Strauss deals with what he calls here a *Depravation* (perversion) of Herzl's political Zionism in the 1923 essay "The Zionism of Nordau."

16. Quotation marks at the end of this sentence are missing in the original.

17. "Dachshund": in German, *Dackel.* The expression *krummer Hund* (crooked dog) also means "dirty dog."

18. See Hans Weinberg, "Zionismus und Religion," 9.

19. In the jargon of the youth movement, the term "decision" is a loaded one that can stand alone, pointing to the act of decision as an end in itself. This attitude is called "decisionism."

20. Literally: "this anticritique, for example, will not leave any remaining doubt."

21. Cf. Weinberg, "Zionismus und Religion," 14: "*daß die nationale Idee allein als ideologisches Fundament für den einzelnen nicht ausreicht,* vielmehr noch eines wie immer gearteten 'Hintergrundes' bedarf. Eine solche Auffassung ist für die Situation, in der sich der Zionismus befindet, recht charakteristisch. Eine ganze Anzahl Zionisten glaubt, daß der Zionismus weder 'wesenhaft' sei, noch seiner Natur nach werden könne. Und damit haben sie ja nicht so unrecht" [*that the national idea does not by itself suffice as an ideological foundation for the individual,* that it rather needs to be augmented by a 'backdrop' of some sort. This kind of view is quite typical for the current situation of Zionism. There are a large number of Zionists who believe that Zionism neither is, nor can—by virtue of its nature—become essential. And in this they are not so very wrong]. (emphasis added). And cf. "Das Camp von Forchtenberg," 198f.: "warf Strauss die Frage auf, ob überhaupt und wie weit die Möglichkeit einer Aneignung der Werte des traditionellen Judentums ohne Rückkehr zur Tradition möglich sei. *Denn geistige Menschen würde ein nur auf das nationale Ehrgefühl begründeter Zionismus nicht befriedigen,* wenn seine tieferen Sphären zu ihm ganz beziehungslos bleiben sollten. Ohne hier endgültige Formulierungen finden zu können, beantwortete er die Frage in mehr negativem Sinn" [Strauss raised the question whether and to what extent it is possible to appropriate the values of traditional Judaism without a return to tradition. *For spiritual people cannot be satisfied by a Zionism that rests exclusively on national honor* if one's deeper spheres remain completely disconnected from it. Unable to advance ultimate formulations he answers the question more in a negative sense] (emphasis added).

Ecclesia militans (1925)

The Jewish Church—as, here and elsewhere, we refer to the separatist Orthodoxy of Frankfurt—is on the offensive. This fact is of interest to us, but it does not frighten us. We know all too well that not all offensives succeed. Perhaps the attack of the Orthodox will run aground on the barbed wire fences in front of our position, so that it may not even be necessary for us to defend the front line, let alone to call for a retreat. As long as we keep cool heads and strong hearts, the evil old enemy [*alt böse Feind*][1] will pose no danger to us. His cruel armor [*sein(e) grausame Rüstung ist*] is the joyful rough-and-ready of his rhetoricians, who surmount obstacles of logic by means of enthusiasm. It is because of the Jewish heart that one does not stand very firm against this sort of impudence.

Let us cast another glance at the arms [*Wehr und Waffen*] of our enemy, our fiercest and most vicious enemy. First, with regard to his war objective—

and forgive me for all the saber-rattling images, but the situation forces them upon us; besides, they lend our enemy's operations a more pleasant sense than they deserve—it is: submission of the Jewish people to the Torah. This objective can be realized without a fight once the existence of God and the divine provenance of the Torah have been acknowledged. Now, the weapon, or the trick, of Orthodoxy is to try to force the acceptance of this demand, without first having to obtain the acknowledgment of its dogmatic presuppositions. One is compelled to resort to this trick because the acknowledgment of these dogmas could never be obtained from the majority of contemporary Jewry. One then makes do with the thoroughly dishonest doctrine that there are no dogmas in Judaism, a doctrine that seems to have been invented just for the purpose of fundamentally destroying any seriousness of the religious decision. As if what mattered was that, among us, the precondition of blessedness is not constituted by the explicit affirmation of propositions of one sort or another, and as if what mattered was not rather the simple fact of the self-evidence with which our prayers refer to the existence and actions of God (a fact that cannot be removed by any amount of enthusiasm), and that they can be said with decency only by such Jews who believe in the existence and actions of God in the sense outlined by the prayers! Further, one does not deem it a robbery [*erachtet es nicht als Raub*][2] when one deduces the necessity of fulfilling the commandments from the legal character of the Torah, whereby "law" is a sort of *canis a non canendo*.[3] Moreover, one makes use of the following line of argument, which is no less shameless: the affirmation of the nation implies the affirmation of the national culture—in our case, however, the national culture is the Torah—hence, it implies the affirmation of the Torah. As if the fundamental question of religion could be decided by a national decree! Finally, one is not ashamed to justify the Torah in a "deeper" way by showing that the politics of the peoples who do not stand under the rule of the Torah—"the Tower of Babel"[4]—leads to world war. This justification too would lead to an observing of the commandments in a manner [that amounts to] a pious fraud, since one would fulfill them for the sake of their pleasant consequences. But does it *prove* anything? Does it lead to a *truth*? As can be proved, truths are not proved by the pleasantness of their consequences.

As I said, Orthodoxy is in the habit of arguing one way or another in the manner described. For the open discussion of theological problems has become a stormy issue ever since the verification of revelation, once customary in traditional theology, was made impossible by the European critique. —As an aside: it may be of interest to the historian of present-day ideas that certain clever minds, who hear the grass grow, have of late been speaking of the

shallowness of the Enlightenment. Endowed with an astonishingly subtle sense
of modernity, they have a lot to say about the soullessness, and so on, of the
nineteenth century. As if the reasonable core that happens to be concealed in
such tirades, or these tirades themselves, could ever be able to blot out once
and for all the critique of religion of the modern era. —It is only when the
futility of all psychological and sociological evasions and tricks will have been
demonstrated to it in every single case that Orthodoxy will consent to start
with a blunt statement of the central dogmas.

If we are not mistaken about certain indications, it is already being re-
called that the question of God and His revelation must be posed quite simple-
mindedly and honestly, without regard to any actual disadvantages involved.
In the end, this is in the highest interest of religion itself. Religion is not
interested in those who fulfill the Law for the sake of their people, or for the
sake of all peoples, and not, or not primarily, for the sake of God. Only when
the question will again be posed in this way, and when the formation of
parties within Judaism will take its shape according to the differences between the answers given to this question, will an argument, indeed a community, of Orthodoxy and non-Orthodoxy be genuinely possible.

In any case, it is an encouraging step forward when, in his most recent
work (*The Jewish National Home*, Frankfurt, 1925), *Isaac Breuer*[5] sees as the
decisive question "whether God and the Torah deserve to have primacy over
the Jewish nation, or whether the historical relation is to be the reverse." It is
no longer a matter of individualism versus typism [*Typismus*],[6] power versus
spirit, high treason versus loyalty to the Law, that is, it is no longer a matter of
interpersonal concerns.

Breuer's writing is encouraging not only for this reason, but also because
it candidly points out the ultimate dogmatic presuppositions. In terms of
presentation, it also differs most advantageously from the author's previous
writings, and indeed from most of Jewish political literature. It is a genuinely
political publication, matter-of-fact [*sachlich*][7] and clear; the dubious poetic
eruptions that made working through Breuer's previous publications a tor-
ment are pushed where they belong, that is, into the corners, as an oasis for
the Jewish heart parched in the desert of politics. To be sure, even now he
cannot get by without bringing in the wrinkled little old mother. Meanwhile, the impression that the author is at home in politics—by the way, in
very aggressive politics—suggests that his poetry is merely a weapon (a mi-
rage gas, if such is technically possible) in the service of the politics. Hence it
must not be judged by its pitiful poetic qualities but rather by its more toler-
able demagogic qualities. This time, the author has dispensed with such popular
numbers, made spicier, without thus having been made "prettier," by the

cut-and-thrust of juristic distinctions that slice through the schmaltz of the street organ. He has reached seriousness.

It so happens that this seriousness is also our own seriousness; or, at least, that this seriousness is a serious matter to us. What even the most shortsighted observer of Orthodox politics may have noticed is practically stated here by the one who has been inspiring this politics: Zionism has a single Jewish enemy, and that enemy is Orthodoxy. To Orthodoxy, we the non-Orthodox are traitors and infidels. This sounds refreshing, even plucky, and so, I suppose, it is quite in order. Breuer keeps these theses in view, yet he moves beyond them without expressing himself in a less ambiguous manner.[8] He deals at great length with certain quarrels that have lately been of concern in Palestine, quarrels that seem to agitate him very much. Lacking expert knowledge ourselves, that is, not having traveled to Palestine, we must leave the practical [*sachlich*] settlement of these quarrels to the Zionist leadership. In this matter, Breuer assumes the peculiar position of a representative of the Jewish nation—which is the bearer of the rights derived from the Balfour Declaration—protesting against the administrative measures of a foreign authority, that is, the government of the Zionist nation that is absurdly the trustee of the rights of the Jewish nation; a knotty situation. Put crudely (and transposed from the key of horse-bell ringing to the key of the Tower of Babel):[9] the point is to pin something on the Zionist organization in the eyes of the English government. This objective stands in an ideal connection with the other one: to cause trouble for those Orthodox who are working within the Zionist organization. From Breuer's standpoint, these Orthodox would likely be seen as Zionist citizens of the Jewish faith. This is essentially an inner-Orthodox argument or, as it were, an international-Orthodox one. We refrain from any interference.

Should we say that we are indifferent to this dismissal from the Jewish people? Today as always, we are concerned about an argument with Orthodoxy, because we hold onto the notion of the historical unity of the Jewish connection. However, this entails certain difficulties that we have already spoken about. Breuer has removed the greatest of these difficulties: the suppression of the actual point of controversy. Yet some difficulties still remain.

One would do Orthodoxy an injustice if one were to charge it with subjective dishonesty. This charge would not only be unjust, it would also be presumptuous, laughable, meaningless, and—a matter of indifference. We do not say this for the sake of extenuation, nor out of halfheartedness. Quite the contrary! —The Orthodox tactics are possible only because Orthodoxy never makes the effort, nor has it ever made the effort, to understand the will of political Zionism. Tagged with the label of *apikorsut* [apostasy], it is not the

topic of serious argument. Why argue at all, if one knows, really and truly
knows, that one is right and that the others are in error? One always and on
principle has a good conscience. . . . But does the unshakable possession of a
good conscience not signify—the loss of one's conscience altogether?

Reading about Herzl, one hardly believes one's eyes: that he "dared to
make a reckless leap among the great powers," a leap that happened to bound
to the national home only through its "miraculous concurrence" with the
World War. Is this fair? Unless we are misinformed, Herzl knew that, if the
peoples render it a political service, then the Jewish people would have to
offer them a political service *in return*. What we are dealing with, then, is not
a "leap," but a playing off of power against power, as is the case in all politics.
Hence the connection between the real foundations of political Zionism and
the real foundations of the World War is not a miraculous connection but a
natural one. We call attention to the fact that the destruction of Turkey, and
the struggle for the minorities, were war objectives of the Entente, and that
the Entente—above all, England—had an *interest* in a favorably disposed Jewish public. The genius of Herzl consisted neither in a "leap" nor in a "cry,"
but in the politicization of the Jewish people.

The refutation of the factual claim would not do justice to our opponent.
One must go further by asking: What is the purpose of Breuer's claim? What
can be gained from it? First: the realization of political Zionism as a consequence of the World War—not a bad way of stigmatizing Zionism in the
eyes of the black-red-and-gold citizen.[10] Second: the Balfour Declaration as
no achievement of Zionism—as a gift of the hour, of history, of providence.
Hence Orthodoxy may also make use of it without scruples.

By a similar logic, it follows that Zionism wants to make the Jewish
people into a people like all other peoples. Years ago one spoke indeed in this
sense of "realization" ["*Verwirklichung*"].[11] Yet the more Herzl's original will
now comes alive, the more distinctly we perceive the will to normalcy as
unmotivated.[12] "A people like all other peoples" cannot be the program of
self-critical Zionism. Rather, its program is only that being the chosen people
need not mean: to be a people of merchants and lawyers. This is not a matter
of a "battle against the rule of God, a battle against the rule of the Torah of
God." We are not talking about a "battle" at all, but at most about distance.
This distance is not rooted in the will to normalcy—Zionism is not a symptom of depression. We protest against any such imputation and, in case of its
recurrence, we shall no longer be able to look at it as an error in good faith.
Rather, this distance is rooted in the fact that, as a result of European critique,
the dogmatic presuppositions of Orthodoxy have been recognized as questionable. If Orthodoxy is resolved to do battle on *this* ground, then Zionism

will not refuse to give battle, even though it cannot appeal to this tradition but only to reason.

NOTES

Source: "Ecclesia militans," *Jüdische Rundschau* (Berlin) 30, no. 36 (8 May 1925): 334, reprinted in *GS*, 2:351–56.

1. *Der alt böse Feind:* here and in the following ("sein Grausam Rüstung ist," "Wehr und Waffen," etc.), Strauss uses words and imagery from Martin Luther's hymn *Ein feste Burg ist unser Gott.* The "Jewish Church" is thus equated with the medieval Catholic Church as perceived by the Protestant Reformation of the sixteenth century. Since not all of the expressions from the hymn can be integrated precisely into the syntax of the English translation, I render the text in idiomatic English and indicate the allusions to the hymn in square brackets.

2. *Erachtet es nicht als Raub:* cf. Luther's translation of Philippians 2:6.

3. Latin: "a dog that is born of something that doesn't bark," that is, an impossibility.

4. Cf. Genesis 11.

5. Isaac Breuer (1883–1946). As a congenial companion piece to Strauss's "Ecclesia militans," see Gershom Scholem "The Politics of Mysticism: Isaac Breuer's New Kuzari," in *The Messianic Idea in Judaism and Other Essays on Jewish Spirituality* (New York: Schocken, 1971), 325–34.

6. Whatever the historical referent of "typism," in contrast to individualism it refers to one of two mutually exclusive trends or points of view, both being purely immanent in historical and sociological thinking.

7. *sachlich:* in the essays from the "phase of reorientation" (1929–30), specifically in "Der Konspektivismus" (1929) and in "'Religiöse Lage der Gegenwart'" (1930), terms such as *sachlich, Sachlichkeit,* and so forth acquire the character of technical terms denoting the program of a "return to the things" *(zu den Sachen)* or to "essentials." Strauss is not alone in borrowing the latter usage from contemporary aesthetics, where one spoke of a *neue Sachlichkeit.* Cf., for example, Franz Rosenzweig, letter of 28 June 1928, to Otto Loewie in vol. 2 of *Briefe und Tagebücher,* ed. Rachel Rosenzweig and Edith Rosenzweig-Scheinmann (with Bernhard Casper) (The Hague: Nijhoff, 1979), 1190. Because of its many and varied connotations, the term can hardly be translated consistently.

8. In the original publication, the word *jedoch* is in the wrong position. I translate the sentence as if it read, "Er überblickt diese Thesen, er geht jedoch über sie hinaus, ohne weiter eindeutig zu werden" instead of "Er überblickt jedoch diese Thesen, er geht über sie hinaus, ohne weiter eindeutig zu werden."

9. That is, translated from fancy language into the language of the ordinary politics of ordinary, self-interested people.

10. *Schwarz-rot-gold:* the colors of the German republic.

11. The term had been coined by Martin Buber. In the early essays, Strauss frequently polemicized against it by countering it with his own variations on the theme of

Wirklichkeit, such as *Einwirklichung* and *Entwirklichtheit*. See "The Zionism of Nordau" and "Paul de Lagarde."

12. Orig.: *die Unmotiviertheit des Normalitätswollens*. What Strauss means to say is that the notion of a will to normalcy is insufficient as a motivation for the political struggle of Zionism. It is not what actually drives Zionism, as Strauss understands it. This is one of the places where the self-understanding of the author can be glimpsed under a thin veil of objective language.

Biblical History and Science (1925)

JEWISH HISTORY: A DISCUSSION
[= *Die Jüdische Rundschau*, editor's introduction to
Leo Strauss, "Biblical History and Science"]

Preliminary note: As has been previously announced, Jüdischer Verlag (Berlin) recently published the second volume of Simon Dubnow's *World History of the Jewish People*. On this occasion Dr. Ernst Simon[1] published a fundamental essay on Jewish historiography in *Jüdisches Wochenblatt* (Frankfurt). The following essay by Dr. Leo Strauß [*sic*] discusses the ideas set out by Simon. We therefore regard it as important for the understanding of our readers to reproduce the key passages of Simon's article. After first praising some of the merits of Dubnow's work, Dr. Simon writes:

> Another methodological attitude of the author, which pervades the presentation perhaps even more deeply, is bound to provoke vehement protest. Dubnow admits that he wants to secularize Jewish history and liberate it from all theological dogmas, which have dominated it until now as much in Jewish as in Christian works. This principle at first sounds plausible. We are used to dating the birth of the sciences from the liberation of the modern mind, which, at the time of the Renaissance, broke the ban of the church and changed scientific inquiry from an "ancilla theologiae" (the "handmaiden of theology") first into her equally legitimate sister and soon into her mistress. The question is, however, whether what Dubnow understands by theology is identical with the claim to spiritual rule of the church, or whether there is not rather in Judaism an intrinsic lawfulness that makes possible an entirely different *concept of science*, and whether, since Judaism is not a "religion" but rather a way of life [*Lebensordnung*], its "theology" needs to be opposed to its "science."
>
> The question raised by these words is the real epistemological problem of any Jewish science. It cannot be solved in this space nor in any newspaper article, since it must be preceded by thorough investigations of the Jewish

concept of truth, of the *concept of time* of tradition, as well as of the entire *doctrine of categories* of Halakhah—that is, of the logic underlying the Oral Teachings [*mündliche Lehre*].[2] Here it merely needs to be stated that it seems strange when a Jewish historian simply glosses over the questions raised hereby by dismissing them as theological questions. This methodological sin of omission directly affects the presentation, for example, in that the actual historical conflict between Samuel and Saul is completely missed when the great struggle between prophecy and kingship is not recognized as a dominant force in the entire early Israelite history. In general, it seems to have escaped Dubnow's notice that the historiography of the Bible is itself one of the most essential historical facts in the course of the historical events themselves. He practices the kind of examination that Ahad Ha'am once referred to (in his famous essay on Moses)[3] as archaeological, in contrast to the truly historical one: he succeeds merely in sorting out the pieces of the mosaic from the picture as a whole, but is unable to reassemble it. One may understand the *coming into being* of historical series of events; but one no longer understands the possibility of their great *effect*.

A true history of Judaism should—like the Bible, and yes, like Josephus Flavius, and Ranke—begin with the creation of the world, which (despite other cosmogonies) is, not by chance, the first of our teachings.

Here our author could perhaps object, on the basis of his methodology, that he did not at all wish to write the history of Judaism as a spiritual truth but that he wrote the *history of the Jews*, who are a people like all others. And with this objection he would, in fact, hit on the core distinction. His work is a necessary expression of that frame of mind which, growing out of modern, nationalistic, clerical, or communist movements, seeks to normalize the Jewish people also with respect to mind, and thus to rob it of its true character, its true right to life. Even purely empirical events, such as the survival of the Jewish people as the only landless nation, will be hard to explain on this basis. In any case, however, the peculiar character of mind that even formed our national body down to the last detail must, as a result, be distorted.

LEO STRAUSS: BIBLICAL HISTORY AND SCIENCE

While discussing the *historical work of Simon Dubnow* (in the last but one issue of the *Jüdisches Wochenblatt*), Ernst Simon protests against Dubnow's program of a Jewish historiography that does not let itself be guided by dogmatic and scholastic concepts. He does so by remarking that Judaism does not put extraneous dogmas ahead of scientific inquiry. Simon assumes that Dubnow still sees himself too much in the role of the "liberator" from the yoke of tradition, which is meaningless today. Indeed, it does seem as if Dubnow's demand forces an open door. Hence, is there any point to this gesture? This gesture is a necessary one; and in what follows, we hope to show that it is so, and why it is so.

If, in the interest of genuine science, Dubnow turns against extraneous dogmas put ahead of science or dragged along by tradition, then, by so doing, he undoubtedly also turns against Jewish tradition. What is at stake is the central dogma of the existence of God and of the actions of God in the world, especially in the history of Israel. Let us not, after all, conceal the essential point of the quarrel. Science *knows* nothing of this dogma, and it does not permit itself on principle to *believe* in it. Now Scripture describes the fortune of Israel—mind you: Israel's external political fortune—as the reward for her obedience, and conversely it describes her misfortune as the punishment for her apostasy. Thus is it written. And one who denies this causal nexus[4] (perhaps denying it exactly on the basis of the deeper Jewish insight that nothing is in our hands regarding the fortune of the wicked and the fate of the pious) also declares by this denial that not everything that is written in Scripture is true. He thus denies the verbal inspiration of Scripture to which the most recent issue of *Israelit* retreated as the stronghold of true belief in its struggle against science, which is fundamentally rebellious because it is autonomous. For "verbal inspiration" not only means that the contents of Scripture derive from God rather than being man-made, but also means that it is true. And so the Orthodox act with complete consistency in protesting against a statement such as the *Jewish Chronicle* made to the effect that one need not view all the stories in Genesis as true.

Now, we all know what this position leads to. Belief is necessarily trivialized into belief in miracles and strange phenomena. The first Isaiah had foreknowledge of the name of the Persian king Cyrus;[5] Jonah actually sat in the belly of the whale; and if it were written in Scripture that the whale had been in the belly of Jonah, and that Jonah, for his part, had spat it out (as the pious Bryan[6] consistently admitted), then this too would have to be believed. Chronological inconsistencies are turned into unfathomable mysteries. We are of the opinion that the Enlightenment laughed this Orthodoxy to death, and if today we good-naturedly laugh at the Enlighteners, then we forget that an Orthodoxy still exists today. After a glance at the *Israelit*, one needs another Voltaire. (Just as the Enlightenment treatment of the figures of Abraham and David is a respectable antidote to many a load of homiletical schmaltz.)

How is Orthodoxy, with its belief in verbal inspiration and miracles, actually still possible today? The answer is that this Orthodoxy is Orthodox not *on account of* but *in spite of* verbal inspiration and miracles. If the Law matters to it, then this is so, for instance, because it asserts that only divine guidance protects humanity from the "madness of genocide," and because it sees in theocracy, which directs man toward the family rather than toward the impersonal state—and here the Jewish heart speaks—the only radical defense against the power instinct that rules the state. (A book that aims to return man entirely to the family bears the title *Elijah* [*Elijahu*]. What a pity that we know so little—indeed, nothing at all—about the family life of this prophet.) For the sake of such a "deeper" meaning of the Law one swallows dogmas whole, unchewed, like pills. One asserts that without inspiration the Law would lose its binding force, and one forgets that one does not base it on inspiration either. "Thus, what is so nauseating is not orthodoxy itself, but a certain squinting, limping orthodoxy which is unequal to itself!" (Lessing).

Let us assume, then, that verbal inspiration has been rendered obsolete, and that this dogma no longer crushes free inquiry. *Nevertheless*, Dubnow's demand is legitimate. Granted that the Bible, and especially the Torah, is the deposit of a centuries-long development (as indeed everyone basically assumes today) and did not have its peculiar origin in a diktat from Mt. Sinai. Still, the central difficulty remains that Scripture speaks unequivocally, adamantly, and compellingly of God's agency: God loves, chooses, rewards, punishes, he is Ruler of the world, also and especially of nature. Science knows nothing, and can know nothing, of all of these things since it does not permit itself to believe. What does science do when it encounters the Bible? It has no right to speak of a factor or an active power called "God." Of course, it must speak of the fact that Scripture speaks of God. But for science the history of God's rule necessarily turns into a history of theophany; it must become psychology. It must understand in what ultimate experiences talk about "God" is grounded. It must analyze "God." God is not a subject; for science God remains merely an object. This is the signature of the Bible science of our time—and that is what Dubnow means, what he must mean, when he refuses to tolerate theological prejudices.

The atheism[7] of present-day Bible science is obvious. If it is not obvious to the point that everyone can grasp it, then this is due to the accidental fact that this science happens to be predominantly in the hands of professors of theology; that the inclination to react to "God," implanted in the human heart from time immemorial, cannot be uprooted overnight; that no atheist emerges unscathed from reading the Psalms and the prophets; mostly, however, that this science has its seat in Germany, the land of "reconciliations" [*Versöhnungen*] and "sublations" [*Aufhebungen*].[8]

As Jews, we are radical; we do not like compromises. Let's bell the cat![9] With this in mind, I addressed the following question to a Jewish Bible scholar: Why does this science not permit itself to believe? It only needs to release itself from that prohibition in order to clear the way for a new biblical theology, for a theological exegesis of the Bible. (Competent people have already cleared the way for themselves: see the journal *Zwischen den Zeiten*.)[10] The answer I received was roughly as follows:

"Respect for a history that stretches over millennia, especially respect for the venerable history of our people, prohibits us today from using the word 'God.' What perhaps was still permissible in the age of Goethe (to call 'God' anything in whose perception one felt blessed) would now—in view of our heightened perception of psychological distances—be an intolerable dishonesty. It is not permissible to speak of God if one does not believe in the power of God over nature. To guide the hearts of men like rivers of water—this, a figment of our imagination could also do, as the history of religion as well as our everyday experience teaches. Without the power over nature God would, in truth, be powerless. I am no brute, I demand no miracles—creation would be enough for me.[11] But who today still dares to teach the creation of the world? (I disregard Orthodoxy, which, in possession of the truth—of neo-Kantianism supported by biblical quotations—can shut itself off from science.) I am not making up this criterion. Hermann Cohen, at least—one of the last of those for whom it was still permissible to speak of God—was enough of a Jew to see precisely in the power of God over nature an indispensable moment, not to say the basic meaning, of the idea of God. This conception seems to me eminently Jewish and rightly so, provided that Heinrich Heine—when speaking of an "existing away through the eternities all"[12]—had a share in Jewish vitality.[13] Even though a thousand essential properties [*Eigentlichkeiten*] of a more naïve religion may live on as symbols, religion becomes a masquerade if the power of God over nature is meant not in a strict sense [*in uneigentlichem Sinne*]."

Thus does Bible science answer our question, and thus does it believe that it brings honor to its name: by being critical and rigorous with itself, by refusing to allow itself any softness or laxity. Whatever one may think of the value of Dubnow's historiography, the intention of this man, which aims at freedom from theological prejudice, redounds to his honor. This intention is still of the utmost urgency even today. The objective of its attack is sharply defined: it is directed against the theological conception of biblical history, which presupposes the rigorous notion of God as the Ruler of the world rather than merely as Ruler of the human world. It is directed neither against the Orthodoxy that believes in every word of Scripture (this battle has been fought out), nor against those who take the name of God in vain by denying (not explicitly, far from it! but tacitly, very tacitly) His power over nature.

The honest exposition of Dubnow's program, therefore, seems to us very topical and very necessary. After what has been said, it is obvious that this program is hardly revolutionary. Hardly any researcher takes seriously [the claim] that events happened in biblical times just as the sources want us to believe: that, because of their piety, the pious judges and kings were successful, and conversely, that the impious ones, because of their lack of piety, were unsuccessful. He is of the opinion that, even in those days, God was for the big battalions; it goes without saying that strength is not identical with superiority in numbers and armaments. For example, "zeal for God" is, objectively speaking, quite an essential factor in the morale of an army, and thus of its strength, regardless of whether God exists and helps or does not. He will be confirmed in this opinion by the observation that a conception of natural causality occasionally shines through in the sources. For instance, if one reads the traditional commentaries on Judges 1:19,[14] one sees what contortions are needed in order to harmonize the literal sense, reminiscent of Frederick the Great,[15] with the traditional conception. Thus, the biblical sources themselves give us the possibility of arriving at a—perhaps not deep, but nevertheless accurate—conception of the beginnings of our people. We are thereby urged to assume that the theological conception of these beginnings may derive from a time in which there was no longer any political life, and therefore also no longer any political understanding. The most topical consequences depend on this. If, for example, the establishment of the kingdom under Saul was stylized as an apostasy only later, that is, in exile; if, as the sources permit to shine through, what originally impelled the establishment of the kingdom was self-evident and elementary needs rather than the theatricality of some hysterical intoxication with normality; if the later stylization was indeed the effect of prophecy, but the effect of prophecy on a people weaned of political responsibility, then the opponents of our political Zionism, who fight us by an appeal to tradition, do not have such an easy position to defend.

NOTES

Source: "Biblische Geschichte und Wissenschaft," *Jüdische Rundschau* (Berlin) 30, no. 88 (10 November 1925): 744–45, reprinted in *GS*, 2:357–61. The editor of *Die Jüdische Rundschau* at the time was Robert Weltsch, but it is not certain that Weltsch wrote the editorial introduction himself.

1. Cf. "Response to Frankfurt's 'Word of Principle'," n. 11.
2. *Mündliche Lehre,* that is, the Oral Torah (i.e., rabbinic tradition).
3. Ahad Ha'am, originally: Asher Hirsch Ginsberg, 1856–1927, Hebrew essayist and leader of the Hibbat Tsiyyon movement. The essay referred to by Ernst Simon is "Moses" (in Hebrew), *Hashiloah* 13, no. 2 (1904), reprinted in Ahad Ha'am, *Al Parashat Ha-derakhim,* vol. 1 (Tel Aviv and Jerusalem: Devir, 1948), 207–22.

4. In the German Protestant theological literature, the technical term for this causal nexus is *Tun-Ergehen-Zusammenhang* (the connection between doing and faring).

5. Cf. Isaiah 45, that is, part of Deutero- or Second Isaiah, a division between sources established on the assumption, rejected by orthodox readers, of a *vaticinium ex eventu*.

6. William Jennings Bryan (1860–1925), three-time Democratic presidential candidate and Presbyterian fundamentalist, famous for his participation in the "monkey trial," a widely noted anti-Darwinist lawsuit in Tennessee (1925). Source: RGG.

7. Cf. Franz Rosenzweig, "Atheistische Theologie," in *Zweistromland: Kleinere Schriften zu Glauben und Denken*, ed. Reinhold Mayer and Annemarie Mayer (Dordrecht and Boston: Martinus Nijhoff, 1984), 687–97, 858.

8. "Reconciliation" and "sublation" are both signal Hegelian terms, although not in the plural. As used here, the terms carry an ironic sense. Germany as the *Land der . . .* (land of . . .) is part of the expression *das Land der Dichter und Denker* (the land of poets and thinkers). This, too, adds to the irony.

9. A well-known expression, in German as in English, meaning "let's do the desirable but dangerous deed."

10. *Zwischen den Zeiten* was a journal of systematic theology founded by Karl Barth, Eduard Thurneysen, and G. Merz in 1922. The term *Zwischen den Zeiten* (between times) stems from Gogarten (in *Die Christliche Welt* 34 (1920): 374–78. Among those who contributed to the journal and, thus, associated themselves with Barth's "theology of the word of God" were Emil Brunner and Rudolf Bultmann. This movement is usually referred to as dialectic theology.

11. "would be enough for me": an allusion to the Passover song "Dayenu."

12. Quotation from Heinrich Heine's satirical poem "Disputation," included in *Romanzero* (1851). The stanza ("Unser Gott, der ist lebendig, / Und in seiner Himmels-halle / Existieret er drauflos / Durch die Ewigkeiten alle") is part of the speech of a rabbi who participates in a Jewish-Christian disputation before the king and queen of Spain. That Heine and the poor son of a rabbi in Heine's poem are invoked in order to point to Jewish vitality, confusing this vitality in turn with belief in a transcendental God (ignoring, also, the difference between hymnic affirmations of divine transcendence and satirical echoes of the same), reveals this speech of "a Jewish Bible scholar" as a specimen of the kind of atheistic theology that Ernst Simon may have (unwittingly) endorsed and that Strauss, here at least, rejects as dishonest. Strauss shares with Franz Rosenzweig the view on the atheism inherent in the ultramodern theology he refers to. See the latter's early open letter to Martin Buber under the title "Atheistische Theologie," reprinted in *Zweistromland*, 687–97.

13. The phrase "had a share in [Jewish vitality]" *(an jüdischer Lebendigkeit teilhatte)* echoes Mishnah Sanhedrin chap. 10, "all Israel have a share in the world to come."

14. Judges 1:19 (KJV): "And the LORD was with Judah; and he drove out the inhabitants of the mountain; but could not drive out the inhabitants of the valley, because they had chariots of iron." The logical subject of v. 19ba seems to be YHWH so that the verse literally reads: "but (YHWH's hand was not with Judah) to inherit the inhabitants of the valley, for they had chariots of iron." Thus YHWH is said to have been unable to overcome a population that availed itself of weaponry superior to that available to the

Judahites. This would be another way of saying that Judah was unable to conquer the valley for perfectly mundane reasons, which implicitly denies the role of any supernatural intervention in the conquest.

15. Frederick II (1712–86), king of Prussia, deist and rationalist, "philosopher of Sans Souci," friend of Voltaire's, and representative of enlightened absolutism. Frederick ("der alte Fritz") was a figure much debated and contemplated in German letters, and his famously irreligious bon mots were handed down for generations.

III

——————————————————————————————————⟨✦⟩

Historical-Philological Writings on Spinoza (1924–26)

In the first essay included in this section, "Cohen's Analysis of Spinoza's Bible Science," Strauss defends Spinoza's *Theological-Political Treatise* against the charges brought against it by Hermann Cohen. Cohen's "Spinoza über Staat und Religion, Judentum und Christentum," a wartime essay from 1915, was Cohen's *j'accuse* against the Sephardic philosopher who, in his view, had committed the "humanly incomprehensible betrayal" of denigrating Judaism while elevating Christianity, providing the subsequent tradition of Continental philosophy with an excuse to ignore and despise the civilizational potential of the sources of Judaism. In Cohen's view, Spinoza had knowingly, high-handedly, and thus unforgivably distorted the record, and he had done so for the selfish motivation of revenge on the Jewish community that had excommunicated him. Strauss's defense of Spinoza was occasioned by the 1924 publication of Cohen's *Jüdische Schriften* that included the 1915 essay. The review was one of six contributions by Strauss to *Der Jude* published in the space of a single year (23 October to 24 October), and it is not without a certain poignancy that his critique of Cohen's apologetics followed on the heels of his defense of the moral integrity of Cohen's old nemesis, Paul de Lagarde.

The rigorous impartiality of Strauss's defense of Spinoza attracted the attention of Julius Guttmann, a dedicated Cohen loyalist, who, as the academic director of the Akademie für die Wissenschaft des Judentums (which had been coinitiated by Cohen and later not only published his *Jüdische Schriften* but also, in 1928, his *Schriften zur Philosophie und Zeitgeschichte*), offered Strauss a research fellowship to pursue his research on Spinoza further. "On the Bible Science of Spinoza and His Precursors," the second text in this section, is Strauss's 1926 report on the progress of his research for the Akademie and was originally published in its *Korrespondenzblatt*. To be sure, the study undertaken by Strauss deviated from what Guttmann had commissioned in that it focused on Spinoza's critique of religion rather than on his Bible science. The tug of war between Guttmann and Strauss is not yet evident in the 1926 report, which is extracted from a longer manuscript begun in 1925 and completed in 1928, but comes to the fore in the compromising title of the book published in 1930: *Spinoza's Critique of Religion as the Foundation of His Bible Science (Die Religionskritik Spinozas als Grundlage seiner Bibelwissenschaft)*. Guttmann's editorial interference prompted Strauss to complain privately about the "conditions of censorship" under which he was compelled to write his first book, conditions that did not prevent Strauss, however, from continuing his official association with the Akademie even beyond his dismissal as an employee, precipitated by a general financial crisis, in 1931.

Cohen's Analysis of Spinoza's Bible Science (1924)[i]

I.

It is typical of Hermann Cohen's style that he couches the critique of an idea in the critique of the possibly accidental expression of that idea.* This is the way of our intensive and penetrating *traditional* art of interpretation, which takes each word seriously and weighs it carefully. Thus, Cohen already objects to the title "Theologico-Political Treatise," where he misses "a reference to philosophy, which may be assumed to contribute to theology as well as to politics." Using the *historical-critical* approach, we shall establish the fact that in the seventeenth century one could dispense with such a reference. On the other hand, Cohen himself needed to give his theological magnum opus

---

[i] Hermann Cohen, "Spinoza über Staat und Religion, Judentum und Christentum" (1915) in *Jahrbuch für jüdische Geschichte und Literatur*, vol. 18, pp. 56–150, now reprinted in volume 3 of the collected *Jewish Writings* of Hermann Cohen, which have just been published by the Akademie für die Wissenschaft des Judentums (Berlin: Schwetschke Verlag).

* [Strauss adds in the margins of his copy:] A further example: Contemplations of the "Society of Ethical Culture" [*Gesellschaft für ethische Kultur*] Cohen criticizes *as follows:* "And yet, the Greek word should have reminded one clearly enough of Socrates and Plato, of the methodological discoverers of ethics, of the founders of morality" *Jüdische Schriften* III, p. 110. (The ethical attitude referred to the simple evidence of the moral.) [Cf. *GS*, 1:363/387 and see *JS*, 3:110 ("Religion und Sittlichkeit").]

the title "The Religion of *Reason* Out of the Sources of Judaism"[1] because, in our century, "religion out of the sources of Judaism" might otherwise suggest something completely different.

The criticism[2] of the title contains in a nutshell the criticism of the book. Philosophy is missing, and without the link of philosophy the joining to gether of theology and politics must appear arbitrary. Thus the examination of the title alone arouses the suspicion that the book may have nonobjective presuppositions.[3] What is applied here is a historiographic method that stems perhaps from the theological science of apologetics: Should a passage by an uninspired author be incomprehensible to the interpreter or should it seem to him objectionable, then he must raise questions about the author's life. In its dark recesses he will find an explanation for the dark passage. There are two such dark recesses in Spinoza's life. First, he "forced"[4] himself to accept an annuity for his political writings in the service of the power of the state— this is the "politics"; and second, his hostile attitude toward the Jewish people makes him look like "the informer, a distinct type characteristic of the history of persecutions of the Jews"[5]—this is the "theology." Cohen only hints at these terrible charges, in support of which he can, incidentally, cite a neutral non-Jewish author—an "unbiased party"[6]—but he hints at them in such a way that no misunderstanding is possible. In any case, Spinoza's life is made to appear here, in an astonishing way, as the mediating agent between ideas that "stand only in a very loose connection with one another."[7] However perfect the enlightenment provided by this explanation, which may be in conformity with Spinoza's life and may do justice to it, we would nevertheless like to attempt to get by without it. Since what is being considered at this point is not the methodology of interpretation in general, may it suffice to contrast the kind of interpretation that focuses strongly on personal circumstances with the historical critical kind. The principle of the latter is expressed, very aptly for our context, by Mommsen's dictum: It is not permissible to refer to "egotistical" motives where motives "in accord with duty" suffice for an explanation.[8]

As we saw, Cohen believes that he must draw on the aforesaid embarrassing facts of Spinoza's life in order to explain the "unnatural"[9] connection between literary critique [of the Bible] and the "publicistic task"[10] of a political pamphlet [*Staatsschrift*] on behalf of the Dutch politician Jan de Witt.[11] If, however, we view the *Treatise* as a work arising from motives "in accord with duty"—as the title reads, the work is meant to demonstrate "that not only can the freedom of philosophizing be granted without detriment to *piety* and *peace within the state*, but its abrogation necessarily entails the abrogation of piety and peace within the state"[12]—then the necessity of connecting the political problem with the philological one follows immediately. The freedom of inquiry was to be protected from the public powers—and there were two public powers, the secular and the spiritual. *The combination of the two heterogeneous problems in the Treatise has a deep root, namely, the context from which the separation of the two powers arises.*[13] That is to say: with respect to the state— and since the reference was to a liberal government[14]—the rational construction would have sufficed. The claims of the church, however, rested less on reason than on Scripture. Therefore it was not enough to prove that reason does not acknowledge such tutelage by the church, it also had to be shown that the church could not rely on Scripture. This proof, however, presupposed the successful refutation of the right of the ecclesiastical interpretation of Scripture. Since it may be assumed that there is a basis for the claims of the church in Scripture, it had to be shown that, according to its own deeper meaning, Scripture cannot be an authority for restricting free inquiry.

Therefore Spinoza, aiming to secure the freedom of inquiry, had to make his argument concerning church and state simultaneously unless he wanted to ignore the historical reality of his time. For the sake of his argument with the church he had to overthrow the supports on which rested the ecclesiastical argumentation, that is, the authority of Scripture and the ecclesiastical interpretation of Scripture. The general disposition of the *Treatise* is that "natural," if one proceeds from its objective tendency [*sachliche Tendenz*]. To be sure, [according to Cohen] the two problems—the problem of political theory and the problem of the critique of the Bible—have "lost" their "isolated objectivity" ["*isolierte Sachlichkeit eingebüßt*"].[15] "Lost"? Can one speak of an objective isolation [*sachliche Isoliertheit*] from one another of the political and ecclesiastical-theological problems in the seventeenth century?

"In fact, the critique of the Bible [*Bibelkritik*] would not have entered this book had it not been prepared by another moment in Spinoza's life."[16] This other moment is the major ban[17] imposed on Spinoza by the Amsterdam Synagogue, or rather, the "protest pamphlet" [*Protestschrift*] written by Spinoza "against the ban imposed on him."[18] Granted that Spinoza would not have written those parts of the *Treatise* that emerged from the "protest pamphlet" if he had not first written the "protest pamphlet"; and that he would not have composed the latter if he had not been banned; and that he would not have been banned if—well, if what? If he had not said and done the things that he justified *in* his "protest pamphlet." This amounts to circular reasoning: Spinoza would not have written his critique of the Bible if he had not held views critical of the Bible [*bibelkritische Ansichten*]. Whether the *Treatise* owes its *existence* in part to a reaction to the ban, or whether Spinoza intended to state the results of his research independently of whatever need he may have had for justification or revenge, is insignificant when it comes to the explanation of its *contents*. This is so because the contents *precede* the ban. He was banned because of "abominable blasphemies against God and Moses." Is it necessary to point out to Hermann Cohen the idea with which the *Critique of Pure Reason* begins?[19] It is doubtful that Spinoza's critique of the Bible begins with the ban; assuming, however, that it begins with the ban, it need not therefore arise from it alone. The essential thing, that is, the contents, would have arisen from Spinoza's own context of thought [*Denkzusammenhang*], while the sense impression of the ban merely provided the occasion. "Thus we see that the ostensibly psychological interest makes a critical substitution [*Unterschleif*] that is *fatal* and *typical*." Thus concludes . . . Hermann Cohen his exposition of the previously mentioned idea on page 97f. of the third edition of his famous work, *Kant's Theory of Experience*.[20]

Appeal to the facts of the life history of a thinker makes sense if it draws on confirmed facts of symbolic value for his lifework.[21] But what is one to think of explanations that draw on facts that are merely conjectured and are of no consequence for the work to be explained, such as the following: Spinoza "apparently refrained from publishing the pamphlet because he wanted to launch the attack on his enemies on a larger scale and from a broader perspective. Perhaps he also derived an ambiguous satisfaction from the idea that he was to conduct his battle against Judaism and its biblical source in combination with the spirit of his politics"?[22] If one wanted to reject this conjecture, then Cohen's explanation of the connection between theology and politics in the *Treatise* would not be sufficient even in the most superficial sense. For if Spinoza had wanted to write a pamphlet of political agitation for Jan de Witt, on the one hand, and a pamphlet against Judaism, on the other, he would not have needed to carry out both plans by means of a *single* book. Thus, aside from its lack of objectivity, Cohen's explanation is supported by pure conjecture.

Therefore:* *in Spinoza's historical context,*[23] *the connection between political theory [Staatstheorie] and critique of the Bible is sufficiently motivated.*[ii]

---

* [Added in the margin:] Cohen himself says something like this in the Halberstadt lecture published in *Korrespondenzblatt*. [Ed.: Cf. *GS*, 1:366/386. The reference is most likely to *JS*, 1:208–10, the addition to the combined reprint of two essays Cohen had previously published in *Korrespondenzblatt des Verbandes der Deutschen Juden*, "Gesinnung" and "Der Nächste" (see *JS*, 1:339–40). In the added paragraphs, Cohen apologizes for not maintaining a strict separation between matters pertaining to the relation between

So much for the problem of the title. Cohen also examines carefully the
table of contents and remarks in this connection that "almost two-thirds of
the entire book deals with biblical theology,"[24] that is, *Treatise*, chapters 1–
11. In addition, the theme of chapters 17 and 18 is: the state and history of the
Hebrews. "The *Treatise* has 20 chapters."[25] A further proof of Spinoza's evil
schemes. Cohen would not go into such statistical pieces of information if he
did not credit them with some demonstrative force in support of the claim
that Spinoza "saved up all his resentment against the ban in order to pour it
out in this work on political philosophy based on philological research into
the Bible."[26]

Cohen does concede that the "philological research into the Bible" is a
precondition for "giving full vent to the old grudge."[27] Therefore, there is a
certain separability of the wicked end from the means that, in and of itself,
Cohen may not object to. This means is put in service of the idea "that the
religion of Judaism, founded by Moses, set, rather, as its sole end the establishment and preservation of the *Jewish state*."[28] And, to Cohen, this idea is satanic—while he certainly would not have considered it satanic but divine if
someone said that the sole end of the religion of Judaism is the establishment
and preservation of the *socialist state*. For all that, this remark is entirely unrelated to the matter at issue; it merely serves to point to Cohen's real tendency
in his critique of the *Treatise*.[29] Put briefly: the sacrilege of Spinoza consists,
according to Cohen, in the politicization of the Jewish religion (in the sense
conveyed above). The motive for this politicization is the will to "destroy the
Jewish concept of religion,"[30] and this will is at least partly determined by the
grudge that Spinoza nursed on account of the ban.

Here, for once, it is advisable that we too draw on the "unbiased party."[31]
It teaches us that "the separation between the spiritual and the secular powers
in the Hebrew state was the standing argument for the presumptions of Calvinist orthodoxy. In reply to this, Spinoza denies that this separation was the
meaning of the Mosaic Law, and seeks to prove that the inevitable result of
priestly independence, and even of the institution of prophecy, was a calam-
ity for the state. *In this respect Spinoza's argument with Judaism is in complete*

God and man (theology) and matters pertaining to the relation between men (morality,
politics). In other words, as Strauss points out correctly, Cohen admits that there may
be perfectly respectable reasons for doing what Spinoza does in *Theological-Political Treatise*.]

ⁱⁱ It may be useful to refer to the treatment of questions concerning biblical criticism in Hobbes's work of political philosophy, *Leviathan* [Ed.: First published 1651].

agreement with the innermost end of the Treatise."[32] Here too, for an objective examination there is no reason to search for motives other than those that are "in accord with duty." Spinoza wants to fight against the damage to political life that arises from the coexistence of the two powers. The defenders of this coexistence [of the powers] supported their claim by the history of the Hebrew nation. Therefore it has to be shown ad hominem that this coexistence was not salutary, that the biblical models of spiritual power were either not "spiritual" or were not models. There is no need to have recourse to the bathos of a thirst for revenge in order to explain this thoroughly clear and self-sustaining context.

We saw above that Spinoza wants, as it were, to win recognition for the neutrality of the philosopher vis-à-vis state and church. How is this to be reconciled with the fact that he now sides with the party of the state and against the party of the church? Is it necessary here to invoke the two hundred guilder? The objective reason for Spinoza's partisanship is that, on grounds of principle, he needs to deny to religious associations the character of a "spiritual *power*" [*geistliche Gewalt*] while, no less on grounds of principle, he needs to emphasize the power character [*Gewaltcharakter*] of the political association [*des staatlichen Verbandes*]. Whatever one may make of the objective justification of this denial [of the character of a "spiritual *power*" to religious associations], it suffices for our critique that there is nothing in Cohen's entire standpoint that he could use to object to this denial.

Thus, it is not Spinoza's fault if his presentation of the contents of the Bible suffers from unscientific ends that are not identical with an elucidation of those contents for their own sake. If Orthodoxy was able to make its political claims bulletproof by means of an appeal to the authority of Scripture, then one could not blame the liberals if they availed themselves of the same means. After all, Spinoza was not the first to look at the Bible from a political perspective, this perspective being self-evident in his age: he merely turned the tables with astonishing energy. It was part of the intellectual landscape from which Spinoza proceeded that, "in political reasoning, biblical analogies were of the strongest demonstrative force."[33] The well-known reason why the Calvinists supported [their political claims] with the [Hebrew] Bible rather than with the New Testament is that in the [Hebrew] Bible there are "spiritual powers" that signify a great deal for concrete political decisions, while the New Testament separates God and Caesar, and commands the Christian to submit to the secular authorities. Hence, if an opponent of Calvinist orthodoxy wanted to deal it a decisive blow, he too had to focus on the [Hebrew] Bible and deprive its "spiritual powers" of their religious halo.

Therefore: *in Spinoza's historical context, the politicizing interpretation of the Bible is sufficiently motivated.*

A further moment in the spiritual situation of the seventeenth century is the Protestant orientation of religion toward faith and toward Scripture. For the Protestant of that time, the Word of God, revelation, universal religion, divine law, and faith—all these were in fact, if not identical, then certainly of equal value. For Spinoza[, on the other hand,] it was, to begin with, self-evident and in accordance with his entire standpoint to give precedence to autonomous knowledge [*Erkenntnis*] over the authority of Scripture. However, he also had to show now, arguing ad hominem,[34] that Scripture does not contain the essential knowledge [*Erkenntnisse*], taught in part also by the Church, that we owe to reason; indeed, even that Scripture, according to its own meaning, does not at all wish to impart knowledge [*Erkenntnisse*]. For Spinoza, knowledge [*Erkenntnis*] is always (mediated or immediate) knowledge [*Erkenntnis*] of God. Given the ontic primacy of God over the created things, delegating the knowledge of God to Scripture and the knowledge of created things to autonomous reason would again lead to an authoritarian dependence of reason [on Scripture]. Hence it is a question of life or death for reason to prove its own priority over Scripture, and even, if possible, to prove the irrelevance of Scripture with regard to matters of scientific validity. Only if God were to have no quality of existence [*Seins-Charakter*], if He were, say, an idea or an ideal,[35] and if therefore true knowledge of existing things [*seiende Dinge*] was possible even without recourse to God (a notion on account of which, in the age of Spinoza, one would doubtlessly have been burnt at the stake and perhaps without Spinoza protesting against it), then only could reason do without the proof that faith and Scripture as the norm of faith have no essential cognitive significance. This is not to rule out the fact that elements of knowledge [*Erkenntnismomente*] contribute to faith or to Scripture. If Spinoza needed to "generate this misconception [*Unbegriff*] of religion by entirely excluding the knowledge of God from faith,"[36] he did so in order that the Orthodox misconception [*Unbegriff*] of science would not prevail, and not in order to damage the reputation of Scripture and of Judaism.

Now what does Cohen say? "The first consequence that follows from this unnatural connection of problems (i.e., that of politics and philology) is that Spinoza does not seek to determine the concept of religion from the point of view of his *Ethics*, but rather he derives it from Scripture, and hence equates it absolutely with the content of Scripture, which constitutes the so-called 'Word of God.' Thus there formed in his mind an identity of the concepts: Word of God, revelation, universal religion, divine law, and faith."[37] As we have seen, Spinoza was not the first for whom this identity formed itself. This identity seems to be no more "unnatural" than the connection of politics and philology if one considers the question: for whose enlightenment did Spinoza write the *Treatise*? and not the question: who paid him and whom did he want to denounce? It may be a matter of unreasonable identifications and connections; but these were just as "natural" in the seventeenth century as the connection and identification of prophecy and socialism in the nineteenth century.

Therefore: *in Spinoza's historical context, the identification of religion and Scripture, and thereby the denial of the cognitive value of religion, is adequately motivated.*

At this point, a comment on a matter of principle may be in order.

We are guided here by the interests of Judaism. These interests are affected in the gravest manner by the question of which image of the biblical world possesses the binding power of the truth. This is why Spinoza, who through his critique contributed more than anyone else to the removal of the traditional image, is of interest to us. Now, it is true that the critical argumentation as such is, within certain limits, independent of the philosophical, political, or selfish motives that occasioned it in its author. But the deeper significance of this critique depends on its point of departure, on the connection of motives that animates it. If this connection is worthless, then the critique is a purely philological[38] enterprise. This was Cohen's claim: Spinoza elaborated "his ideas toward achieving a literary effect, indeed an effect on contemporary issues."[39] He even topped this claim by seeking to make plausible the insincerity of the entire critique by pointing to Spinoza's hatred of Judaism. He arrives at this result: "Such a man may have been able to elucidate the age and the order of the biblical scriptures. These merits are fully comprehensible. But biblical criticism [*Bibelkritik*] would be in bad shape if it exhausted itself in such *philology*, if its *understanding* of the Bible, its understanding of the prophets, truly and inwardly rested on Spinoza's shoulders."[40] Much depends on the tenability of the claims leading to such a judgment. We were able to invalidate the second claim, and to take the edge off the first. We did this by showing that, in Spinoza's historical context, the "unnatural" connection of politics and philology, the politicizing tendency of the interpretation of the Bible, and the denial of the cognitive character of religion necessarily emerge from the striving for the liberation of science and the state from ecclesiastical tutelage. *Spinoza was compelled to engage in the critique of the Bible by legitimate motives, whether or not he was full of hatred toward Judaism.*

II.

The topical[41] and historically conditioned end of the *Treatise*, as legitimate as it may be, is a source of errors for a genuine comprehension of the contents of the Bible.[42] To be sure, the striving for the liberation of science and the state from ecclesiastical tutelage is, in this respect, no more dangerous than an interpretation of Scripture that supports ecclesiastical claims to power. However, such a confrontation merely excuses, but it does not surmount, the lack of objectivity in Spinoza's Bible research [*Bibelforschung*]. Spinoza must argue ad hominem.[43] Thus he runs the risk of being diverted from the deeper connection of philosophical motives that constitutes the *Ethics,* and of eventually contradicting this connection. If one could prove such a contradiction, the charge of a lack of objectivity would gain considerably in weight. If, on the other hand, we showed the inadequacy of *one* such attempted proof, we still would not have secured the objectivity of the *Treatise,* which, in this context, means: its inner connection and harmony with the philosophical system of the *Ethics.*[44] Perhaps other contradictions could still be proven! At this point, however, the positive problem of deriving the fundamental principles of Spinoza's Bible science from the system of the *Ethics* can only be posed. With its solution, the topicality of the *Treatise* would be freed from the gravest suspicions.

From now on, Cohen is concerned with proving a contradiction between philosophical theses. This being so, the plane occupied in the hitherto discussed part of the analysis is abandoned: we breathe again the pure air of philosophical argumentation.

Cohen had reproached Spinoza for "seeking to determine the concept of religion not from the point of view of his *Ethics,* but to derive it from Scripture."[45] He saw this as the consequence of the publicistic and denunciatory tendency.[46] We have seen that Spinoza argues ad hominem. Whether this argumentation leads to an "utter contradiction . . . with the Spinoza of the *Ethics*"[47] seems, therefore, to be of little importance.[48] The contradiction could be explained as an external accommodation to ecclesiastical teachings, an accommodation not uncommon in the age of the Enlightenment. But the contradiction would remain, and it would give new life to the suspicion. Hence we will have to take a closer look.

Cohen's first philosophical objection refers to the contradiction between the concept of the will in the *Ethics* and that which is presupposed in the teachings of the *Treatise* on the philosophy of religion, or rather, on theology.

"According to Spinoza, faith is obedience to God. Consequently, faith establishes and signifies not a theoretical relation to God but merely a practical one."[49] Why does Spinoza dispute the theoretical character of faith? First, he does this for the sake of safeguarding the autonomy of reason. But second, he also does so in order to overcome the dependence of blessedness on belief in all of the views and events handed down in the Bible. Now Cohen, however, substitutes his (as it were)[50] Maimonidean-Kantian *rational faith* for the Protestant *faith in Scripture*—for which, one may presume, there is a Jewish analogue, as is shown, for example, by the justification for the ban on Spinoza. It is this Protestant faith in Scripture whose theoretical value is attacked by Spinoza. On the other hand, the norm of Cohen's Maimonidean-Kantian *rational faith* is not what is said about God in *Scripture* inasmuch as it is Scripture, but rather it is the *concept* of God—and he is surprised that Spinoza excludes knowledge of God from faith *in spite of this*. Spinoza does not know of the "faith" that Cohen substitutes for the discussions of the *Treatise*.* Rather, first and above all, he knows of faith in Scripture as the norm of truth and the criterion of a pious state of mind [*Gesinnung*], faith that was then an actuality of the highest order. Therefore, Spinoza's thesis cited in Cohen's words means none other than this: faith in the "truth" of all passages of Scripture has no significance for knowledge. To be sure, Spinoza substructs *his own* concept of faith beneath the Orthodox one.[51] Faith is not faith in a content for the sake of this content, but rather faith, insofar as it makes one blessed [*selig*], can only be the expression of the very turn of mind [*Gesinnung*] whose reward is, or which itself is, "blessedness" [*Seligkeit*].[52] This turn of mind is obedience to the divine commandment of love of the neighbor. Spinoza examines the [Hebrew] Bible and finds that the only sense in which faith is commanded in Scripture is the sense in which he understands it, not, however, as faith in the opinions and actions reported in Scripture.

At this point, Cohen brings in the "sharpshooting guns of the *Ethics*":[53] "How, then, is human action possible if it is not guided by reason, which, in Spinoza, is in any case synonymous with the will?"[54] Because the norms of moral action are inscribed in every human being,[55] even in one not guided by reason, and because everyone can accept them from Scripture. "The will is thus to be moved by Scripture even if it remains unmoved by reason!"[56] Indeed, those whose will cannot be moved by reason are brought to moral action by obedience alone. The will of the unwise is identical with his obedient reason, just as the will of the wise is identical with his autonomous reason. In any case: *intellectus et voluntas unum et idem sunt* [intellect and will are one and the same].[57] Therefore, it is not possible to speak of a contradiction between the doctrine [in Spinoza's *Treatise*] of the merely practical character of faith and the doctrine of the *Ethics*. The deeper cause of the misunderstanding

---

* [Added in the margin:] "The cultural historical significance of Protestantism consists in the detaching [*Ablösen*] of religion from science, of science from religion." (Jüd. Schr. III 114). [Cf. *GS*, 1:372, 387 and see *JS*, 3:114.]

is that Cohen overlooks the *hierarchy* that is acknowledged here as well as elsewhere in Spinoza's system, according to which obedience to God is a lower form, legitimate in itself, of the human relation to God, whose highest rung is the *amor Dei intellectualis* [intellectual love of God]. Instead, Cohen finds in the *Treatise* an "irreconcilable *opposition* between religion and philosophy."[58]

The truth can be comprehended by autonomous, theoretical reason alone. The salvation of one's soul, however, must not be made dependent on knowledge or else it would be unattainable for most human beings.[59] Truth can only be known, it cannot be believed in. One has attained it only when one understands it; if one does not understand it, one has but words. Truths that are not understood but merely believed in can endanger the salvation of the soul (e.g., the doctrine of predestination, if misunderstood, can lead to the most lax morality); and untruths that are inwardly accepted and shape the heart of a human being can contribute to the salvation of the soul (e.g., the belief in the existence of angels). We therefore understand Spinoza's thesis, which Cohen expresses thus: Spinoza "put religion altogether outside the pale of truth."[60] He quotes, full of indignation: "Dogmas of this kind could be regarded as pious in one and as impious in another; this is because they are merely to be judged according to their works."[61] For Cohen, "it cannot be doubted that this theory must dissolve itself in contradictions."[62] We shall see.

In order to create an authority removed from the confusion of opinions about religious doctrine of his century, Spinoza establishes a number of dogmas that are the logical presupposition of obedience to God and love of the neighbor.[63] We are not concerned here with truth, or with validity on the highest level of the human mind, that is, on the level of autonomous and philosophizing reason. For reason, after all, there is no category of obedience to God! Cohen especially objects to the fact that the uniqueness of God is mentioned in this context. "And is the uniqueness of God not supposed to rest on knowledge? The specialist in Jewish philosophy of religion does not mention at all that uniqueness is a problem of knowledge alone. . . ."[64] It was unnecessary for Spinoza to raise a big fuss about the fact that uniqueness, in a legitimate and ultimate sense, is accessible only to thought. But it is not accessible to everyone's thought, and [yet] everyone who wants to lead a decent life must, at least according to Spinoza, believe in this uniqueness. "Because devotion, veneration, and love spring only from the preeminence of the one above all others."[65]

In a similar manner, Cohen discusses yet another of Spinoza's dogmas. Here, too, he fails to appreciate the, so to speak, sociopedagogical character of Spinoza's dogmatics—which, by the way, is none other than the perhaps most conscious, at least the most upright and disinterested, form of the *pia fraus* [pious fraud]. Cohen takes it for a "philosophy of religion."[66]

Cohen: If knowledge, rather than religion, points "the way even toward practice," "then Scripture could not attain its identity with faith. Scripture in regard to its 'proper' content, however, is supposed to be authenticated here as the 'Word of God.' We know that this is the main topic of the *Treatise*."[67] We know that this presentation reverses Spinoza's train of thought. He proceeds from the historically actual "identity" of faith and Scripture. This identity points toward the possibility of a moral practice that is not founded on knowledge.

Cohen's second philosophical objection is much weightier. It is no longer leveled against a contradiction between Spinoza's individual theses but rather directly against the core of the system: ethical idealism is made impossible by the complete integration of the ethical into the Unity of Nature [*die Eine Natur*]. Since our concern here is only with Bible science, we content ourselves with merely mentioning this fundamental philosophical opposition. We shall comment on only one point. Cohen calls Spinoza a "sophist,"[68] namely, with respect to his complete elimination, within the Unity of Nature, of oppositions of value [*Wertgegensätze*] that belong under the purview of reason, "for Nature's bounds are not set by the laws of human reason."[69] Spinoza expresses this idea in yet another way: Our knowledge is only partial.[70] That is the profound idea of Job, chapter 38. We understand[71] that Cohen feels repelled by it, Cohen who asks: "How can nature, how can God answer for this difference among human beings"[72] (*scil.* the difference between those who are designated by nature to live according to reason and those not so designated)? Meanwhile he puts Spinoza among the "mystics" who are "not satisfied with the transcendence of God"![73]

Cohen views Spinoza's political doctrine [*Staatslehre*] with great antipathy. We distinguish between two moments in this doctrine. 1. The foundation of the state on egoism and prudence, on "eternal truths"[74]—as Spinoza says seriously and Cohen ironically. Just as easily as he did for the sentence that the reward of virtue is virtue itself,[75] Cohen could have certainly indicated the source of this doctrine in *Pirkei Avot*: "But for the fear of government, men would swallow each other alive."[76] 2. The demand, based on the actual situation in the seventeenth century, for a superordination of the power of the state over the church. In our context, this second point is more essential. I quote the main passage from Spinoza: "However, because human beings usually err the most in religious matters, and because they compete with each other inventing all sorts of things according to their respective casts of mind (as is abundantly confirmed by experience), so surely the right of the state would be made dependent on the various judgments and affects of individuals if no one were legally required to obey the supreme power in matters that he himself imputes to religion."[77] We note that behind this judgment stands the historical reality of seventeenth-century Netherlands, with its plethora of sects, and that, in any case, it refers to this historical reality rather than to any Jewish matters. However worthless its reasons, the clergy that wished to rebel against the secular authority could do so, with the most effective pretense, by appealing to the Hebrew prophets. In light of this situation, Spinoza's judgment—a judgment that is to be understood as thoroughly ad hominem—to the effect that the prophets "stirred up the people more than they improved them," and that they were "often found intolerable even by pious kings,"[78] is not wholly incomprehensible.[79] In any case, we need not suspect that behind this judgment lies the satanic[80] consciousness of opposition to ethical idealism or, even less, an indirect proof of the ethical idealism of the prophets.

We maintain: *the moral principle of the Treatise does not contradict that of the Ethics. Spinoza's general way of proceeding in the Treatise can be justified also from a systematic perspective, because the fundamental necessity and the objective [sachlich] legitimacy of the argumentatio ad hominem (in the unusual extension of its application that is important to the Treatise) follows from the principle of hierarchy that is fundamental to the Ethics.*

III.

We have attempted to show that the purpose and disposition of the *Treatise* can be easily understood from the general intellectual climate of the seventeenth century. In this attempt it has been unnecessary to stress Spinoza's Jewish connections, aside from the more technical question of his knowledge of language and literature. At least it should have become clear that an objective understanding of the purpose and disposition of the *Treatise* is entirely possible without regard to the "personal" motives stressed by Cohen. Now, it is conceivable that Spinoza's general attitude shows itself more in the *implementation of his investigation*, namely, in that it directed his research in Bible science [*bibelwissenschaftliche Forschung*] toward those facts whose disclosure amounted to an attack on Judaism. Therefore we now turn to Cohen's objections to Spinoza's theses of Bible science [*bibelwissenschaftliche Thesen*]. Above all, we ask how the result of the investigations of the *Treatise* concerning the comparison between the religions, that is, the superiority of Christianity over Judaism, is to be assessed with regard to Cohen's repeatedly mentioned charge.

The first chapter of the *Treatise* deals with prophecy and the second with the prophets. "Yet already in connection with prophecy it says: 'A prophet is someone who . . .' If this writing is to constitute the beginning of the more recent Bible science [*Bibelwissenschaft*], then this beginning is still quite primitive. For we might surely expect that, when it comes to the concept of prophecy, one would have to start with a distinction between literary documents and prophecy in the form of oracles. Here, however, prophecy is defined as a 'certain knowledge revealed by God to man.'"[81] With equal right "we might expect" the Copernican revolution [to have been initiated] in [the works of] Thales, or the infinitesimal calculus in [the works of] Pythagoras. Spinoza needed to start from a determination of the cognitive value of prophetic knowledge, because he was concerned with securing the perfect self-sufficiency of rational knowledge vis-à-vis revealed knowledge. Only on the basis of this determination could he establish all of the following: the superiority of reason over Scripture in terms of scientific value; the measuring of doctrines taught on the basis of Scripture by a standard independent of Scripture; the necessity of a psychological explanation of deviations from this standard; and the impartial evaluation of distinctions such as that between preliterary and literary prophecy.

Spinoza characterizes prophecy according to his "fundamental exegetical rule": Scripture is to be explained by Scripture alone, on the basis of Scripture.[82] In addition, he had no other choice, as he states not without irony, "for nowadays, so far as I know, we have no prophets."[83] Despite the crudeness [*Primitivität*] of his Bible science he is thus more critical than, say, present-day American psychology of religion.[84] On the basis of Scripture then, he distinguishes between revelations through words, through visions, and through both words and visions.[85] Words and visions can be: 1. real; or, 2. "imaginary" (merely envisioned). Cohen objects. "The literary point of view is here not taken into account at all.[86] For how can a revelation or any communication occur other than through words into which visions as well as apparitions must immediately translate themselves? This classification cannot be arrived at impartially. It must aim at a distinction."[87] The distinction Cohen has in mind is that between biblical prophecy and the prophecy of Christ.[88]

Does the classification adduced above really depend on love of Christianity or, rather, on hatred of Judaism?[89] No. Because even if a vision must "translate itself immediately" into words—one can very well contest this "must": of course the prophets' visions, as far as we know of such, must have certainly translated themselves somehow into words, but this did not necessarily occur "immediately"—a vision is distinguished clearly and distinctly from an aural revelation [*Audition*], especially from an aural revelation [*Audition*] of words. Even without evil intentions one would arrive at this distinction, or at one objectively related to it, if one were to think of the variety of revelations in, say, Amos 7:1 and 4 Hosea 1, and Isaiah 6.[90]

Cohen: "The prophets heard *a real voice;* even Moses is no exception here."[91] This is supposed to be Spinoza's conception. In Spinoza we read: "Therefore there can be no doubt that other prophets did *not hear a real voice,*"[92] while Moses, however, did hear such a voice. —Cohen: "He wants to demonstrate from Exodus 25:22, which he quotes in Hebrew, 'that God availed himself of a real voice.' *Likewise in 1. Samuel 3.*"[93] Regarding this passage, Spinoza says: "However, since we must draw a distinction between the prophecy of Moses and that of the other prophets, *we must necessarily state that the voice heard by Samuel was imaginary.* This can already be gathered from the fact that it was similar to the voice of Eli. . . ."[94] To be sure, it must be admitted that nothing depends on the inaccuracy of the representation of Spinoza's ideas in this context.[95] For it suffices for Cohen that Spinoza opines that, in numerous passages, Scripture clearly teaches the corporeality of God, and that he elucidates this opinion by the further assertion that the prohibition of graven images does not imply the commandment to believe in the incorporeality of God. On this point, Spinoza concurs with Rabad,[96] the great opponent of the Rambam[97] (highly revered by Cohen), who objected to the Rambam: Greater and better men than he had followed the view of God's corporeality in accordance with what is taught in Scripture.[98] This remark [of Rabad] proves that the view that Spinoza derived from his reading of the Bible can also be derived from a reading of it without harboring evil intentions.

We now come to the main point. Spinoza teaches: Moses spoke with God face to face, hence as body to body, whereas Christ spoke with God as mind to mind.[99] Obviously, this thesis is not an immediate consequence of Spinoza's method of Bible science, which is based on the "fundamental exegetical rule." This method is no more refuted by the possible lack of objectivity in the thesis by which Spinoza compares religions than is the law of causality by a failed experiment. According to this method [of Bible science], the New Testament would have to be investigated in exactly the same way as the [Hebrew] Bible, and if, in fact, it does not speak of Christ as having seen or heard God, well, then we will just have to accept it. In fact, this thesis would imply no disparagement whatsoever of Judaism, for Judaism is not at all identical with the more primitive stages of the Bible; rather, the "important as well as interesting clarifications" made by the Talmud and by the theologians are just as pertinent to it. Besides, the spirituality of the images in the New Testament was made possible solely by the spiritualizing tendency of prophecy. If, however, Spinoza's thesis in question is not sustainable vis-à-vis the New Testament, well, then Spinoza was misled by his "reverence for the life of Christ" (Cohen).[100] This "reverence" can perhaps be more accurately determined by noting that it was because of considerations of a philosophical nature that Spinoza gave precedence to Christianity over Judaism; in which respect he may, of course, have erred as well. In any case, if one thinks of the absurdity of the Christian dogmas often stressed on the Jewish side, then, from his point of view, such judgment was not as unfounded as one might think. Spinoza did not associate these dogmas with Christianity at all. He concerned himself with the simple teaching of the Gospels according to which the fulfillment of the commandments to obey God and to love one's neighbor is the mark of true piety (rather than the fulfillment of "essentially indifferent" ceremonies); he concerned himself with Paul's deeper struggle against the Law. The ecclesiastical development of the Protestant sects pointed toward a Christianism [*Christlichkeit*] in which the dogmas and ceremonies of Christianity lost their essential significance. At that time, there was no development of Judaism that aimed to abolish the Law. If Spinoza now rejected the Law as the heart of religion, if he regarded it as religiously possible to transgress the Law, then he was putting himself outside of Judaism in the only historical form in which it then existed. Appeal to Scripture was not possible, because Scripture contains the Law and requires its observance; for the Christian, in possession of the New Testament, and especially of the Pauline Epistles, an appeal against church and dogma was always possible (whether or not legitimate). Spinoza's preference for Christianity is absolutely sustainable, first, if one conceives of the Law as religiously irrelevant and, second, if one concedes that Judaism is not thinkable without the Law. (Here I understand by "Law" that which one traditionally understands by it, and this means neither social measures for the improvement of the common welfare, nor personal taste for religious form.) In this context, it is not improper to point out that when Spinoza incurred the ban of excommunication by his law-transgressing and law-denying conduct, and thus experienced in his own life the identity of Judaism and the Law, he was certainly not disposed to appreciate the philosophical justifications and sublimations of the ceremonial law. One must also (to quote Cohen) "consider that the doctrines of Zwingli must have been known to him,[101] and that, in his circle of Rhynsburgers, he flattered himself with the illusion that the dogmatic conception of the Trinity had been generally overcome."[102] If this is an "illusion," then, as the more fair-minded Mendelssohn would have said, we are dealing with an error of the intellect rather than with malice of the heart.

Therefore: *Spinoza's preference for Christianity is motivated by objective considerations* (whether these objective considerations are sound is a separate question), and hence we need not have recourse to Spinoza's sentiments in order to understand this preference.

The philological consequence of this attitude toward Christianity is that Spinoza views the [Hebrew] Bible and the New Testament as a "uniform Scripture." However, that does not forestall the judgment of Bible science on this matter. For it proceeds by dividing the pretended uniformity of the canon into its actual layers, and for this procedure it is irrelevant whether one *starts from the premise* of the homogeneity or the heterogeneity, of the uniformity or the divergence, of the two documents. According to the "fundamental exegetical rule," everything depends on the *outcome* of the investigation. Briefly stated, Spinoza's conclusion is as follows: uniformity of the prophetic-Christian-Pauline line in the struggle against external works, with this line representing an ascent; divergence of the two documents insofar as the heart of the [Hebrew] Bible is the Law and the heart of the New Testament is the requirement, flowing from a pious conviction, of a loving conduct toward one's neighbor.

Now, as for the [Hebrew] Bible as such, without regard to the New Testament, Spinoza's Bible science stresses just those themes which are readily covered up [*bedecken*], in part already by tradition but especially by liberalism. These themes are mainly the following.

1. *The primitive-numinous as opposed to the rational*, spiritualized, moderated: the passions, the zeal, the corporeality of God. Cohen: "Since [according to Spinoza] 'at no point does Moses teach that God is free of passion or emotion, we can evidently infer that Moses believed this himself, or at least that he wished to teach it, no matter how much, in our view, this pronouncement is opposed to reason.' Thus Scripture is interpreted contrary to the meaning of monotheism."[103] Which monotheism? Cf. the words of Rabad quoted above.

2. *The cultic as opposed to the humanitarian:* the Sabbath is viewed as a morally indifferent ceremonial institution rather than a social-ethical one.

3. *The naïve-egotistical as opposed to the moral:* the hope of the pious for temporal reward, God's blessing as temporal prosperity.

4. *The national as opposed to the humanity-related [das Menscheitliche]:* the biblical God is the God of the Hebrew people, God's enemies are the enemies of the Hebrew people, the Hebrew people is a people like any other. While "like any other" implies a limitation on nationalism, it obviously lies in a direction diametrically opposed to tradition and to liberalism. Cohen sees a contradiction between Spinoza's referring to particular passages in the Bible for proof of the religious particularism of Judaism, and, on the other hand, his

appealing to universalist passages, that is, passages speaking of God's love for all people, in order to contest the chosenness of the Hebrew people. This contradiction, however, leads back to the Bible. Cohen recognizes this himself when he says that, "fundamentally," biblical religion's "national particularism must turn into a universalism of humanity."[104] Presumably, if Spinoza had had at his disposal the logical means of Hegelian dialectics, he would have resolved this contradiction in the same way as Cohen. Unfortunately, the Hegelian system presupposes that of Spinoza.

With regard to religious nationalism, Spinoza should not have referred to 2 Chronicles 32:19; as Cohen states correctly, this passage hardly proves what it was meant to prove.[105] Rather, he should have referred to Deuteronomy 4:19–20, Judges 11:24, and Jeremiah 2:11. It is all but self-evident that, in the context of Abraham's blessing (Genesis 12:3), *venivrekhu* [106] must be interpreted in the passive voice.

5. *The political as opposed to the religious:* the history of religion is a function of political history, which here, however, is understood in the narrower sense: religion is a means for political ends. Cohen sees a contradiction in Spinoza's "taking as direct prophecies" the announcements of the destruction of the Hebrew people, and taking them as fulfilled prophecies at that, while nevertheless trying to account for the continued existence of the people in the Diaspora as contrary to those announcements. This contradiction is resolved if one calls to mind Spinoza's view that, given the destruction of the Hebrew state caused by political mistakes of the people, the continued existence of the people has become politically meaningless, and thus altogether meaningless—for true religion is not national—and that it has its sole reason in the separation of the Jews and the hatred of the Gentiles.

These conclusions of Spinoza's Bible science are the occasion for Cohen's aggressive defense. In a few successful instances this defense rebuts some of Spinoza's exaggerations that are not the result of his method, and, therefore, concerning which it is irrelevant whether they were due to objective errors or evil intentions. If one focuses on the essential results, one can say that one would have had to arrive at them even without evil intentions. Even if Spinoza saw in these results a crushing judgment on Judaism; even if he discovered and presented them with the intention of crushing Judaism; even if it were true that only a mind sharpened by a "humanly incomprehensible" alienation[107] could have arrived at them; even so, the truth of these results is independent of such personal presuppositions.

Therefore: *the essential conclusions of Spinoza's Bible science are sufficiently motivated by the actual nature [Beschaffenheit] of the object of this science.*

IV.

We had to resist Cohen's appeal to Spinoza's Jewish connection because, as matters stood, Cohen saw the objectivity of Spinoza's Bible science encumbered by this connection. It had to be shown that the *purpose*, the general *disposition* of the problems, and the *result* of the investigations in the *Treatise* can be understood without any reference to Spinoza's empirical connection to Judaism. In this respect, the *Treatise* is a Christian-European, not a Jewish, event.

The *method* of the *Treatise*, however, is another matter. This is not to say that, in its final and developed form, it is non-European. What points more deeply toward Jewish contexts is merely the origin of the method that unfolds most of all in the polemic against that of the Rambam. Here the battle against the "Pharisees" seems to be more than a veiled attack on the teachings of Christianity. Even this need not be seen as an inner Jewish debate: perhaps the Rambam's interpretation of the Bible seemed to Spinoza the most obvious one in accordance with his education, or perhaps it seemed to him the most consistent form of the kind of interpretation of the Bible that is common to all churches. In any case, here we would like to address the antithesis between Rambam and Spinoza only insofar as it is a special case of the antithesis between the *traditional-ecclesiastical* interpretation of the Bible and the *critical-scientific* interpretation of the Bible. Only because of that more general antithesis did Spinoza's method acquire significance for Christian Europe. Moreover, as has been pointed out above, the struggle against the ecclesiastical form of the interpretation of Scripture was a necessary moment in the struggle against ecclesiastical claims vis-à-vis science and the state. Therefore, in our consideration of the method of the *Treatise* we move along the same line as we did in our replies to Cohen's attack. However, this line will lead us to an even deeper formulation of the question.

The inner progress of a living religion, if such a religion is based on holy scriptures, occurs only through the reinterpretation [*umdeutende Auslegung*] of these holy scriptures. Thus, as is well known, sensuous representations of the divine are spiritualized and harsh features are mitigated. In particular, the progress of cognitive reason [*erkennende Vernunft*] is communicated in this way to religion. However, in contrast to this kind of interpretation, which further developed religion in, as it were, a straight direction, there arose the idea (in the Protestantism of the first centuries of the modern era, from very specific, religiously conditioned presuppositions) of a return to the layer on which tradition ultimately rests, the layer of "pure doctrine." This is Spinoza's starting point. Aided substantially by the humanist elements in the thinking of his time, he now develops the interpretation of the Bible as a pure science, that is, as a science that is no longer, from its very outset, subservient to religion. This is not contradicted by the fact that the creation [*Erzeugung*] of this science is due to, or at least codetermined by, the objective of fighting against ecclesiastical claims. The science itself is, in its [inherent] meaning, separable from this motive, even though it may initially determine the direction of the inquiry.

Hence, a return to Scripture that was hostile to tradition existed already before Spinoza. It must be asked: How did he find a way from his Jewish foundations to it? Why does he refuse to interpret Scripture in such a way as to make it conform with his religious and rational persuasion, so as to integrate himself into the framework of Judaism, he "on whose lineage, whose mind, and whose learning the Jews had vested the greatest hopes"? Why does he interpret "honestly" in this far from self-evident sense? What should have been more obvious to him than fidelity toward the community for which his fathers had sacrificed without hesitation life, homeland, and possessions? What drove him to "destroy the beautiful world"?

This is but to pose the question. With respect to Cohen, the following can be advanced. It matters not *why* Spinoza was "honest"—what his religious, moral, or selfish motivations were; suffice it that he was, and that the image of the Bible discovered on the basis of this "honesty," if and insofar as it is true, maintains and supports itself and deposes its opposite. For according to the *Ethics*, truth is the norm of itself *and* of the false.[108]

The need that had to give rise to Spinoza's enterprise, that is, the struggle for the independence of science and state from the church, was hardly perceptible in Cohen's time: it had been resolved by the efforts of the previous centuries. Now, Cohen is, among his contemporaries, the one who has the deepest inner connection with the spirit of the great age of the Enlightenment. Nevertheless, in his review of Spinoza's critique of the Rambam's principle of interpretation, Cohen misses the decisive sentence: "If Maimonides had been convinced by reason that the world is eternal, *he would not have hesitated to twist and to interpret Scripture* until it would have *seemed* finally to teach the same thing."[109] Here the honesty and sincerity, for which Cohen gladly and often praises the Enlightenment, turns against the traditional method of reinterpreting and reshaping [*umdeutende Fortbildung*] of biblical doctrines. What prevents Cohen in this case from being just is less a traditionalist than an apologetic interest. His interest in bringing out clearly what is actually written in the Bible is weakened by his consideration of the Christian attacks against Judaism—in other words, by an interest of "life."[iii] In Spinoza this apologetic interest is, of course, absent. Blame it on human frailty—the objectivity of the investigation of Bible science may no more be endangered by the skeptical coldness of the apostate than by the apologetic love of the faithful.

We shall not discuss the question of Spinoza's attitude toward Judaism. Its resolution would not contribute anything decisive to an objective understanding of the *Treatise*. As to a "human" assessment of Spinoza's coldness and alienness toward Judaism, this would presuppose an assessment of the conduct of the Jews toward him: not an assessment of the ban of excommunication (against which, naturally, nothing can be objected) but, rather, of the expressions of private attitudes that were presumably not above criticism to the same extent as the ban of excommunication itself. We would rather not be drawn into this difficult business.

It was possible to reach an understanding of the purpose, the disposition, the conclusions, and the method of the *Treatise* on the basis of Spinoza's motives that were "in accord with duty," because we refrained from considering the Jewish interest. It is conceivable that a critique of the Bible that results from even the most objective and hate-free attitude is not in the interest of Judaism. Indeed, since Spinoza's method was applied by him and justified by its application only in connection with his alienation from Judaism and his entrance into the Christian-European context, its significance for Judaism was not established from the outset. We may point ad hominem to the greater "honesty" of this method, as against Cohen, who knew of no fundamental reservations about the right of science. From our standpoint, however, it must be asked in all seriousness how this "honesty" relates to possible higher needs of Judaism, whether it bestows a right to destroy the beautiful world of tradition? What does the struggle for the autonomy of science and the state have to do with the interest of Judaism? What interest can Judaism have in knowing what the dawn of its history was *actually* like?

[iii] "On the other hand, when Spinoza, with uncharitable harshness, not only makes his tribe contemptible (just when Rembrandt, residing in his alley, immortalizes the ideality of the Jewish type) but also mutilates the unique God whose confession was the reason for his and his father's fleeing Portugal and the Inquisition, no one opposes this humanly incomprehensible act of treason. Hence, there is but one explanation for this, one that is highly welcome: that for once a Jew of importance has renounced his stubbornness . . ." [*JS*, 3:360–61]. "The pithy sayings in which Spinoza discharged his vengeful hatred of the Jews can still be found today almost literally in the daily newspapers of certain political leanings" [*JS*, 3:363].

Therefore, another investigation would be needed to ask how the interest of Judaism relates to Spinoza's Bible science. We may define this task more precisely by asking: *Which Jewish impulses are alive in Spinoza's Bible science?*

Based on this question, it is possible to reach a fundamental judgment on Cohen's analysis of Spinoza's Bible science. Cohen is right when he establishes (although not explicitly) the interest of Judaism as the highest authority for assessing this science; he is wrong when he determines the interest of Judaism by the external consideration of the purposes of theologico-political apologetics, rather than determining it on the basis of the inner need of the spirit of our people [*Volksgeist*]. He is right when he seeks to measure Spinoza's thought about Judaism, and his conduct toward Judaism, by Jewish standards. But would it not be more conducive to the self-knowledge of the Jewish spirit if one asked what motives of Judaism led to Spinoza's thought and conduct with regard to Judaism if one conceived of his argument with Judaism as a Jewish argument? Be that as it may, even this narrower formulation of the question testifies to the exemplary seriousness of Hermann Cohen, who was not satisfied with the image of the "God-intoxicated man," an image drawn by German romanticism and copied by Jewish romanticism.

NOTES

Source: "Cohens Analyse der Bibel-Wissenschaft Spinozas," *Der Jude: Eine Monatsschrift* (Berlin) 8, nos. 5/6 (May–June 1924): 295–14, reprinted in *GS*, 1:363–86. Strauss quotes from Hermann Cohen, *Jüdische Schriften* (Berlin: Schwetschke Verlag, 1924). The editor of that collection, Bruno Strauß, was aware of Leo Strauss's plan to publish "Cohen's Analysis" in *Der Jude*. See *JS*, 3:375. The essay on Cohen and Spinoza caught the attention of Julius Guttmann, then director of the Akademie für die Wissenschaft des Judentums, which was to provide Strauss first with a fellowship and then with employment as an editor and specialist in Jewish philosophy. Cf. the introduction to the present volume.

The term "Bible science" is as odd in English as the word *Bibelwissenschaft* is in German. It seems to juxtapose its two heterogeneous parts in unmitigated opposition. In "Spinoza über Staat und Religion, Judentum und Christentum" (*JS*, 3:290–372), Cohen uses a variety of terms referring to biblical scholarship, such as *Bibelkritik*, *theologische Wissenschaft*, *biblische Theologie*, *Bibelforscher*, *Bibelforschung*, *Wissenschaften* (as opposed by Spinoza to obedience required by the laws of Moses), *Bibelexegese*, *Theologie* (as opposed to philosophy), *biblische Geschichte*, and once also the term *Bibelwissenschaft* (p. 313: "Da diese Schrift den Anfang der neueren Bibelwissenschaft bilden soll"), a passage quoted by Strauss in "Cohens Analyse der Bibel-Wissenschaft Spinozas," 307. Strauss uses the expression *Bibelwissenschaft* in the title and four times (once as an adjective referring to more recent scholarship) in section III of this essay, where it appears mostly in the context of an adumbration of his own nonpolemical understanding of Spinoza's contribution. In the essay "Zur Bibelwissenschaft Spinozas und seiner Vorläufer" (1926), Strauss explores the subject matter independently of Cohen's views and consistently employs the somewhat unusual term *Bibelwissenschaft*. Since, in his collaboration with Elsa Sinclair, Strauss approved of the expression "Bible science" as the English equivalent of *Bibelwissenschaft,* the present translation follows this precedent and prefers the perhaps intentionally jarring expression to more common terms such as "biblical science," "biblical scholarship," and so on.

1. Hermann Cohen, *Die Religion der Vernunft aus den Quellen des Judentums* (Leipzig: Gustav Fock, 1919), posthumously published in a series of "Schriften herausgegeben von der Gesellschaft zur Förderung der Wissenschaft des Judentums." *Religion der Vernunft* was commissioned in 1904 by the Gesellschaft (cofounded by Cohen in 1902) as the volume on "Jewish philosophy of religion and ethics" in its series "Grundriss der gesamten Wissenschaft des Judentum." Cohen was in the process of revising and editing it when he died in April 1918. In 1924, when Strauss wrote the present essay, he quoted from the only edition in existence at the time, which appeared under the erroneous title *Die Religion der Vernunft.* The problematic definitive article, suggesting an exclusivism alien to Cohen's thought, was dropped only in the second edition, edited by Bruno Strauß and published by Kauffmann in Frankfurt am Main in 1929.

2. While the word *Kritik* can be translated either as criticism or as critique (see "On the Bible Science of Spinoza and His Precursors," note 5), the preposition *am* makes it unambiguous: *Kritik am Titel* and *Kritik am Buch* mean, respectively, "criticism of the title" and "criticism of the book," whereas the earlier phrases *Kritik eines Gedankens* and *Kritik des Ausdrucks* (simple genitive, no preposition) are best rendered as "critique of an idea" and "critique of the expression," respectively.

3. In the opening paragraphs of "Spinoza über Staat und Religion, Judentum und Christentum," Cohen distinguishes between the "logical disposition" indicated in the title of Spinoza's *Theological-Political Treatise* and the significant effects the *Treatise* had on "cultural history." As for its cultural historical effects, Cohen (in the manner of a *captatio benevolentiae*) emphasizes the significant contributions of the *TPT* to the history of the Enlightenment before proceeding to criticize it. See Cohen, "Spinoza über Staat und Religion," in *JS,* 3:290.

4. The phrase *hat es über sich gebracht* is meant ironically. To make this unambiguous in English, I added quotation marks to "forced." Generally speaking, the opening paragraphs in this essay, defending Spinoza against attacks informed by Cohen's deeply offended sensibility, may be characterized as ironic.

5. Cohen, "Spinoza über Staat und Religion," 292, refers to the ban (i.e., the excommunication) imposed on Spinoza by the Amsterdam Jewish community. He says that, in addition to a more specific reason discussed later on in the essay, the community would have been justified to pronounce a ban as a measure of self-protection against Spinoza as a *malshin,* that is, as an informer or collaborator who betrays his fellow Jews to the non-Jewish authorities. The importance of this concept can be gleaned from the fact that a special benediction cursing the informer was inserted into the Eighteen Benedictions (a centerpiece of Jewish liturgy) after the first Jewish revolt against Rome, which culminated in the momentous event of the destruction of the Herodian Temple (66–70 C.E.).

6. *unparteiische Seite:* Cohen, "Spinoza über Staat und Religion," 295. The reference is to Carl Gebhardt's 1908 translation of *Thelogical-Political Treatise,* Philosophische Bibliothek, vol. 93 (Hamburg: Felix Meiner, 1908). See Cohen, "Spinoza über Staat und Religion," 291 n. 1. This edition of Gebhardt's translation was not available to me. I used the fifth edition, 1955 (reprint: Darmstadt, 1965), which is identical with the fourth edition, 1922. P. xxxvi of this edition lists Cohen's essay on Spinoza in its updated bibliography.

7. Cohen, "Spinoza über Staat und Religion," 294, quoting Carl Gebhardt.

8. Mommsen's dictum is reminiscent of William of Ockham's principle of economy ("Ockham's Razor"), according to which the simplest explanation for a thing, if sufficient, should be considered as the true one.

9. Cohen, "Spinoza über Staat und Religion," 291: "da diese Verbindung unnatürlich ist. . . ."

10. Ibid. distinguishes between a "publicistic task," which consists in (in Gebhardt's words) a "Dutch state paper [*Staatsschrift*] in accordance with the politics of Jan de Witt" and a "purely *philological* task" (emphasis in the original), which consists in determining dates and authorships of the biblical books.

11. See Cohen, quoting Gebhardt, in "Spinoza über Staat und Religion," 291: "daß dieses Werk in seinem praktischen Teile nichts anderes ist als eine holländische Staatsschrift im Sinne der Politik Jan de Witts" [in practical respects this work is nothing but a political pamphlet advocating the politics of Jan de Witt]. And cf. Strauss, "Cohen's Analyse," 296, where quotations from Gebhardt are not distinguished from quotations from Cohen.

12. Spinoza, *Theological-Political Treatise,* ed. Gebhardt, prints this sentence on the title page. The full text, in the context of Spinoza's preface to the *Treatise,* runs as follows: "Now since we have the rare good fortune to live in a commonwealth where freedom of judgment is fully granted to the individual citizen and he may worship God as he pleases, and where nothing is esteemed dearer and more precious than freedom, I think I am undertaking no ungrateful or unprofitable task in *demonstrating that not only can this freedom be granted without endangering piety and the peace of the commonwealth, but also that the peace of the commonwealth and piety depend on this freedom*" (Baruch de Spinoza, *Theological Political Treatise,* trans. Samuel Shirley [Leiden: Brill, 1989; reprint, Indianapolis: Hackett Publications, 1998], 3; emphasis added). In a letter to Heinrich Oldenburg, conjectured to have been written in the year 1665, that is, five years before the publication of the *Treatise* in 1670, Spinoza describes his motivation to write on Scripture as threefold: "I'm now writing a treatise on my views regarding Scripture. The reasons that move me to do so are these: 1. The prejudice of the theologians. For I know that these are the main obstacles which prevent men from giving their minds to philosophy. So I apply myself to exposing such prejudices and removing them from the minds of sensible people. 2. The opinion of me held by the common people, who constantly accuse me of atheism. I am driven to avert this accusation, too, as far as I can. 3. The freedom to philosophise and to say what we think. This I want to vindicate completely, for here it is in every way suppressed by the excessive authority and egotism of preachers" (Letter 30 in *Spinoza: The Letters,* trans. Samuel Shirley [Indianapolis: Hackett Publications, 1995], 185f.). Given the clout of censorship, Spinoza was forced

to publish the treatise anonymously and, for this reason alone, the defense of the philosopher against the charge of atheism appears only in passing and in general terms.

13. That is, if one agrees, as Cohen is here assumed to have agreed, that church and state should be separated, one must, with Spinoza, also affirm that Scripture provides no support for religion's claim to a rational grounding. In other words, the very combination of the theological and the political indicates the rational coherence of Spinoza's attack on Scripture.

14. The original *da es sich um eine liberale Regierung handelte* is ambiguous and could refer either to the actual government or to the one advocated in *Theological-Political Treatise*. Since, at the time of Spinoza, the government of the Netherlands was not in fact a liberal one, at least not one that was even close to tolerating the kind of freethinking Spinoza advocated, Strauss more likely refers to the liberal government that is advocated in the *Treatise*, not the one that actually existed at the time of Spinoza.

15. Cohen, "Spinoza über Staat und Religion," 291: "At least one of the two tasks lost its *isolated* objectivity." The emphasis indicates that Cohen, too, acknowledges objective connections between theology and politics but nevertheless charges Spinoza with a reductionist caricature of religion, or politics, or both.

16. Ibid.

17. Cf. ibid., "mit dem großen Bann belegt," and Strauss, "der . . . über Spinoza verhängte Große Bann." The reference is to a *herem qlali*, a ban of excommunication, as opposed to a minor ban, *herem zuta*, which is usually referred to by the form of punishment it imposes, such as fines, stripes, and boycotts.

18. Cohen, "Spinoza über Staat und Religion," 292.

19. Cf. I. Kant, *Kritik der reinen Vernunft*, ed. Karl Rosenkranz, 2d ed. (Leipzig: Voss, 1838), 695: "Dass alle unsere Erkenntniss mit der Erfahrung anfange, daran ist gar kein Zweifel . . ." [There is no doubt, that all our knowledge begins with experience . . .]. Strauss echoes this phrase in the following sentence.

20. Hermann Cohen, *Kants Theorie der Erfahrung* (1918), 3d ed., in vol. 1, pt. 2 of *Werke* (Hildesheim: Olms, 1987), 99f. The emphasis is Strauss's, not Cohen's. In the original, the sentence summarizes a discussion on English sensualism that is adduced as an example of a common psychological misunderstanding of Cartesian philosophy. According to Cohen, sensualism "took 'lively' feelings for 'impressions' of things, and ideas as the 'copies' of those impressions." Cohen articulates Kant's "transcendental method" as a direct conversion of the "substitution" that is the "fatal and typical" flaw of sensualist theory of cognition. What sensualism represents as the "processes of cognition" [*Vorgänge des Erkennens*] must instead be interpreted as "concepts that concern the value and contents of cognition" (99). By referring to this passage, Strauss portrays Cohen as falling short of his own methodological postulate when he looked for extraneous psychological motivations to explain why Spinoza combined political philosophy and criticism of the Bible. The added emphasis poignantly turns the adjectives "fatal and typical" against Cohen, their author.

21. *für das Werk des betreffenden Lebens* (the work of the relevant life). The unusual turn of phrase is derived from the term *Lebenswerk*.

22. Cohen, "Spinoza über Staat und Religion," 292. Cohen assumes that, when Spinoza wrote the *Theological-Political Treatise*, he aimed to make an argument for politi-

cal liberty that was in keeping with the principles of his *Ethics*. What Strauss calls a conjecture is the assumption that Spinoza may have decided not to publish his *Apology* (which Cohen calls a "protest pamphlet") because it may have provided him less satisfaction than the more sophisticated argument presented in the *Theological-Political Treatise*, where the argument against Jews and Scripture is less personal but all the more profound, and where his protest is embedded in an elaborate political theory.

23. Cohen, too, refers to Hobbes in this context, albeit not with the same purpose. Cf. "Spinoza über Staat und Religion," 293.

24. See ibid., 293, and cf. the emphases in the original here omitted.

25. Ibid., 292.

26. Ibid., 294.

27. Ibid.

28. Ibid., 293. In the original, only the words "religion" and "state" are emphasized. Strauss highlights the word "Jewish" as preparation for the point he is about to make in the next sentence.

29. What Strauss implies is that Cohen's critique is hypocritical in that he himself has a hidden political agenda, that is, Strauss turns around Cohen's psychological and political objections to Spinoza to reveal Cohen's own psychological and political motivations.

30. Ibid.

31. Cf. note 6, above. The following lengthy quotation is from Carl Gebhardt's introduction to *Theological-Political Treatise* (1908).

32. See Gebhardt, introduction to Spinoza, *Theological-Political Treatise,* xvii. The emphasis is added by Strauss.

33. Ibid., xvi.

34. Cf. ibid., xvii, xxf. The *argumentatio ad hominem* that Gebhardt sees at work in Spinoza echoes Spinoza's imputation of the like rhetoric to Ezra as the hypothetical author of the Book of Deuteronomy and of the books of Joshua through Kings. So, for example, toward the end of chapter 8 of *Theological-Political Treatise.*

35. A dig at Cohen who, in keeping with the principles of critical idealism and drawing on the Maimonidean doctrine of attributes, emphasized that essential attributes of reality, existence, life, and so on cannot apply to God. The "idea of God" is prominently introduced in Cohen's 1904 *Ethik des reinen Willens* (1904; 2d ed., 1907; 5th ed. in vol. 7 of *Werke* [Hildesheim: Olms, 1981]), chapter 9, and again in *Die Religion der Vernunft aus den Quellen des Judentums,* 1st ed., 186f. (chap. 9, "Das Problem der religiösen Liebe"), where Cohen responds to the charge that a mere "idea of God" cannot be the object of religious love: "*How can one love an idea?* To this one should answer: How can one love anything but an idea?" (*Die Religion der Vernunft,* 1st ed., 187). The concept of the "ideal" prepares the way for the chapter on the idea of God in *Ethik des reinen Willens* (namely, chap. 8).

36. Cohen, "Spinoza über Staat und Religion," 296.

37. Ibid., 295f. (cf. the various emphases in the original, which Strauss does not reproduce here).

38. Cf. ibid., 291: "eine rein *philologische* Frage."

39. Ibid., 297. Strauss alters the syntax of the original, creating the impression that

Spinoza was the sole target of this charge, whereas, in the original, Cohen muses on a certain recklessness in the literary style of "spirits who, like Spinoza, elaborate their ideas toward achieving a literary effect on contemporary matters."

40. Ibid., p. 295: *"Philologie,"* Strauss's emphasis. In the original, the German word for "prophets" is also emphasized.

41. *Der aktuelle . . . Zweck,* that is, the immediate historical purpose that Spinoza pursues in *Theological-Political Treatise* and from which the work arises. In the following, Strauss differentiates between the possibility of deriving Spinoza's Bible science from topical *(aktuellen)*—that is, circumstance-driven—motives that may lead him to contradict the principles of his *Ethics,* and that of tracing the principles of his Bible science back to the *Ethics,* and thus proving the political independence and rational coherence of Spinoza's work.

42. Here Strauss raises the larger question of the legitimacy of Spinoza's critique of the Bible, adumbrating, in a nutshell, the problem dealt with in the essay "On the Bible Science of Spinoza and His Precursors," as well as, more exhaustively, in Strauss, *Die Religionskritik Spinozas also Grundlage seiner Bibelwissenschaft: Untersuchungen zu Spinozas Theologisch Politischem Traktat,* Series: Veröffentlichungen der Akademie für die Wissenschaft des Judentums, Philosophische Sektion, Zweiter Band (Berlin: Akademie Verlag, 1930), translated into English as *Spinoza's Critique of Religion,* trans. Elsa Sinclair (New York: Schocken, 1965).

43. "ad hominem": see note 34, above.

44. It should be noted that Strauss problematizes the philosophical coherence of *Theological-Political Treatise* with Cohen and against Gebhardt. According to the latter it is the very *argumentatio ad hominem*—namely, the political purpose of the *Staatsschrift* in favor of the policies of Jan de Witt—that makes it impossible for Spinoza to argue from a position congenial to his *Ethics.* While avoiding unconscionable contradictions to his philosophical convictions, Spinoza advocates the position of the aristocratic regents or the "neutralists." Cf. Gebhardt, introduction to *Theological-Political Treatise,* xviiif. Like Cohen, however, Strauss is interested in the question of the relation between the philosophical *Ethics* and the critique of the Bible in the *Treatise,* a problem Gebhardt dismisses when he states that the *Treatise* includes quite a few sentences that contradict the *Ethics* and none that contradict the "neutralist" creed (xix).

45. Cohen, "Spinoza über Staat und Religion," 295.

46. Cf. ibid.: "How does Spinoza determine the concept of religion? It is the first consequence that follows from this unnatural connection of problems: that Spinoza does not seek to determine the concept of religion from the point of view of his *Ethics,* but that he derives it from Scripture instead . . ." (emphases omitted).

47. Ibid., 299.

48. Strauss is here in agreement with Gebhardt. But cf. note 44, above.

49. Cohen, "Spinoza über Staat und Religion," 297.

50. *sit venia verbo:* Strauss cautions that the expression "Maimonidean–Kantian *rational faith*" must not be taken to insinuate that he accepted the tenability of Cohen's synthesis of Maimonidean and Kantian notions. He merely uses this expression in order to describe placatively what Cohen substitutes for the Protestant faith in Scripture that Spinoza, according to Strauss, actually attacked. One should bear in mind that, to Strauss,

trust in revelation (Maimonides) and trust in reason (Kant) represent irreconcilable opposites.]

51. "Nun substruiert Spinoza allerdings *seinen* Glaubensbegriff dem orthodoxen." Instead of paraphrasing and interpreting the term *substruiert*—as does the French translation ("Spinoza, quant à lui, construit son concept de foi en subvertissant le concept orthodoxe de la foi")—I offer the literal translation of the term *substruiert*, which is no less rare in the German dictionary than its equivalent in the English one. Yet the meaning is quite clear, as is Strauss's intention. The word, deriving from the Latin *substruo* (to lay a foundation, build beneath), is meant to indicate that, while Cohen inadvertently imputes to Spinoza an alien concept of faith, Spinoza consciously establishes his depiction of orthodox faith on the foundation of his own concept of faith and thus in accordance with the principles of his *Ethics*.

52. Cf. Cohen, "Spinoza über Staat und Religion," 334: "Und in diesem höchsten Gute der Erkenntnis besteht unsere Seligkeit."

53. Ibid., referring to Spinoza: "Und das gesamte Scharfgeschütz der Ethik wird hier aufgefahren. . . ."

54. Cohen, "Spinoza über Staat und Religion," 297.

55. "Weil die Normen sittlichen Handelns jedem Menschen eingeschrieben sind . . .": cf. chap. 5 of Spinoza, *Theological-Political Treatise*, trans. Gebhardt: "daß das göttliche Gesetz, das die Menschen wahrhaft glücklich macht und das wahre Leben lehrt, allen Menschen gemein ist; ja ich habe es so aus der menschlichen Natur hergeleitet, daß es danach aussieht, als sei es dem menschlichen Geist eingeboren und sozusagen eingeschrieben" [that the divine law that leads to the happiness of the people and teaches them the true life is common to all people; I even derived it from human nature, making it seem as if it were native to the human spirit and, as it were, inscribed in it].

56. Cohen, "Spinoza über Staat und Religion," 298.

57. Ibid., 299. And cf. Spinoza, *Theological-Political Treatise*, ed. Gebhardt, 84.

58. Cohen, "Spinoza über Staat und Religion," 303. The emphasis is added by Strauss.

59. Cf. Spinoza, *Theological-Political Treatise*, chapter 15, last paragraph.

60. Cohen, "Spinoza über Staat und Religion," 299. This sentence is quoted again prominently in Strauss's preface to *Spinoza's Critique of Religion* (Chicago: University of Chicago Press, 1997), 18.

61. Cohen, "Spinoza über Staat und Religion," 300. There is no sign of indignation in the text close to this quotation. Rather, Cohen comments on the quote from Spinoza by adding ironically: "This then is the deeper meaning of the sentence: 'Dogmas are merely practical rules of obedience.' Unfortunately, what is missing is the exposition of the spiritual bond that establishes a connection between such works."

62. Ibid.: "It cannot be doubted that this theory must dissolve into absurd contradictions."

63. Cf. Spinoza, *Theological-Political Treatise*, chapter 14: "On Faith"; in the Shirley translation, p. 167.

64. Strauss: "die Einzigkeit nur ein Problem der Erkenntnis." Cf. Cohen, "Spinoza über Staat und Religion," 300f.: "die Einzigkeit *durchaus* nur ein Problem der Erkenntnis" (emphasis added). As evident from the continuation in the original, the "specialist in

Jewish philosophy of religion" is none other than Spinoza himself, who—according to Cohen—remains silent on a salient point of the Jewish philosophical tradition, namely, on the idea of God's uniqueness, an idea that, to Cohen, is the main source of compatibility and congeniality between the Jewish and Greek philosophical traditions. See Cohen, "Spinoza über Staat und Religion," and cf. idem, *Der Begriff der Religion im System der Philosophie* (Giessen: Töpelmann, 1915), pt. 2, paras. 26–37, 58–59, as well as the essay "Einheit oder Einzigkeit Gottes" (1918), in *Jüdische Schriften*, 1:87–99, chapter 1 of *Religion of Reason*, and elsewhere. The insinuation Strauss picks up on and rejects is that Spinoza shows his bad faith by ignoring the meaning, which Cohen alleges to be obvious, of this core doctrine of Jewish religious thought.

65. Spinoza, *Theological-Political Treatise,* trans. Shirley, 167. Shirley, incidentally, translates the heading of the second of Spinoza's universal doctrines of faith ("eum esse unicum") as "God is one alone," whereas Gebhardt reads "Gott ist einzig," as quoted in Cohen, "Spinoza über Staat und Religion," 300.

66. Cohen, "Spinoza über Staat und Religion," 301. Referring to chapter 14 of Spinoza, *Theological-Political Treatise,* ed. Gebhardt, 256, Cohen uses the phrase *diese Art von Philosophie der Religion* in a mocking tone. While Strauss attempts to portray all of Cohen's rhetoric in this essay as driven by righteous indignation, and his judgment as clouded by passion, Cohen's style is in fact much more nuanced and needs to be examined on its own terms. In his preface to *Spinoza's Critique of Religion,* Strauss's assessment of Cohen's critique of Spinoza is much more balanced and less polemical.

67. Cohen, "Spinoza über Staat und Religion," 302.

68. Cf. ibid., 304: "so tritt damit der alte sophistische Gegenbegriff der Macht als Natur auf, und die sittliche Grundkraft der Natur verschwindet. . . ." And ibid., 273, with reference to *Theological-Political Treatise,* ed. Gebhardt: "Der sophistische Charakter dieses Naturbegriffs bezeugt sich bei Spinoza schon dadurch, daß er 'die Grundlagen des Staates' im 16. Kapitel zu begründen beginnt am 'natürlichen Rechte des Einzelnen, ohne vorerst auf Staat und Religion Rücksicht zu nehmen'. . . ." And cf. Cohen, "Spinoza über Staat und Religion," 307. Cohen's emphasis on the opposition between the Platonic method of deriving the particular from the universal and the Sophists' method of proceeding from the particular to the universal—wherein natural philosophy and science are respectively made the point of departure for the respective determination of the problem of rights—is echoed in Strauss's essay "Spinoza's Bible Science" as well as in *Spinoza's Critique of Religion,* where Strauss takes the analysis a step further when he asks for the prephilosophical motivation of the critique of religion in the Epicurean tradition. In the latter tradition, the school of choice in natural philosophy is that of Democritus who, like the Sophists and Spinoza, proceeds from the particular to the universal.

69. Strauss, "Cohens Analyse der Bibelwissenschaft Spinozas," 305: "denn die Natur wird nicht durch die Gesetze der menschlichen Vernunft begrenzt." Cf. *Theological-Political Treatise,* ed. Gebhardt, 275: "Denn die Natur ist nicht zwischen die Gesetze der menschlichen Vernunft eingeschlossen." Our translation follows *Theological-Political Treatise,* trans. Shirley, 180.

70. Strauss: "Unser Wissen sei Stückwerk." Cf. *Theological-Political Treatise,* trans. Gebhardt, 276: "weil unsere Kenntnis von den Dingen Stückwerk ist." Shirley translates: "our knowledge is only partial" (*Theological-Political Treatise,* 180)

71. *Wir begreifen* . . . : cf. Cohen, "Spinoza über Staat und Religion," 371 (from whence the quotation, later in this paragraph, is also taken): "Es kann nun zwar begriffen werden. . . ." . And see note 73, below.

72. Cohen, "Spinoza über Staat und Religion," 306, and cf. Strauss, preface to *Spinoza's Critique of Religion* (1997), 19, where the sentence is quoted again.

73. Cohen, "Spinoza über Staat und Religion," 371: "Es kann nun zwar begriffen werden, daß *Mystiker* von der *Transzendenz* des einzigen Gottes nicht befriedigt werden. Dagegen hat die Geschichte gelehrt, daß der *Pantheismus* an sich nicht im Widerspruch steht zum Monotheismus" [While it may be understandable that *mystics* are dissatisfied with the *transcendence* of the unique God, history has taught us that *pantheism* as such does not necessarily contradict monotheism]. This passage, partially quoted by Strauss, explicitly points to the possibility of finding redeeming qualities in pantheism, which Cohen holds to be "not intrinsically opposed to monotheism." Whatever the meaning of Cohen's reference to "mystics who are not satisfied with the transcendence of God," Strauss defends Spinoza's respect for divine transcendence by pointing to his insistence on the "fragmentary" nature of human knowledge.

74. Ibid., 307, and Spinoza, *Theological-Political Treatise*, trans. Gebhardt, 277: "daß man es unter die ewigen Wahrheiten rechnen muß, die niemand verkennen kann." Shirley translates: "This law is so deeply inscribed in human nature that it should be counted among the eternal truths universally known" (*Theological-Political Treatise*, 181).

75. Mishnah Avot 4:2, *s'khar mitsvah mitsvah* (The reward of a commandment is a commandment) is quoted—without indication of the source—in *Theological-Political Treatise*, chapter 4. Gebhardt translates: "*der höchste Lohn des Gesetzes* ist das Gesetz selbst" (83), which Cohen cites: "As the fourth characteristic [*scil.* as the fourth distinction of the "natural divine law"] he points to the sentence: 'the highest reward of the divine law is the law itself' [footnote: *Summum legis divinae praemium esse ipsam Legem*]. Here, adding merely the word 'highest,' he took a sentence from the Mishnah, from the famous *Ethics of the Fathers*. . . . But, of course, he denies being indebted in any way to the Pharisees" ("Spinoza über Staat und Religion," 336). Strauss points out that Cohen's demand of a disclosure of rabbinic sources cited by Spinoza appears one-sided and apologetic in that it ignores that even Spinoza's "foundation of the state on egoism and prudence"—something Cohen opposes on ethical grounds—can be said to have its source in the Mishnah.

76. Mishnah Avot 3:2, quoted also in Strauss, preface to *Spinoza's Critique of Religion* (1997), 22.

77. Strauss, "Cohens Analyse der Bibelwissenschaft Spinozas," 305f., quoting *Theological-Political Treatise*, trans. Gebhardt, 290. Cf. Shirley (*Theological-Political Treatise*, 189): "But in matters of religion men are especially prone to go astray and contentiously advance many ideas of their own devising, as is abundantly testified by experience. It is therefore quite clear that, if nobody were bound by right to obey the sovereign power in those matters which he thinks to pertain to religion, the state's right would then inevitably depend on judgments and feelings that vary with each individual."

78. Cohen, "Spinoza über Staat und Religion," 312, quoting *Theological-Political Treatise*, trans. Gebhardt, 327. Cf. *Theological-Political Treatise*, trans. Shirley, 214.

79. "Incomprehensible." Cf. Cohen, "Spinoza über Staat und Religion," 329, in a

different context, but still related to the discussion of prophets and prophecy: "It should nevertheless remain incomprehensible how it could become possible for Spinoza to generalize the necessary particularism of the political laws [*Staatsgesetze*] to apply to the *entire* content of the Mosaic and Old Testament laws in general."

80. Cf. Cohen, "Spinoza über Staat und Religion," 333, in a different context, but still related to the discussion of Spinoza's determination of the value of the Hebrew religion and the reasons for its longevity even after the demise of the ancient state: "How the latter political point of view [*scil.* the possibility of a renewed election of Israel as implied in a renewal of Jewish nationalism; cf. *Theological-Political Treatise*, ed. Gebhardt, 75; *Theological-Political Treatise*, trans. Shirley, 47] goes along with his religious notion of a divine governance of the world is hardly comprehensible without recourse to a demonic sense of irony."

81. Cohen, "Spinoza über Staat und Religion," 312f. Strauss (*GS*, 1:376): "dem Menschen"; Cohen ("Spinoza über Staat und Religion," 313): "den Menschen"; Spinoza (*Theological-Political Treatise*, ed. Gebhardt, 15): "den Menschen." Cf. *Tractatus theologico-politicus*, ed. J. Van Vloten and J.P.N. Land (The Hague: Martinus Nijhoff, 1913–14), 1:357, cited in Cohen, "Spinoza über Staat und Religion," 313 n. 1: "certa cognitio a Deo hominibus revelata."

82. See Spinoza, *Theological-Political Treatise*, trans. Gebhardt, 18; and cf. Cohen, "Spinoza über Staat und Religion," 314.

83. Spinoza, *Theological-Political Treatise*, trans. Gebhardt, 18.

84. The reference is most likely to William James, *Varieties of the Religious Experience*, first published in 1902 and translated into German by G. Wobbermin (second edition: 1914). Guided by a positivist understanding of science, this influential school initially emphasized the extraordinary religious experience, such as conversion and mystical experience, and the empirical data it analyzed consisted mostly of autobiographical writings, diaries, and so on. Hence, Strauss's critical aside. Almost a century later, the American academic study of religion continues to be preoccupied with the methodological opposition implied in this brief aside. See, most recently, David Ray Griffin, "Religious Experience, Naturalism, and the Social Scientific Study of Religion," *JAAR* 68, no. 1 (March 2000): 99–125, and the responses and rejoinders in the same issue, pp. 127–49.

85. *JS*, 314–15, citing Spinoza, *Theological-Political Treatise*, ed. Gebhardt, 19.

86. What Cohen means to say here, and explicitly says a few lines before, is that Spinoza does not take into account the possibility that the prophets themselves, at the stage at which their oracles were fashioned into the literature that alone is available to us, acted as the authors of this prophetic literature; in other words, Spinoza seems to assume naïvely that he is dealing with immediate and unreflected representations of sense impressions (aural and visual) rather than with literary formations of such representations. We can claim that even Cohen's assumption of the possibility of inferring from the text the creative genius of its prophetic authorship is overly confident. Strauss advances a similar objection in the parenthesis below.

87. Cohen, "Spinoza über Staat und Religion," 315.

88. That is, the distinction that Cohen correctly identifies as underlying Spinoza's classification of prophecy into real and imaginary. Cf. ibid., 314–18, which follows and

paraphrases the argument of chapter 1 of *Theological-Political Treatise,* ed. Gebhardt, 19–25; cf. *Theological-Political Treatise,* ed. Shirley, 11–14.

89. Strauss's equation of love of Christianity and hatred of Judaism stretches the point. While Cohen imputes to Spinoza a certain "piety for the teachings of Christ" ("Spinoza über Staat und Religion," 318), he neither condemns this sentiment nor associates it with a "hatred of Judaism." Rather, Cohen associates this piety with the philosophical pantheism of the *Ethics,* which, as Spinoza himself concedes, is far from the accepted Christological doctrine of "some" churches. What Cohen criticizes with regard to the prophetology in the *Theological-Political Treatise* is that Spinoza allows for a philosophical interpretation of the revelation in/to Christ yet denies such a possibility to the interpretation of the Mosaic revelation. This charge is, to Cohen, aggravated because elsewhere (in his *Ethics*) Spinoza does recognize an adumbration of his pantheistic philosophy among "some Hebrews." Cf. Cohen, "Spinoza über Staat und Religion," 320, and see Cohen, *Religion der Vernunft,* 2d ed. (Frankfurt am Main: Kauffmann, 1929), 83, 122, 124, 126f., 190, 260.

90. Amos 7:1 and 7:4 are examples of parabolic visions "shown" to the prophet; Hosea 1 is an example of words spoken directly to a prophet; Isaiah 6 is the prophet's account of a theophany. And cf. Maimonides, *Guide* II:45.

91. In Cohen, "Spinoza über Staat und Religion," 315, only the word *Stimme* (voice) is emphasized.

92. Spinoza, *Theological-Political Treatise,* trans. Gebhardt, 23. The emphasis is Strauss's. My translation here is adapted from *Theological-Political Treatise,* trans. Shirley, 14.

93. Cohen, "Spinoza über Staat und Religion," 316.

94. Spinoza, *Theological-Political Treatise,* trans. Gebhardt, 19.

95. Cohen's report of Spinoza's opinions is, indeed, inaccurate and, as Strauss readily concedes, the major point of Cohen's argument does not hinge on the distortion of the details in question. Still, I know of no other case where Cohen ascribes to an author, whose work he parses with as much care as he does Spinoza's *Treatise,* an opinion as blatantly contradicting the actual text.

96. R. Abraham ben David of Posquières (c. 1125–98), philosophically educated and widely respected Provençal halakhist. Rabad authored, among many other works, a critical scholion *(hassagot)* on the *Code* of Maimonides that, since the earliest printed editions, has been a standard companion to the latter. (Cf. *EJ,* s.v. "Abraham ben David of Posquières," by I. Twersky.

97. Rabbi Moshe ben Maimon, or Moses Maimonides (1135–1204). Cohen's well-known appreciation of Maimonides is manifest in many of his writings. See in particular the essay "Charakteristik der Ethik Maimunis," in *Moses Ben Maimon: Sein Leben, seine Werke und sein Einfluss: Zur Erinnerung an den siebenhundertsten Todestag des Maimonides,* ed. W. Bacher, M. Brann, D. Simonsen, and J. Guttmann for the Gesellschaft zur Förderung der Wissenschaft des Judentums, vol. 1 (Leipzig: Fock, 1908), 63–134.

98. Note that Rabad was himself a rationalist interpreter of Scripture and hence far from asserting divine corporeality. Yet he criticized the more theoretically oriented Maimonides for going too far when, in his *Code,* he found those asserting corporeality deserving of excommunication.

99. Strauss: "wie Geist zu Geiste"; cf. *Theological-Political Treatise*, ed. Gebhardt, 25: "von Geist zu Geiste"; *Theological-Political Treatise*, trans. Shirley, 14: "mind to mind." And see Cohen, "Spinoza über Staat und Religion," 317f.

100. Cf. Strauss: "'seine Pietät für Christi *Leben*' (Cohen)" (= Spinoza's reverence for the life of Christ); and Cohen, "Spinoza über Staat und Religion," 318: "seiner Pietät für dessen *Lehren*" (= Spinoza's reverence for the teachings of Christ). Emphases added. Cf., however, Cohen, "Ein ungedruckter Vortrag Hermann Cohens über Spinozas Verhältnis zum Judentum," with an introduction by Franz Rosenzweig, in *Festgabe zum 10jährigen Bestehen der Akademie für die Wissenschaft des Judentums, 1919–1929* (Berlin: Akademie Verlag, 1929), 42–68, which is the printed version of a speech Cohen gave in 1910. On p. 58 of this text, which Strauss references in the notes to his preface to *Spinoza's Critique of Religion*, we find a passage that may have been on Strauss's mind when he wrote of Spinoza's piety, alleged by Cohen, for the "life of Christ" instead of for the "teachings of Christ:" "Also nicht allein die sogenannte Lehre Christi nach der hergebrachten Fiktion, sondern die Lebensgeschichte Christi nach den Aposteln soll man menschlich leicht begreifen können" [Hence not just the so-called doctrine of Christ according to the traditional fiction is supposed to be humanly and easily comprehensible, but also the biography of Christ according to the apostles]. This passage was not yet published in 1924 and, unless another, similar passage can be identified in Cohen's published work, Strauss may be assumed to have had access to the manuscript. It is possible, of course, that he inadvertently switched "life" for "doctrine" (*Leben* instead of *Lehre*) due to the alliteration as well as the closer association between piety and life (a *lectio simplicior*) than between piety and doctrine.

101. Cf. Cohen, "Spinoza über Staat und Religion," 319: "bekannt geworden"; and Strauss, "Cohens Analyse der Bibelwissenschaft Spinozas," 309: "bekannt gewesen."

102. Cohen, "Spinoza über Staat und Religion," 319.

103. Cohen, "Spinoza über Staat und Religion," 353, quoting chapter 7 of Spinoza, *Theological-Political Treatise*, trans. Gebhardt, 139.

104. Cohen, "Spinoza über Staat und Religion," 329.

105. Cf. ibid., 325, and see chapter 2 of Spinoza, *Theological-Political Treatise*, trans. Gebhardt, 50.

106. Genesis 12:3b. Cf. KJV, "and in thee shall all families of the earth be blessed," and *Tanakh* (JPS): "And all the families of the earth / Shall bless themselves by you."

107. Cohen, "Spinoza über Staat und Religion," 361: "diesen menschlich unbegreiflichen Verrat." Instead of Spinoza's "betrayal" *(Verrat)*, Strauss speaks here of his "alienation," a term that later, in *Spinoza's Critique of Religion*, is used to describe Spinoza's psychological condition. See, for example, *Spinoza's Critique of Religion*, 174. In the last footnote here, however, as well as in the 1962 preface to *Spinoza's Critique of Religion*, 19, Cohen's view is cited fully and without this modification. In footnote 39 of the preface to *Spinoza's Critique of Religion*, the most strongly negative epithets Cohen applied to Spinoza are documented by no less than six references.

108. See Spinoza, *Ethics* pt. 2, proposition 43, scholium.

109. Chapter 7 of Spinoza, *Theological-Political Treatise*, trans. Gebhardt, 156; cf. Cohen, "Spinoza über Staat und Religion," 353f.

On the Bible Science of Spinoza and His Precursors (1926)

The following essay is meant to provide a programmatically brief orientation—as appropriate for the purpose of the *Korrespondenzblatt*[1]—on the guiding question of the investigation I am undertaking on behalf of the Academy for the Science of Judaism.[2] The subject of the investigation is the Bible science[3] of Spinoza and of some of his precursors (Uriel da Costa, Isaac de La Peyrère, and Thomas Hobbes), who worked under similar conditions toward the establishment of this discipline. Spinoza's Bible science has not been the theme of adequate, and certainly not of productive, monographic treatment since 1867, when Carl Siegfried's article "Spinoza als Kritiker und Ausleger des Alten Testaments" was published. The present attempt to produce a new exposition is amply justified by the many changes in our conception and judgment of Spinoza due to studies that have been published in the meantime, studies dealing with his biography, with the development of his doctrine, with the intellectual history of his time, and with the general history of Bible science. I owe the idea for my work to the critical study of Hermann Cohen's article, "Spinoza über Staat und Religion, Judentum und Christentum" (reprinted in the third volume of his *Jüdische Schriften*),[4] which, in terms of the radicalism of its questioning and the forcefulness with which he calls Spinoza to account, is simply paradigmatic and which, in this very respect, is peerless in the recent literature on Spinoza. To be sure, while few of Cohen's contemporaries were as inspired as he was by the spirit of the great age of the Enlightenment, to which he zealously testified in many important passages of his writings, when it comes to his criticism[5] of Spinoza, apparently diverted by his insight into the deeper opposition, he failed to recognize Spinoza's true objective (which is essentially identical with that of the Enlightenment) as well as the immediate target of his attack. Spinoza did not turn against the "monotheism of Judaism" or against the "social ethics of the prophets" but rather against revealed religion in all its forms. In view of Cohen's radicalization of the question, one must again undertake an analysis of the *Theological-Political Treatise* as a radical critique of revealed religion.

I.

Spinoza's Bible science is first of all a fact in the history of the sciences. Spinoza has the undisputed merit of having established Bible science as a science "free of presuppositions."[6] In the pertinent chapters of the *Theological-Political Treatise* he determined the fundamental objectives and methods of research of the new discipline and advanced to fundamental results that have never been challenged throughout the further development of the field. Bible science forms a part of the whole of the hermeneutic disciplines. In regard to its insight into the demands of hermeneutics as such, however, the achievement of the *Treatise* falls short of what, for example, Erasmus of Rotterdam conceived as necessary.[7] Thus the total achievement of the *Treatise* in the history of the sciences would seem to be the constitution of a specialized science. This remark clearly misses the true meaning of Spinoza's achievement, because the constitution of Bible science is of deeper significance than, say, the constitution[8] of the specialized sciences concerned with the study of Egyptian or Assyrian antiquities. Indeed, this deeper significance of the *Treatise* does not consist at all in its contribution to the history of science. Once it is presupposed that, with respect to its origin, the Bible is in principle just a literary document like any other, it follows that it must be dealt with scientifically just like any other document, that from the outset it forms a part of the subjects of the humanities with their essentially coherent methodology, and that there are no further difficulties in principle that hinder the constitution of Bible science. Therefore, the constitution of Bible science is preceded by the justification of its presupposition, that is, the critique of the opposite presupposition made by revealed religion and the critique of revealed religion in general. Due to these preconditions, Spinoza's Bible science is endowed with a greater interest than that which it would have earned as a mere fact in the history of the sciences. It is an important moment in the universal movement called the Enlightenment's critique of religion. Is this critique, and in particular Spinoza's critique of revealed religion, something other than scientific and theoretical critique? In Spinoza's view it is not. This view must be taken seriously and weighed carefully, but it must not be binding on us. An immanent analysis might be sufficient if we were dealing with an interpretation of the *Ethics*. However, when Spinoza reaches beyond the context of his own life and thought and when he embarks on the critique of another context, he is subject to a norm other than the one immanent in him. By undertaking this critique he subjects himself to the judgment implicit in the question of whether he hit or missed the criticized context. Only when this question is posed do the specific presuppositions of his critique emerge. At the same time, Spinoza's general conception of his critique as theoretical, or even as potentially theoretical, is called into question.

The presupposition of Spinoza's Bible science is the critique of religion, and the critique of religion, in turn, is the result of the system developed in the *Ethics*. Strictly speaking, the critique of religion cannot be distinguished from the system, because truth is the norm of itself and of falsehood. Religion is refuted and its claims are proven to be erroneous by the positive construction of the system. Thus, the ultimate presuppositions of Spinoza's critique of religion are identical with the definitions and axioms of the *Ethics* (or with equivalent propositions). Although it is not his habit to uncover the errors of others, Spinoza makes an exhaustive effort to refute religion, because its claims are prejudices that can obstruct the understanding of his proofs. The claims of religion are necessary errors, rooted in human nature, and are impossible to eradicate from the minds and hearts of most human beings. Hence the errors of religion (of superstition, as Spinoza likes to say)[9] and the truths of philosophy are of a kind that cannot be evaded by the human being. Rather, the human being's original and sole striving, that of persisting in his being, forces him either toward these truths or toward those errors. The striving for self-preservation generates the very passions in which it runs aground and negates itself.[10] The passions endanger our being. The situation in which the striving for self-preservation loses itself in the striving for sensual happiness and temporal goods gives rise to religion. On the other hand, the radically understood striving for self-preservation fulfills itself in theory.[11] Theory and religion are opposite possibilities for the human being that are as diametrically opposed to each other as strength and impotence, freedom and bondage, a spiritual and a carnal attitude.

There is a difference between the religion of the multitude, superstition, and the official doctrine of the theologians, on the one hand, and the teachings of the prophets, the Psalms, the Proverbs, the Gospels, and the Pauline Epistles, on the other. In his fight against the "superstition" that completely dominated the contemporary churches, Spinoza relied on the doctrine of the "*ancient* religion," usurped and disfigured by priests out of greed and vanity. Thus Spinoza's own conception was that he did not fight against religion but against superstition (which, however, is just positive revealed religion in all its forms), and not against Scripture but against the conception and use of Scripture by revealed religion. He regards his criticism of religion as an immanent critique.

Spinoza's position, and the critique of religion that comes with it, asserts itself in the biographical context as well as in that of the *Treatise* through his critique of the position of Maimonides. Now, Maimonides' position implies a criticism of a "more naïve" position, which is the very position Spinoza denigrates as superstition and which Maimonides judges no more leniently. In the course of his critical dismemberment of the whole of Maimonides' position into its component parts, Spinoza discovers the "naïve" position that had been "overcome" ["*überwunden*"] by Maimonides, and he makes it the object of a criticism sharply distinguished from his critique of Maimonides.

The "naïve" position presents itself to him independently in the form of the Calvinist orthodoxy of his time. Accordingly, Spinoza's critique of religion occurs in two phases: first, as a critique of the position of Maimonides; and second, as a critique of the position of Calvinist orthodoxy (or of a corresponding Jewish form of the same).

The Critique of Maimonides' Position

The critique of Maimonides' position is a scientific critique of scientific claims, and as such it is immanent in Maimonides' position. This is so because in justifying his doctrine, Maimonides relies not so much on Scripture as on reason. He simply derives the true meaning of Scripture by interpreting it on the basis of objective truths that reason knows without regard to Scripture. This makes reason seemingly independent of Scripture. True, it becomes impossible to object to the results of rational investigation on the basis of individual passages of Scripture, however numerous. But the operative presupposition in Maimonides' interpretation of Scripture—that Scripture is true because it is revealed—directs theological speculation toward a certain concept of God. The fact of revelation is presupposed.

Spinoza argues against this presupposition in two ways. First, he denies the revealed character of Scripture and the factuality of revelation through a philological and historical critique of the canon and the tradition. And second, he refutes the possibility of revelation through a philosophical critique of the concept of God of revealed religion by demonstrating that it contradicts God's essence to reveal a law. But it is just this more radical part of his critique that is not immanent. Even if we suppose that, in Spinoza's mind, his position is derived from Maimonides' position by means of a further immanent development, and thus by strict inference, and even if we further suppose that he invariably believes that rigorous deduction from (as he claims) generally accepted theological propositions yields results that negate [*aufgehoben wird*][12] the position of revealed religion, [we must conclude that] this belief is not grounded in the facts.

Spinoza's critique of the possibility of revelation follows from the proposition that in God intellect and will are one and the same. This proposition is equivalent to a denial of creation, of the giving of the Law, and of miracles. This proposition is also encountered in Maimonides. This fact seemed to justify the belief that there was an essential agreement between Maimonides and Spinoza—a fact that does not redound to Maimonides' credit. Nevertheless, on closer inspection it becomes apparent that what Maimonides advances and what Spinoza makes the foundation of his critique of religion are not the same proposition. Thus, the theology of Maimonides is not the basis of Spinoza's critique of revealed religion. If one looks for such a basis, then one must return to those presuppositions of the aforementioned proposition of identity by which Spinoza undermines Maimonides' position, that is, the belief in a God who freely creates and acts graciously. These presuppositions are developed in the *Ethics*.

The extensive discussion in the *Treatise*, however, points to another, more immediate presupposition that also has the advantage of being explicitly acknowledged by Maimonides. I am referring to the conception of *theory* common to Maimonides and Spinoza. Theory as presupposition and element of the knowledge of God and thus of *beatitudo* [blessedness] is the highest interest of human beings, and it absorbs or depreciates all other interests. Proceeding from the character of theory as such, Spinoza brings to light the tension between theory and Scripture (more precisely, between theory and Torah): the Torah directs itself to a group of human beings, a special group of human beings, while theory is in principle the concern of each human being as an individual. Maimonides avoids this consequence by his doctrine of the *divine law*. According to this doctrine, the divine law has the function of determining the means that serve the heterogeneous goals in life of the wise few and the unwise many through a *single* legal order. The Torah aims at the highest perfection of the few, that is, theory. At the same time, it aims at the social organization of the many and at their civilizing [*Sittigung*], which serves this secondary purpose. Thus, the purpose of revelation, insofar as it is not simply identical with theory, is the social organization of the multitude. For Maimonides, the relation of care for the multitude vis-à-vis theory is not just the relation of a means to an end, in the sense that social organization and external security of life are together the *conditio sine qua non* of the theoretical life. Rather, he is vitally concerned that the fundamental truths be recognized as such by the multitude, ignoring the function of these truths in the organization of society. All human beings, the wise and the foolish,[13] are to be united by the recognition of *one* truth.

Spinoza is not moved by the interest that all human beings recognize the truth, an interest not entailed by the interest in truth. These heterogeneous interests are united only by the identification of theory with revelation, and thus by the identification of the acceptance of untruth with idolatry. For Spinoza, the multitude is an *object* of theoretical interest; he enjoys the contemplation of the multitude [whose members] are enslaved by their passions. This attitude toward the multitude is the ultimate presupposition of Spinoza's theory of the state. In the final analysis, his interest in the social organization of the multitude proves to be a consequence of his interest in theory. Thus the radicalization of the theoretical interest turns out to be an essential moment in the opposition between Spinoza and Maimonides, and an essential presupposition of Spinoza's critique of religion. This presupposition is immanent in Maimonides' position.

This state of affairs is not altered by the overt connection that Spinoza establishes between the unlimited supremacy of theory and the denial of both divine and human freedom, that is, the conviction that all human affects and actions are a product of the one Nature that is always and everywhere the same; for the supremacy of theory is recognized by Maimonides under the presupposition of totally different objective convictions. In this regard, Spinoza's critique only confirms the objections, advanced from within revealed religion, to the attempt to elevate theory, under the assumption of revealed religion, to the [level of] highest human interest. Thus it is a truly immanent critique.

Interest in radically conceived theory demands that everything that is should become the object of theory, and that one should adopt a theoretical attitude in approaching everything that is. Thus Spinoza must take exception to the special status that Scripture is assigned in the work of Maimonides. It too becomes an object of theoretical interest, and every other interest in it is devalued in principle. This has decisive consequences for the interpretation of Scripture. Scripture must not be *presupposed* to be true. It is only on the basis of an unbiased examination that one can pass judgment on its truth. It is true that Maimonides cannot demonstrate the truth of Scripture on the basis of Scripture, that is, on the basis of its literal sense, because his understanding of Scripture presupposes his conviction of its truth. This conviction, however, is authenticated by the tradition of its revealed character. At this point, we may disregard the philological and historical critique by which Spinoza defends himself against this conviction. What is of fundamental importance is that the way in which Maimonides interprets Scripture—namely, he does so on the basis of his conviction of its truth—is seen by Spinoza as failing the elementary demands of the theoretical attitude. He marvels at how unscrupulously Maimonides negates or falsifies all of the most obvious opposing judgments, and at how unrestrained he is in adapting Scripture to his opinions.

Just like Spinoza's doctrine of the divine law, his doctrine of prophecy contains proof of a fundamental inner difficulty in Maimonides' position. Here too the starting point of Spinoza's prophetology in the corresponding doctrine of Maimonides has long been evident and was firmly established by M. Joël.[14] Maimonides' prophetology arises from the difficulty that the belief in the truth of Scripture runs into when it faces the manifest untruth of numerous scriptural passages. For example, according to Aristotelian physics, changes in the movements of the celestial bodies such as those in the miracle of Joshua [Joshua 10:12–14] are impossible. The distinction that presents itself here—between a meaning of Scripture that is literal, inappropriate, and imaginative and one that is appropriate and true—makes it necessary to represent the act of prophetic perception in such a way that it simultaneously explains the inner truth and the imaginative expression of prophetic speech. Thus Maimonides teaches that prophecy is an emanation from God that, mediated through the active intellect, first unfolds in the intellect and then in the imaginative faculty of the prophet. The intellect and the imaginative faculty cooperate in the prophetic act; in fact, each of these capacities is enhanced beyond ordinary measure.

Spinoza's decisive objection states that, given the opposition of intellect and imaginative faculty—an opposition recognized also by Maimonides—an extraordinary enhancement of the imaginative faculty must lead to an extraordinary reduction of the capacity for pure intellection. This objection is aimed at an inner difficulty in Maimonidean prophetology. In this case, the criticism does not affect Maimonides, because Spinoza has a totally different conception and valuation of the "imaginative faculty" and thus misses the point of Maimonides' prophetology. Apart from this, what is of fundamental significance is that the theological arguments derived from Maimonides' philosophical doctrine of God and His attributes are of little account for the discussions in the *Treatise*. In contrast to Spinoza, the concept of God characteristic of Maimonides has a voice in his prophetology only insofar as, according to this doctrine, God can prevent at His discretion the actualization of the prophetic potential. In all of Spinoza's critique this characteristic reservation is never mentioned.

Closer examination of the misunderstanding implied in Spinoza's criticism[15] of Maimonides' prophetology brings to light a deeper presupposition that, though favoring the radicalization of the theoretical interest, cannot be derived from this interest itself.[16] According to Maimonides' doctrine, the cooperation of intellect and imaginative faculty in the prophetic perception does not detract from the theoretical dignity of prophecy, because the imaginative faculty does not influence, and therefore does not hinder and interfere with, the intellect. Rather, the imaginative faculty is ruled and controlled by the intellect and put in its service. As I said, Spinoza fails to perceive this point in Maimonides' prophetology. Besides, his conception of the imaginative faculty compelled him to deny the possibility presumed by Maimonides. It goes without saying that a decisive role in this opposition between

Maimonides and Spinoza is played by the opposition between their conceptions—the Aristotelian and the Cartesian—of truth and knowledge.

In and behind this opposition, however, there appears a moment that is even more characteristic of the critique of revelation. According to Maimonides, theory operating by means of the intellect alone is in principle *surpassable*. This is so in two respects. First, philosophical knowledge can be, and has actually been, surpassed by prophetic knowledge. Secondly, an essentially unsurpassable and essentially perfect philosophical knowledge exists historically in the doctrine of Aristotle. Thus all theoretical investigation moves in a horizon ruled and limited by *authorities*. Maimonides' attempt to identify theory and Scripture presupposes the conviction that theory has arrived at its essential completion and perfection in the investigations of Aristotle. This is so because, if Scripture is to be made accessible only by its interpretation that aims at objective truth, perfect truth must be available. Revelation is to be identified only with a perfect and complete theory. It is impossible to undertake this endeavor vis-à-vis the "new science," which admits infinite progress, and thus admits essential incompleteness and imperfection at each concrete stage. The type of theory envisioned by Maimonides offers less resistance to identification with revelation than the type present to Spinoza. The overthrow of the authority of Aristotle by the new physics discredited the *contents* of Maimonides' interpretation of Scripture. The liberation of science from every tie to authority and the rise of a positive science with an unlimited horizon of future tasks and discoveries made the *principle* of Maimonides' interpretation untenable.

At this point, the question we must put to Spinoza's critique of Maimonides and, accordingly, to Maimonides himself calls for a more accurate formulation. We proceeded from the fundamental agreement between the two philosophers' conception and valuation of theory. Based on this agreement, Spinoza's criticism presented itself as an inner critique of the position of Maimonides. It urges the opposition between theory and Scripture and argues against the possibility of *harmonizing* theory and Scripture. More radical than the question of whether theory and Scripture can be harmonized, however, is the question of their coordination—that is, assuming the supremacy of theory, the question of what an *interest* in revelation really means. More accurately, if the interest in theory is the highest interest of human beings, absorbing or depreciating all other interests, and if the intellect as the natural organ of theory is adequate for the perfection of theory, what then is the purpose of revelation? This question is not directed to the *belief* in revelation, which can support itself by a great many arguments drawn from theology, from the economy of salvation, and from history, but to the issue of whether it is possible, in principle, for the theorist to lead his life in disregard of revelation. If this possibility is granted, then the belief in revelation may become a constituent of the intellectual convictions of the theorist, a constituent from which, incidentally, the most important consequences for the contents of his theory, and especially for a specific concept of God, may, or even must, follow. Revelation, however, has no significance for his life, for his highest and exclusive interest, and for the consummation of his theory. He does not *need* revelation. If it is claimed that the theorist's own thought is unsurpassable, or even just adequate, for the perfection of theory, then it follows that this possibility must be admitted.

It can be shown to be typical of the theory that arises in the context of revealed religion that it calls into question the legitimacy in principle of unaided human thought, while it also attempts to secure its own theory, determined even in its contents by the tradition of revealed religion, against the unbelieving theory of the philosophers. This holds true for Maimonides as well. His speculative practice suggests the following general view of the relation between reason and revelation: the truths of revelation are identical with the truths of reason, that is, they are accessible to human reason. This is not to say that unguided human reason left to its own resources could have discovered all fundamental truths. Even Aristotle, *the* philosopher, could know only the sublunar world in its essential truth. It is not by accident that the decisive correction Maimonides made to Aristotelian-Neoplatonic theology, namely, the claim that the world has been created, is a correction of this theology that accords with Scripture. Of course, Maimonides provides reasons for the dogma of creation. He proves that the creation of the world is more plausible than its eternity. But he is aware that human capacity does not suffice for solving this question perfectly. When it comes to a fundamental question, on whose resolution depends the being or nonbeing of revealed religion, unaided human reason is in principle subject to error. In the face of this limitation of human thought, Maimonides demands caution and distrust of human thought and refers to the tradition founded on prophecy. We may therefore perceive that the characteristic presupposition of Spinoza's critique of religion is the conviction of the sufficiency of human thought for the perfection of theory. One might object that the opposite conviction, that is, distrust of human thought, is not truly characteristic of Maimonides the "rationalist." This objection draws its strength from a comparison of Maimonides' position with other potential and actual positions within revealed religion. But this approach is inappropriate if we are asking about the characteristic difference between

Spinoza as the one who denies revealed religion and Maimonides as the one who affirms it. The necessity of revelation is to be legitimized solely by doubting or limiting the right of sovereign human thought.

The following considerations speak in favor of locating the core of the opposition between Spinoza and revealed religion (and, accordingly, of the opposition between Spinoza and Maimonides) in the antithesis of belief in sufficiency and belief in insufficiency. All objective arguments against the doctrines of revealed religion presuppose the conviction that human thought, following its own directives, is competent and qualified to judge revelation. Hence the justification of this conviction must precede the critique of the doctrines of revelation. At the very least, any doubt as to the sufficiency of human thought must first be removed. Furthermore, if the belief in a God who revealed a law could be destroyed or even had been destroyed by philosophical critique, or if the belief in the revelation of the Mosaic law could be destroyed or even had been destroyed by historical critique, this still would by no means render destructible, or actually destroy, the interest in revelation grounded in the conviction, or in the insight, that human life in itself is either completely directionless or lacks adequate direction. Hence the critic—having shaken himself free of the belief in a revelation accommodated to human interest, or in a superhuman revelation that first awakens this interest, and therefore having set himself the task of understanding the alleged revelation of God as merely a work of man and deriving it from the laws of human nature—is likely to begin the analysis of revealed religion with the fact that appears, even from the perspective of revealed religion, to be the human correlate of a superhuman revelation, namely, with the fact of man's inadequacy for the guidance of his own life. Thus we understand why Spinoza prefaces with a critique of the interest in revelation, that is, a critique of the insufficiency experience of revealed religion, the *Theological-Political Treatise,* which, in its most fundamental parts, is dedicated to the critique of revealed religion.

In summary, we may characterize Spinoza's critique of Maimonides as follows. On the basis of theory, Spinoza argues against the possibility of harmonizing theory and Scripture. His critique aims at the separation of "philosophy" from "theology" and of theory from Scripture. What appears in this process is in part the inner difficulties of Maimonides' position and in part its historically conditioned character. The primary condition for the possibility of harmonizing theory and Scripture proves to be the belief in the dependence of human reason on superhuman guidance for the achievement of the perfection of theory. Therefore, the central task of Spinoza's critique of revealed religion must be to criticize the belief in the insufficiency [of human thought].

The Critique of Calvin's Position

The object of Spinoza's critique is not Maimonides' doubt about the sufficiency of man—a doubt that just barely subsists, is hardly ever actually operative, and indeed appears in his thought very infrequently—but the emphatic denial of human sufficiency and the claim that human nature is radically corrupt. Spinoza's attack is directed not against Maimonides but against Protestantism, more precisely against Counterremonstrant Calvinism.[17] In order to comprehend clearly, if possible even more clearly than Spinoza himself succeeded in doing, Spinoza's critique of revealed religion, we must confront the ultimate presuppositions of Spinoza with those of Calvin.

Calvin begins his theology with an exposition of what it is to know God. After all, for him too the ultimate goal of the *vita beata* is the knowledge of God. The contents of the knowledge of God—God the creator, sustainer, and ruler of the world, omnipotent lord, just judge, and merciful father of human beings, in short, the biblical idea of God—is here at first not even called into question but rather presupposed as true. Knowledge of God thus understood is implanted in the human heart, and is furthermore manifest from the structure of the world and from its steadfast governance. The fact that human beings nevertheless criticize this idea of God is a sign that natural knowledge of God is all too easily obscured, and that human knowledge is not sufficient for the knowledge of the true God. Therefore the human being is in need of a support better than the natural light: he needs the word of God as the witness borne by God about Himself offered in the Holy Scriptures of the Old and the New Testaments. The human being is convinced of the authority of the Holy Scriptures by the inner testimony of the Holy Spirit. The same spirit who spoke through the mouth of the prophets vouches for the truth of the Scriptures by being effective in us. The living unity of Scripture and spirit convinces us of the truth of the idea of God that Spinoza contests.[18]

The positions of Calvin and Spinoza seem to be directly opposed to one another without the possibility of agreement or, what amounts to the same thing, without the possibility of genuine critique. Spinoza appeals for his theology to the natural light just as uncompromisingly as Calvin appeals for his theology to Scripture, vouched for and made accessible by the inner testimony of the Holy Spirit.[19] These positions are not defensive positions, impregnable by virtue of a fundamental circularity but therefore also unfit for attack. Rather, the passionate faith in the justice and truth of one's cause compels each of the two opponents (indeed it could not be otherwise) to attack. *Every* right is denied to the opponent's position. As yet, neither side is ready to accept a clean separation between religion and theory. Rather, revealed religion and enlightenment fight a life-and-death battle on the same plane of the one and eternal truth. Let us find out about the two opponents' offensive weapons.

For his doctrine Spinoza relies on his own judgment. He speaks scornfully of those who deem it pious not to trust reason and their own judgment. To Spinoza this is not piety but sheer folly. The only way he can understand the skepticism of his opponents is to suppose that they fear that religion and belief cannot be defended unless human beings deliberately keep themselves in complete ignorance and entirely take leave of reason. On each occasion he is reassured by what the intellect reveals, without in any way suspecting that he may have deceived himself. It is possible that this trust is justified by the deeper presuppositions of Spinoza's system. However, in the context of the critique of religion, all concrete objections to it have as their primary condition the trust in one's own reflections, the high-minded faith in the human being and in reason as his supreme power.

Calvin's radical critique is directed against this confidence and against the readiness to be satisfied with human capacities. He sees the typical obstacle to human self-knowledge in the natural tendency of human beings to flatter themselves, their completely blind self-infatuation. From this natural tendency arises the conviction held by almost all human beings that "man is abundantly self-sufficient to live well and in happiness" *(hominem sibi abunde sufficere ad bene beateque vivendum)*. Human beings tend to be reassured by their gifts, to be at peace with themselves, and to be satisfied with themselves. But only he can be satisfied with himself who does not know himself and whose conscience is not sufficiently tender, he who does not prostrate himself before the majesty of God in confusion and distress of mind. Calvin sees the inability and unwillingness to have one's conscience radically shaken as stemming from self-confidence, from faith in the sufficiency of human beings, which is the precondition for disinterest in revelation.

This critique smacks of theological polemics. Calvin coarsens the opponent's opinion by the way he reports it *(hominem sibi abunde sufficere,* etc.); by making a state of mind that the philosophers see as the goal in life of a few noble spirits the actual achievement of almost all human beings; and by reducing an intention of the philosophers that is anything but vulgar—at least in their own minds—to a very vulgar tendency. This character of the critique should be strongly emphasized. Just as Calvin attributes the belief in human sufficiency to vulgar self-satisfaction, to carnal self-love, Spinoza attributes the belief in human insufficiency to the vulgar incapacity to plan, to immoderate carnal desire. Just as Calvin scornfully points out the shameful multiplicity *(pudenda varietas)* of philosophies, Spinoza refers to the great multiplicity and changeability of "superstition." One cannot dismiss this critique as mere abuse of one's opponent. At the very least it has to be taken very seriously as an indication of how little the critic is interested in *understanding* his opponent's position. Can there be true critique on this level of discussion, a level at which one sniffs out on the ground of the disputed stance only those fundamental facts about the human being that one's own conception requires, and at which one disregards the self-conception of the opponent [by viewing it] as a rationalization of his carnal mind? Can there be true critique so long as faith in the rightness of one's cause is not limited by any insight into its conditionality, and so long as the critic can rely on something absolute (either on revelation or on reason common to all human beings)? On the other hand, is radical critique— such as is evident in Calvin or Spinoza, which denies every right to the opposite position—possible under the conditions of the historical consciousness?

In any case, in our context it suffices to show that Spinoza's critique of revealed religion is an external challenge rather than a true critique. Spinoza associates interest in revelation with fear, namely, with the fear of danger. In the literature of revealed religion, however, a distinction is always drawn between fear of God and profane fear. Paying no heed to a distinction that [in his view] amounts to a [mere] protest,[20] Spinoza deduces revealed religion from profane fear. The question that is very much suggested by this deduction is whether he knew what the fear of God, and the stirring of conscience entailed by it, actually is. His conception of the law shows rather distinctly that he does not understand human beings who fear not out of fear of punishment and who obey not out of a slavish attitude. In this context nothing is less justified than Spinoza's appeal to Paul's criticism of legalism. In Paul, the deepest awareness of sin rebels against legalism, while Spinoza's rejection of the Law rests on the rejection of obedience as such, and rests ultimately on the absence of any awareness of sin. Spinoza is a *homo liber* and a *homo fortis*, to whom radical stirrings of conscience and moments of ultimate despair are unknown. He either did not know or deadened in himself the characteristic experiences that are connected with the interest in revelation. In any case, he did not subject them to critique.

The inadequacy of the critique follows from the character of the critique. Spinoza wants to criticize religion by means of theory. Since and insofar as religion, as he saw it, is founded on obedience and belief, on distrust and suspicion of human capacities, especially of theory, his criticism is essentially transcendent. It does not arise out of obedience and belief. Every critical argument, any presupposition made by Spinoza, is preceded by the conviction that one can judge the truths of religion from a theoretical stance outside of the domain of obedience and belief. In the context of the critique of religion and of the critical question it entails, what becomes problematic is the will to theoretical critique and the readiness for it as well as for theory in general. The question of "Why theory?" is posed as the question of "Why disobedience and unbelief?" This "Why?" precedes all theory. Rather than a theoretical insight or a conviction, it is a motive.

The question "How is critique of religion at all possible?" makes it necessary to distinguish between theory and motive. The internal division of Spinoza's critique of religion also points to this distinction. As Spinoza noted explicitly, he needs one method for the critique of revelation and another for the critique of miracles. The critique of revelation is a "theological" problem, while the critique of miracles is a "philosophical" problem. But this means that the critique of religion is divided in two: theoretical critique of the theoretical claims of religion; and critique of the presupposition of religion that casts doubt on the legitimacy of theory itself, a critique that is immanent in religion and relies on Scripture. The Enlightenment's critique of religion was crowned with a considerable and lasting success in spite of the fact that it confronted the actual intention of revealed religion in almost complete blindness. This historical fact can be understood only on the basis of the distinction between motive and theory.

One is led to this distinction, alien to Spinoza's thought, only by reflection[21] on the conditions of the possibility of a critique of religion. If it is granted that the motive of the critique of religion and the motives of revealed religion itself are unrelated, then this deprives the critique of religion of its decisive weight. Nevertheless, there are various motives that may compel one to the critique of religion, and these may be differentiated according to their rank and force, and especially according to their relation to theory and to the critique of religion that is theoretically justified. For the sake of a fundamental ranking of the questions posed by Spinoza's critique of religion, one is well advised to be guided by the Epicurean type of criticism of religion. Rather than being attained by virtue of an idealizing abstraction, this type of criticism, both as a historical fact and in terms of its historical effectiveness, proves to be an extreme case of the critique of religion mainly because here the primacy of the motive is evident, conscious, and explicit. The theory of the Epicureans essentially serves the purpose of liberating human beings from the fear of the gods and from the fear of death. The Epicurean motive is the interest in a life of tranquility and absence of terror. This interest rebels against the fear of the gods and against the fear of death. It wants to reach its goal through knowledge of actual causes. This enterprise has a chance of success if and only if the true being of the gods and of the cosmos is such that knowledge of them does not lead to newer, and even greater, anxiety and disquiet. In this respect, the Epicurean critique of religion likewise presupposes a primary theoretical conception. The stability [*Fixierung*] of this type of critique of religion and of the analysis of religion associated with it is the condition for an understanding of the critique of religion and thus also of the Bible science of the seventeenth century. This must not be taken to mean that the influence of the Epicurean motive reached as far as the influence of the Epicurean analysis of religion. As for Spinoza himself, he is not in every respect influenced by this motive, but rather by the Epicurean conception and explanation of religion alone: religion as a figment of fear and dream.

Along with the doctrines of the analysis of religion, the motives of the critique of religion are the ultimate presuppositions of Bible science, at least insofar as the Bible is considered primarily as a religious document. The way in which the primary efforts at criticizing religion are concretized in Bible science is not completely described by the general relation between critique of religion and Bible science. We shall trace this process of concretization in Uriel da Costa,[22] a precursor of Spinoza who took up the fight against religion by means of Bible science under similar preconditions. Da Costa shares one specific precondition with Spinoza, namely, that of being of Jewish origin or, more precisely, of Marrano origin.

II.[i]

If we assume that the affiliation of the Marranos with Christianity was based on nothing but coercion by the church and by the Iberian monarchies that were then in the process of consolidation, then their criticism of Christianity appears to be fully understandable. To be sure, the fact that their ancestors had at one time been forcibly converted to Christianity did not prevent the descendants from being devout Christians. This being so, what could have led a devout Christian and son of a devout Christian to criticism of Christianity? It was more likely a Christian difficulty than an objection raised by Jews,

---

[i] For the following I have used: *Die Schriften des Uriel da Costa. Mit Einleitung, Uebertragung und Regesten*, ed. Carl Gebhardt (1922).

never mind by Jewish ancestors. It is only following his loss of faith in the church, brought on by the experience that the doctrine of works of the church is not sufficient for salvation, that da Costa adopts Jewish arguments against Christianity. Is the criticism that leads him to Judaism connected with his being a Marrano? Da Costa himself does not answer this question. He mentions his Marrano descent and describes his path from Christianity to Judaism without indicating any connection between the two. Doubtless such a connection exists. The life of the Marranos within the Christian church and within Christian society lacks all naturalness. Thus they are predisposed to a criticism of Christianity. Now, if a Marrano's criticism of Christianity leads him to Judaism, then it is natural to regard the critical attitude of the Jew toward Christianity as the characteristic condition of his criticism. Marranos of da Costa's type, uncertain and insecure Christians, were pointed toward Judaism, of whose contents they knew little or nothing, by virtue of the traditions of their families. Their criticism is not Jewish; at most it is criticism based on the critical attitude of the Jew toward Christianity, and hence is devoid, or almost devoid, of specifically Jewish contents.

Of course, this is not how da Costa saw himself. He points to doubts about the truth of Christianity and to good reasons for the truth of Judaism. These reasons are reminiscent of the discussion, more than a century old, between the Spanish Jews and Christianity: the Old Testament is more rational than the New Testament; furthermore, the Old Testament is more trustworthy than the New because the Old Testament is an undisputed authority for both Jews and Christians while the New Testament is so only for Christians (Da Costa, p. 106; cf. Judah Halevi, *Kuzari* I:10; Joseph Albo, *Sefer Ha'iqqarim* I:11 and 24). To this context also belongs the reference to the idea of the Noahide commandments. These specific arguments would not have enticed da Costa away from Christianity, and indeed he would not have arrived at these arguments, without the earlier and more radical critique of the Catholic doctrine of works. This critique is preceded by the general condition of the Marrano readiness to criticize Christianity. But does this *condition* of all Marrano criticism produce da Costa's critique? Is it its sufficient cause and its inner *motive?* If we answer this question in the negative, then we find ourselves in agreement with da Costa himself who, in his autobiography, mentions his being a Marrano as a circumstance of his life but not as critical to his spiritual decision. In order to determine the motive of his critique we will follow his own account.

Born the son of a good Catholic, da Costa grows up in the Catholic milieu. He strives to follow meticulously all the behests of the church out of fear of eternal damnation. As an adult he experiences the impossibility of gaining remission of sins through confession and, furthermore, the impossibility of fulfilling the demands of the church. Thus he despairs of his salvation; he faces eternal damnation in all its horror. Da Costa's being and essence are revealed in the way in which he responds to this situation: he challenges the truth of what was usually taught about the hereafter (p. 106). Thus fear of eternal damnation drives da Costa to deny the immortality of the soul. If death is the end of everything, then the terrors of hell cease to exist. The *Epicurean* motive is unmistakable. The extent to which it influenced da Costa can be gleaned from several of his pronouncements. "What weighed him down and tormented him most in this life" was the idea of eternal bliss [*einem ewigen Gut*] and eternal woe [*einem ewigen Übel*]. This is a tormenting idea, because it means something uncertain. Eternal bliss is a "wager against long odds" (p. 101). The Epicurean aspiration after certain happiness stands in the way of so great a risk. Above all, it prohibits the belief in eternal damnation because of the original preference for joy over pain. Religion is contested as a source of "the gravest terrors and fears" (p. 120). Da Costa charges religion with defaming God by "virtually presenting him to the eyes of men as the cruelest hangman and most terrible torturer" (p. 121). However, he cannot adopt the Epicurean theology. For him as the heir of millennial religious traditions, the connection between God and the world is much too vital. For him, too, God is the *autor naturae* [the author of nature] (p. 110). Therefore, his battle is directed not against the idea of an active God but solely against the idea of eternal damnation and immortality of the soul. The Epicurean motive itself is unchanged by this limitation of its field of application. Incidentally, da Costa explicitly advocates the vindication of Epicurus, whom he does not know directly through his works but only through his doctrines and through the judgment of certain men who are lovers of truth (p. 108f.). Predestined by his nature, da Costa has his place in the Epicurean movement of his time, a trend against which the religious institutions no longer offered absolute protection.[ii]

The predicament in which da Costa was caught at the age of twenty causes him therefore to examine, on the basis of his own reflection, the precondition of this very predicament, that is, the Catholic ideas of afterlife. Since his rational examination of Catholic dogmas deprived him of the spiritual support he had once found in the Catholic Church, he is dominated by the desire to find such support elsewhere. Thus he begins to read the Torah

---

[ii] Da Silva, whose criticism was more justified than he realized, called him "one who resurrects the disgraceful and long buried sect of Epicurus." See Gebhardt, p. 174.

and the prophets; the tradition of his family pointing toward Judaism had likely showed him the way. He finds here less serious difficulties for reason than in the doctrine of the new covenant. It is thus by his own reflection that he comes to trust Moses more than the New Testament, and *consequently* to acknowledge the duty of obedience to the Mosaic law.

Soon after joining the Sephardic community in Amsterdam he notices that the community does not conduct itself according to the letter of the Mosaic law. He comes into conflict with the community. This was unavoidable; after all, the concrete context of Judaism had long since vanished from the horizon of the Marranos, a context that had given rise to his and his ancestors' critique of Christianity, yet one that was not at all represented in this critique. His return to Judaism is rooted in this critique, which, in his case, has its deepest and most personal root in the Epicurean motive; indeed, it is this Epicurean motive that determines his "Judaism." Therefore, on his first encounter with concrete Judaism he finds it necessary to extend to Judaism the critique that he had hitherto directed only at Christianity. More precisely: first, he argues against the law of the Jewish tradition on the ground of the law of Moses ("Theses against the Tradition," 1–32); and second, he argues against the dogma of immortality advocated by Judaism on the grounds of both reason and Scripture ("On the Mortality of the Human Soul," 33–101). The conflict with the community opens fully the way for critique. From now on, positive religion and natural law (i.e., the Noahide commandments) are antithetically opposed to one another. The value of the ceremonies, the election of the Jewish people, the divinity of the Mosaic law, the miracles, and the right of ecclesiastical jurisdiction are denied. The critique of the Marrano ends in that century's common European movement of critique of religion, which was sustained, just like his own critique of religion, by the horror at the consequences of the *ira theologorum* [the wrath of the theologians]. As he can say about himself: *circa religionem passus sum in vita incredibilia* [I have suffered unbelievable things in life because of religion]. This motive is identical with the Epicurean one. What can be learned from the religious upheavals and struggles of that century concerns only the intensity of the effect of the Epicurean motive, but not, however, its inner essence.

At this juncture it must be borne in mind that, because of the very fact that they fought, the Epicureans of that age evidently no longer lived according to the precepts of Epicurus. Epicurus was no fighter. Nothing could make him risk his life and happiness. True to his ultimate intention, he submitted to the dominant cult and recognized it. When Lucretius sings the praises of Epicurus as the first to have dared to oppose religion *(obsistere contra)*, he describes his own attitude rather than that of his master. The more active and manly attitude characteristic of the men of the Enlightenment who agree with Epicurus's primary intention—an attitude that distinguishes them from Epicurus himself and that they share with Lucretius—expresses itself also in that they fight religion (like Lucretius) not only as the source of the greatest terrors and anxieties, but also as the origin of the most heinous crimes (Gebhardt, p. 120f.). Religion is not only harmful but also evil. Thus da Costa feels that he is not just a fighter pure and simple but a fighter for truth and freedom against falsehood and enslavement. Honor forbids the evasion of this combat. To evade it might be useful, but it would be shameful (p. 115ff.).

However, in his critique of religion, and especially of the idea of eternity, da Costa refers to the riskiness and fearfulness (or even evil) of this idea, but relies just as much on reason and Scripture. He makes it seem as if he arrived at a denial of immortality only because he submitted to Scripture:

> Post cæptum opus (sc. a study of the Bible) *accidit* etiam (. . .) ut (. . .) accederem sententiæ illorum, qui legis veteris præmium et pœnam definiunt temporalem, et de altera vita et immortalitate animorum minime cogitant (. . . .) (P. 108)

> [After a study of the Bible it also *happened* . . . that . . . I adopted the propositions of those who defined the reward and punishment of the old law as temporal, and thought little of another life and of the immortality of souls. . . . (P. 108).]

This, however, is contradicted by the fact that, at the very first, da Costa took exception to the traditional doctrines regarding another life. Da Costa wants to create the impression that the road he traversed, from the most unreasonable of all religions to an undisguised Epicureanism, was determined by reason and Scripture alone. In contrast to the Epicurean motive, da Costa's radicalism toward the Bible and his rationalism are both of secondary nature. It is true, however, that these two tendencies represent a single integrated authority for the critique of religion, an authority that cannot simply be derived from that motive.

Thus da Costa regards himself as impelled to criticize religion not only by the Epicurean motive but also by doubt about the reasonableness of religious dogmas and their conformity with Scripture. This doubt, then, is evidently of a different character than the Epicurean motive. If these truly heterogeneous efforts nevertheless come together in the same result, then we are dealing not with an external coincidence but with an inner harmony, whose analysis would lead us far beyond the limits of this study. Here it suffices to note that in the case of da Costa, just as undoubtedly as in the case of the philosophy of Epicurus, the "practical" motive is the primary one. Thus da Costa turns the insights that provide a basis for the doubts into means toward his "practical" ends. He owes these insights to the *physiology* of Michael *Servetus.*[iii]

Servetus[23]—who discovered the pulmonary blood circulation—undertook to illuminate the doctrines of Scripture on the basis of his physiological insights. This doctrinal matter is part of a theological system whose original motives are not very clear. This much, however, seems likely: that Servetus's denial of the immortality of the soul (if one can speak at all of such a denial in Servetus),[iv] rather than flowing directly from his interest, is a mere consequence of this interest, and not even a very emphatic one. Servetus is not concerned with liberating himself from the fear of eternal damnation by denying the existence of hell. The doctrine of Servetus that da Costa adopts teaches that the soul (the vital spirit) springs from a union of the air, breathed in by the lungs and transported to the heart, with the finest and thinnest blood that is transported from the liver to the heart. The finer it becomes, the more the vital spirit strives upward toward the brain, where it is transformed into a psychical spirit *(spiritus animalis).* Hence it is one and the same force that acts in breath, blood, the vital spirit, and the soul.[v] Just like the souls of animals, the souls of human beings are propagated by procreation.[vi] From

---

[iii] It was Professor Julius Guttmann who brought the relation between da Costa and Servetus to my attention.

[iv] H. Tollin, *Das Lehrsystem Michael Servet's genetisch dargestellt,* esp. vol. III (Gütersloh, 1878), 283ff.

[v] Servetus, *Christianismi Restitutio* (1553), p. 169: *"In his omnibus est unius spiritus et lucis Dei energia"* ["In all of these there is a uniform spirit and the energy of God's light"]. On p. 170: *"Hinc dicitur anima esse in sanguine, et anima ipsa sanguis, . . . ut docet ipse Deus Gen. 9, Lev. 17 et Deut. 12"* ["Thereupon it is said that the soul is in the blood and the soul itself is blood, . . . as God himself teaches in Genesis 9, Leviticus 17, and Deuteronomy 12"]. On p. 178: *"Ecce totam animae rationem, et quare anima omnis carnis in sanguine sit, et anima ipsa sanguis sit, ut ait Deus. Nam afflante Deo, inspirata per os et narcs, in cor et cerebrum ipsius Adae, et natorum eius, illa caelestis spiritus aura, sive idealis scintilla, et spiritali illi sanguineae materiae intus essentialiter iuncta, facta est in eius visceribus anima. Gen. 2, Esa. 57, Ezech. 37, et Zacha. 12"* ["See the whole reason of the soul and how the soul of all flesh is in the blood and the soul itself is blood, as God asserts. Because it was breathed by God into Adam's own heart and brain and into those of his offspring, inspired through mouth and nostrils, and that aura of the heavenly spirit, like a scintillation of the ideal, and out of spiritual and bloody matter that is essentially combined within, the soul is made in their bowels. Genesis 2, Isaiah 57, Ezekiel 37, and Zachariah 12"]. On p. 179: *". . . Idipsum*

this the assertion follows by necessity that the soul is mortal. This is also the teaching of Scripture: it regards the grave and hell as one and the same. Numerous passages dwell on life's brevity and vanity, and most of all, however, on the basic hopelessness of human life. Servetus limits this proposition by the statement that Christ's descent into hell has rendered the despair expressed

---

probat litera Geneseos. Nam non simpliciter dicitur halitus ille Dei esse anima: sed inspirato illo halitu facta est intus anima vivens" [This is proven by the letter of Genesis. Namely it does not simply say that the breath of God is the soul but, rather, only once that breath was breathed a living soul was made within]. On p. 216: *"Nisi hæc vis, ac eliciendæ et producendæ animæ virtus elementis inesset, non dixisset Deus, Producant terra et aqua animalia"* [God would not have said "Let the earth and the water bring forth animated creatures" if it were not for that force and that strength inherent in the elements that elicits and produces the souls].

In da Costa, p. 65: "Thus, we say, the human soul is and is called the vital spirit, through which the human being lives, and the said vital spirit is in the blood, . . . Accordingly, the soul of the beast is its blood filled with spirit, as the Law states and it is in the blood that the soul dwells." On p. 76, da Costa refers to Genesis 2:7 to prove "that the animals have the same vital spirit as the human being because when God created them He said: Let the earth bring forth the living being and afterwards, when creating the human being, who was already animated by the vital spirit that He breathed into them, it says: and man became a living being; and thus he used the same word in both passages, . . ." On p. 77: "Had Adam been alive when God gave the vital spirit into him we could say that this spirit was something distinct and separate from the breath of life of the animals since Adam was already alive. However, Adam did not move before the vital spirit entered into him. It follows that the vital spirit that was breathed into Adam was the animal spirit and this very animal spirit was the rational soul and all is one and the same namely in that, at the moment the animal soul entered into the human being, reason and reflection are also in him, i.e., what one calls the rational soul." Incidentally, in his doctrine of animal souls Descartes also refers to Deuteronomy 12:23 and to Leviticus 17:14. See Henri Gouhier, *La pensée réligieuse de Descartes* (Paris, 1924), p. 225.

[vi] Servetus, p. 179: *"Ex semine manifeste eliciuntur animantium aliorum animæ, ac etiam humanæ, accedenti ipsi homini divinæ mentis halitu, . . ."* [The souls of the other animated beings are elicited from manifest semen, and indeed also the human ones, being like humans from the breath of the divine mind, . . .]. On p. 260: *"Si constat brutorum animas elici ex semine, et nobis esse cum eis plurima communia, constabit quoque nostras ex semine quodammodo elici"* [If it is settled that the souls of the animals are elicited from semen, it will be certain that our souls are also elicited in a certain manner from semen].

In da Costa, p. 65: "It is crystal clear that the human being begets the soul of another human being by natural procreation in the same manner as an animal begets the soul of another animal of its kind, . . ." On p. 66: ". . . the divine order and institution that, by force of the divine word, puts all by means of the semen into each particular creature; each begets its own kind, and thus the kinds continue and increase."

in these very passages untenable. Through Christ the souls became immortal.[vii]
Pursuing his own intent (namely, that of uprooting the doctrine of eternal
damnation and of the immortality of the soul in order to liberate the human
being from the gravest terrors and anxieties), da Costa disregards this qualification, and thus reaches a conception of human life that corresponds very
little to the intent of Servetus. To be sure, it is impossible to tell whether, and
to what degree, da Costa was himself affected by the mood expressed in the
biblical passages that he adduces.

Reliance on reason and reliance on Scripture work together in da Costa's
argument against immortality. At first, both authorities are, in fact, identical.
They contrast with each other only gradually, until finally they face one
another as enemies. In this process a tendency reveals itself that dominates da
Costa's thought as if it were its law. This tendency—one still potent then but
destined to die soon—can be historically determined by the category of "Renaissance."

There is a conviction, inherent in the striving of the Renaissance for a
rebirth of life from its origins, that regards the present state as the corruption
of an original perfect state. What applies here is the formula: truth is in the
beginning. This belief was nourished by revealed religion, with its idea of a
first and perfect revelation that occurred in primordial times and that defini-
tively disclosed, at least for the present state of the world, the true goal and
the true norm of life. Within revealed religion, and in relation to it, this belief
attained its most radical application in the Protestant Reformation. The original
revelation is contrasted in its purity with all things of later origin, which are
falsifying additions, fictions, lies, and the mere work of man. The pure doc-

---

[vii] Servetus, p. 235f.: *"Qui ante mortem Christi mortui sunt, ad infernum ducti sunt, quasi
a Deo oblitioni traditi, exceptis paucis, quos futuri Christi fides fovebat. Hinc sepulcrum vulgo
dicebatur terra perditionis et oblivionis, ps. 88. Idem sacris literaris erat sepulcri et inferni nomen,
ut simul ad sepulcrum, et infernum iretur . . . Ut corpus peccato animam traxit, ditionique subiecit:
ita cum corporis sepulcro sublicitor anima tenebris, morti et inferno"* [Those who died before the
death of Christ were led to hell, as if handed by God to obliteration, except the few
whom faith in the future of Christ maintained. From this cause, the grave is commonly
called the land of perdition and of oblivion (Psalm 88). In the Holy Scriptures, grave
and hell had the same name, so that one went at the same time to grave and hell. . . . Just
as the body pulled the soul into sin and subjected it to its force, so the soul is brought
under the dominion of darkness, death, and hell when the body is put in the grave]

Da Costa, pp. 68f., quotes Psalm 88:11–13, and comments: "Hereby it is denied
that the dead give praise to God and that they can rise again for that purpose because,
where they are, there is no life nor is there spirit in the tomb, the land of decay the land
of gloom and of oblivion, and only the living can praise God. . . ."

trine was corrupted and befouled by the priests' lust for power and greed for wealth. Hence the worst aspersion cast in the polemics of this age is the reproach of innovation. In da Costa, this dominant tendency is controlled by the Epicurean motive.

We see that for da Costa turning to the truth is returning to the original. Thus: first, he returns to the Old Testament as against the New Testament, next he returns to the Torah as against the Jewish tradition, then he returns to the Torah as against the other parts of Scripture,[viii] and finally he returns to the Noahide commandments as against the Torah. The Noahide law is the *lex primaria* [primary law] that existed from the beginning and that will always exist. It is innate and common to all human beings, the root of all laws and the source of all rights. Any deviation and any addition is already a corruption. The natural original law commands mutual love. The positive religions lead to mutual hatred. The state brought about by religion is contrary to human nature. It is rooted in wickedness, in thirst for honor and gain, in the aim of holding human beings in terror (da Costa, pp. 107 and 118ff.). The return to the original is accomplished by recognizing the original revelation in reason. God reveals Himself in the law of nature. Every later revelation needs to be measured by this standard. Insofar as Scripture contradicts reason, it is human invention (ibid. p. 110).

Since reason decides the truth of the doctrines of Scripture, it decides at the same time their genuineness. Thus the equation true = genuine determines da Costa's criticism of the Bible. The doctrine of immortality is untrue because it contradicts the Law. Thus the passages of Scripture that, according to the critic's opinion, actually speak of immortality (namely Daniel 12:2 and 12:13) are excised as inventions of the Pharisees. *Critique of dogma guides the critique of the biblical text; critique concerning the truth guides the critique concerning genuineness*, although it does not consistently determine the latter. Da Costa relies, at least in a subsidiary manner, on a reference to the Sadducees, who did not recognize the Book of Daniel. Since it is attested to only by the Pharisaic tradition, the genuineness of that book collapses. This thesis is then extended to the whole of Scripture, without further specific justification (pp. 85 and 95). What is typical about this procedure is that, for the purpose of a

---

[viii] The report in the first book of Samuel of Saul's necromancy is "absolutely *opposed* to the doctrine that follows from the *Law*," therefore "necessarily *false*," stemming from the Pharisees, i.e., not genuine. "We have the Law as a guide and fundamental basis, and through the Law we must judge and distinguish false from true" (da Costa, p. 81f.).

critical examination of the canon in its traditional form, one relies on such evidence from the time of the compilation of the canon that, reported by the tradition itself, is of authoritative character for it.

NOTES

Source: "Zur Bibelwissenschaft Spinozas und seiner Vorläufer," *Korrespondenzblatt des Vereins zur Gründung und Erhaltung einer Akademie für die Wissenschaft des Judentums* 7 (1926): 1–22, reprinted in *GS*, 1:389–414. The essay "Zur Bibelwissenschaft Spinozas und seiner Vorläufer" is a short companion piece to the monograph *Die Religionskritik Spinozas*, published by the Akademie für die Wissenschaft des Judentums in Berlin in 1930. According to the preface to the English translation (*Spinoza's Critique of Religion*, [New York: Schocken, 1965]), Strauss wrote the book between 1925 and 1928. The English version by Elsa M. Sinclair was authorized by Leo Strauss. Sinclair had previously translated the manuscript of *The Political Philosophy of Hobbes: Its Basis and Its Genesis* (Oxford: Clarendon, 1936). The essay "Zur Bibelwissenschaft Spinozas" often agrees verbatim with passages in the larger composition. Hence, in working on the present translation, it was possible to compare and consult the authorized translation of *Die Religionskritik Spinozas*. Where the literal meaning of the text could be rendered more accurately, but no less elegantly, I allowed myself to deviate from the 1965 translation. The same is true in cases where Sinclair seems to have missed the intended meaning of the original.

1. According to its masthead, the *Korrespondenzblatt* not only had the purpose of publishing the annual reports of the activities of the Akademie and of the society that supported it but also of allowing "learned work" to have an effect "on the broader public through generally accessible essays growing out of the work of the research institute."

2. On Strauss's affiliation with the Akademie für die Wissenschaft des Judentums, see the introduction to this volume and the eulogy on Franz Rosenzweig ("Franz Rosenzweig and the Academy for the Science of Judaism").

3. *Bibelwissenschaft:* rendering the German *Wissenschaft* as "science," the translation adopted by Sinclair and presumably approved by Strauss, is somewhat confusing to the Anglo-Saxon reader. The critical and methodologically grounded scholarship that is intended by the term *Bibelwissenschaft* seems rendered more elegantly in terms such as "critical study of the Bible," "biblical scholarship," and the like, while "Bible science" (as consistently used throughout *Spinoza's Critique of Religion*) seems clumsy, but perhaps it is intentionally retained because of its specifically Germanic connotations. The difference in terminology (the German *Wissenschaft* applies to both the sciences and the humanities) points to a deeper taxonomic difference between the systems of classification prevalent in the German and the Anglo-Saxon academic traditions, respectively. Since this taxonomic matter involves the question of to what degree the paradigm of scientific knowledge can be legitimately applied to the humanities, the problem must have been for Strauss more than a relatively indifferent terminological matter.

There are, in fact, strong indications that Strauss used the term *Bibelwissenschaft* deliberately, a term that, compared to *biblische Wissenschaft* and the like, occasionally sounds awkward even in German. Strauss himself already uses the expression *Bibelwissenschaft* in the title, as well as four times in section III of his essay "Cohen's Analysis of Spinoza's Bible Science" (1924). There it occurs exclusively in the context of an adumbration of Strauss's own nonpolemical understanding of Spinoza's contribution to the study of the Bible rather than in the context of his critical paraphrase of Cohen's views on Spinoza. When he paraphrases Cohen, he sticks to the latter's terminology, using expressions such as *Bibelkritik, biblische Wissenschaft,* and so forth. In the essay "Zur Bibelwissenschaft Spinozas und seiner Vorläufer," Strauss explores the subject matter independently of Cohen's perspective and consistently employs the somewhat unusual construction *Bibelwissenschaft.* That this usage was deliberate is confirmed by Strauss's approval of "Bible science" as the English equivalent of *Bibelwissenschaft.* It may not be farfetched to regard the term as ironic in that it combines the very attitudes (revelation and theory) whose difference has been muddied by modernity, a difference Strauss sets out to restore. Bible science in Spinoza's sense is shown to be grounded in the assumption of a sufficiency of reason, whereas the Bible and, with it, revealed religion is founded on distrust in the sufficiency of reason and, hence, is founded on faith. Therefore, wherever possible, the present translation strives to render the expression *Bibelwissenschaft* literally, except where such literalness would give rise to syntactic and stylistic awkwardness absent in the original.

    4. "Cohens Analyse der Bibel-Wissenschaft Spinozas," *Der Jude* 8 (1924): 295–314, translated in this volume as "Cohen's Analysis of Spinoza's Bible Science." Hermann Cohen's "Spinoza über Staat und Religion, Judentum und Christentum" (1915) was first published in *Jahrbuch für jüdische Geschichte und Literatur* 18 (1915): 56–150, and reprinted in *JS,* 3:290-372.

    5. The word *Kritik* can be translated either as "criticism" or as "critique." Deriving from the Greek κρίσις, which originally refers to a court of law or to judgment, *Kritik* is the act of examining or investigating an issue either with the intention of establishing its true nature or character ("critique") or (if convinced of its inferiority, guilt, etc.) with the intention of achieving a condemnation ("criticism"). Because of the latter possibility, *Kritik* is frequently associated with an inherently prejudicial bias toward finding the object of scrutiny guilty in the sense of the accusation, and criticizing someone or something falls itself under the critical verdict of revealing preconceived notions. In German, when used with the preposition *an* (as in the phrase *in seiner Kritik an Spinoza*), the meaning is unambiguously that of criticism in this negative sense. In philosophical literature, on the other hand, *Kritik* often takes the first, constructive meaning of "critique." As introduced by Immanuel Kant in his *Kritik der reinen Vernunft* [Critique of pure reason] (Riga: Hartknoch, 1781) critique refers to a method of philosophical inquiry aiming to establish the range and grounds of legitimate judgments of reason. Some of the differences over the interpretation of Kant's First Critique can be illustrated by this ambivalence in the term *Kritik.* While to Moses Mendelssohn, for example, who took *Kritik* to mean criticism, Kant was the "all-destroying" *(der Alleszertrümmernde),* to Hermann Cohen, interpreting *Kritik* as a constructive act of rational *Grundlegung,* Kant was the founder of a method of critical idealism in the sense of a constructive idealism. Today "critique" is commonly used in the context of applied aesthetics, literary theory, and so on, where it hovers between hermeneutics of suspicion

and Kantian critique. Thus, for example, to "critique" a painting, a novel, or a musical composition involves the critical examination of its presuppositions as well as a judgment on whether or not it accomplishes its objective.

In the present essay, Strauss takes a specific moment in the long-standing tradition of *Religionskritik* (critique of religion) and subjects it to a critical investigation as to the legitimacy of its methods and motives. On the basis of this examination, Strauss decides whether *Kritik* is constructive, based on the inherently agreed-upon presuppositions, and hence critique, or whether it is mere external or polemical criticism. Critique reveals something essential about the examined object, whereas criticism reveals something about the intentions of the examiner without revealing something essential about the examined object. Since Strauss himself examines the examinations of others, he cannot always immediately indicate whether what he is looking at is a case of critique or criticism. In most cases, this ambiguity is simply hidden, because the same word stands for both meanings.

"The Bible Science of Spinoza" derives considerable suspense from this ambiguity, which itself is nowhere stated. Yet to the translator this presents the difficulty of having to decide in each case what Strauss is referring to, whereas author did not need to make this decision. He simply used the same word for both, and made it unambiguous only in a few cases, either by the use of a preposition or by the context. Since making this decision on behalf of the author amounts to interpretation, I have taken advantage of the contemporary usage of critique, which by now has become similarly ambiguous. Only where context or construction make it unambiguously clear that criticism is the intended meaning do I use the latter term.

Strauss's theoretical interest in the problem of the legitimacy of the critique/criticism of religion harks back to his dissertation on Jacobi (see "On the Problem of Knowledge"), where he describes a fundamental tension between the attitude of belief and the critical attitude instantiated by the Cartesian tradition, to which Spinoza belongs. In the present essay, a related opposition is presupposed—namely, that between belief in the sufficiency and the belief in the insufficiency of the human intellect. The latter is the attitude at the root of religious faith; the former is the attitude at the root of the Epicurean criticism of religion, revived (as Strauss assumes at this time) by Spinoza. The essay examines Spinoza's critique/criticism of Maimonides and of Calvin. In each case, Strauss tries to determine whether Spinoza's examination amounts to critique or criticism, that is, whether it points to difficulties inherent in the examined position and merely radicalizes it to the point that contradictory first assumptions become visible, or whether the assumptions at the root of Maimonides' and Calvin's respective positions are misjudged by Spinoza. In this sense, Strauss reads Spinoza as using his own critical method and examines in which case he uses it appropriately and in which cases he fails to do so.

6. In the original: "'voraussetzungslose' Wissenschaft." Cf. *Spinoza's Critique of Religion*, 130, 263/*Die Religionskritik Spinozas*, 110, 260.

7. For a curious yet instructive comparison, see *Spinoza's Critique of Religion*, 35/ *Die Religionskritik Spinozas*, 1–2. However, although the German original is similar to our essay, it is clear that the English version has been reworked by Strauss (or at least by Sinclair).

8. *Konstitution* refers here either to the establishment of a science, to its justifica-

tion, or to its disposition. By reiterating the term, Strauss remains vague and thereby draws attention to the possibility that a discipline as well established as biblical scholarship may be haunted by unsettled questions of justification or disposition.

9. For Strauss on Spinoza and superstition, see *Spinoza's Critique of Religion*, 252–53/*Die Religionskritik Spinozas*, 248–49.

10. Literally "in denen es sich selbst aufhebt." It is sometimes unclear what Strauss has in mind when he uses the Hegelian term *aufheben*. In an almost identical passage in *Spinoza's Critique of Religion*, 203/*Die Religionskritik Spinozas*, 193, Sinclair translates *aufheben* as "sublate," but we find that in this case her choice of words is somewhat misleading. See the next note.

11. From this and the following sentence it is clear why Sinclair chose "sublate" as the equivalent of *aufheben* in the previous sentence (see previous note). Strauss's distinction between the origin of religion and the origin of theory can be understood to mean the following. The striving for self-preservation generates passions that obviate the preservation of the self. This "situation" can be overcome by two diametrically opposed cultural strategies, namely, religion and theory. The common origin of religion and theory consists in the conflict between the striving for self-preservation and the passions that are generated by this striving. Strictly speaking, only theory qualifies as the result of a sublation in the Hegelian sense, for only in theory is the striving for self-preservation purified and carried through to its "radical" (as Strauss likes to put it) conclusions. Theory could not have emerged as the consistent pursuit of self-preservation without the antithesis of the passions. To what degree religion is likewise the result of a genuine synthesis in which self-preservation and the obviating passions it engenders are both sublated into a different synthesis is unclear. Whether or not all this accurately represents Strauss's intention, it explains why Sinclair may have felt compelled to opt for the Hegelian term. Self-preservation and passions are related like thesis and antithesis. The fact that two syntheses are possible to this dialectic and that these syntheses constitute antagonists in an eternal struggle (as "diametrically opposed" possibilities) propels Strauss beyond the orbit of Hegelian thought and closer to Carl Schmitt. On Carl Schmitt and Leo Strauss, see Heinrich Meier, *Carl Schmitt and Leo Strauss: The Hidden Dialogue*, trans. J. Harvey Lomax (Chicago: University of Chicago Press, 1995.

12. See note above.

13. *die Weisen und die Unweisen:* see *Spinoza's Critique of Religion*, p. 171/*Die Religionskritik Spinozas*, p. 156: "the wise and the foolish."

14. Manuel Joël: for the specific reference, see *Spinoza's Critique of Religion*, 152 n. 188/*Die Religionskritik Spinozas*, 134 n. 188.

15. While "critique" would work here in English as well, or even better than "criticism," the construction *Kritik an* unambiguously refers to "criticism," not "critique."

16. From this sentence alone it remains unclear what, to Strauss, constitutes such a "deeper presupposition" and whether it resides in Maimuni or in Spinoza. It is not until two pages further down in the inquiry that this presupposition is identified as that of "the conviction [on Spinoza's part] of the sufficiency of human thought for the perfection of theory."

17. Counterremonstrant Calvinism refers to the traditional faction of Reformed

ministers and theologians that prevailed over the Arminian faction at the Synod of Dordrecht (held from 13 November 1618 to 29 May 1619). The Arminians (including the humanist and natural law theorist Hugo Grotius) argued for tolerance in nonessential dogmatic matters, and unsuccessfully petitioned the state for the recognition of their creed. The main dogmatic disagreements concerned the doctrine of predestination, and the question of whether faith is entirely preordained or whether human beings contribute to their salvation by an element of faith that originates in them rather than in God. The Arminians presented their suggestions for an amendment of the Heidelberg Catechism in a document called "Remonstrantie" (1610), which was countered by a "Contra-Remonstrantie" (1611). After the Synod of Dordrecht expelled the Arminians, they organized themselves in the "Remonstrantsche Broederschap."

18. Cf. *Die Religionskritik Spinozas*, 182/*Spinoza's Critique of Religion*, 193, for a series of almost identical sentences. *Die Religionskritik Spinozas*/*Spinoza's Critique of Religion* adds the reference to Calvin, *Institutio* 1.3–8.

19. Emphasizing the parallel elements in this sentence, Strauss later added quotation marks to the expressions "natural light" and "inner testimony of the Holy Spirit." See *Spinoza's Critique of Religion*, 195/*Die Religionskritik Spinozas*, 184.

20. That is, Spinoza dismisses the distinction between two kinds of fear as a mere outcry of protest, grounded in apologetics rather than in a substantive difference.

21. Cf. "Reflektiertheit" in the opening sentence of "Paul de Lagarde," and cf. the introduction to this volume. While in the early essays Strauss regards "reflection" as an important philosophical device, around 1929/30 it begins to appear to him as the quintessential expression of the beholdenness to historicism—or to the past as "fate"—that, in his phase of reorientation, he identifies as that which needs to be overcome.

22. For Uriel da Costa or Acosta (1585–1640), cf. *EJ*, s.v. "Costa, Uriel da," by Richard H. Popkin. Below, Strauss relates some of the relevant biographical information about da Costa. More importantly, however, his analysis of the development of da Costa's critique of religion—that is, the development of da Costa's views critical of Christian doctrine prior to his turning to Judaism—has been confirmed by historical evidence from documents of the Inquisition. See the Popkin article just cited, and see also chap. 2 of Leo Strauss, *Spinoza's Critique of Religion*, 53–63.

23. Michael Servet, Servetus, or Miguel Serveto, also known under various forms of the name Villanueva, born 1511 in Tudela (Spain), was burned alive as a heretic in Champel (Switzerland) in 1553. Originally trained as a lawyer, Servetus became an innovative physician who was the first in the West to describe pulmonary circulation. He published several scientific works (1535: on comparative geography; 1537: on digestion; 1538: on medical astrology). Nominally a Catholic, this humanist thinker and correspondent of many Protestant reformers aroused the ire of both the Inquisition and of Calvin because of his anti-Trinitarian theology based on an intensive study of the Bible and on a Neoplatonic cosmic-pantheistic Christology. Servetus's main theological works are: *De Trinitatis erroribus libri septem* (Hagenau, 1531); *Dialogorum de Trinitate libri duo* (Hagenau, 1532); *Biblia Sacra ex Santis Pagini tralatione . . . recognita et scholiis illustrata* (Lyons, 1542–45); *Christianismi restitutio* (1553).

IV

―――――――――――――――――――――――――――――― ⟨⟨⟨⟩

Reorientation
(1928–32)

The late twenties and early thirties were for Strauss a time of reorientation. The rethinking of his positions is evident in his letters and in publications of the mid-1930s, especially in the introduction to *Philosophy
and Law* (1935). In the few writings he published at the time, however,
he only hints at some of the concerns he expressed more freely in lectures to learned audiences at the Lehranstalt für die Wissenschaft des
Judentums and to the Zionist youths he continued to address on occasion. The notable exception is the 1928 review of Freud's *Future of an
Illusion*. Published in *Der jüdische Student*, the widely disseminated publication of the Zionist students' organization Kartell jüdischer Verbindungen
(K.J.V.), the essay presents an argument for a radically atheistic conception of political Zionism, a position that, to the majority of Strauss's
readers, was as unacceptable on principle as on pragmatic considerations.
In the second half of the 1920s, German Zionism had largely outgrown
the theoretical and diasporatic orientation of the youth movement and
had turned "Palestinocentric" instead (see Lavsky, *Before Catastrophe*, cited
here in the introduction). The shared pragmatic goals of increasing and
supporting the Jewish colonization of Palestine brought with it a careful
avoidance of ideological conflict between the left-wing Hapoel Hatzair
and the organization of religious Zionism, Mizrahi. Strauss's argument
violated this tacit agreement. The strongly negative response to it had
the effect of ending his career as a political theorist of Zionism. Zionism
had changed, and the radical honesty of the youth movement was out.
Strauss was not immediately deterred. Over the course of the next few
years Zionist youth groups still provided the setting for some of his unpublished ruminations on the "religious situation of the present" and
similar themes, yet these ruminations were increasingly less straightforward, more ironic and double-edged, and ever more self-conscious in

style. Rereading Lessing, Strauss became mindful of the exoteric character of all theological-political writing, and he began to practice it himself.
But this somewhat playful writing soon gave way to the earnest and
open recognition of his disenchantment with Zionism as the ultimate
resolution to the Jewish problem caused by the dissolution of the ghetto,
the only Jewish problem he was truly interested in. He had turned from
practical involvement in a political movement to the theoretical examination of premodern political philosophy and its implications for modern man.

Sigmund Freud, *The Future of an Illusion* (1928)

The following remarks are meant as a call to develop the Zionist ideology in
a direction in which it is not commonly developed. They follow *The Future
of an Illusion* by Sigmund Freud, which appeared a year ago.[1] They do so
neither in order to cloak themselves in the authority of a man of European
fame (no authorities exist in the field in which they move), nor because what
they imply could not have been known without Freud. Rather, they do so
merely because the clarity and simplicity of the Freudian manner of speaking
(a clarity and simplicity not very common in Germany) help to prevent beat-
ing around the bush on the essential questions. To be sure, such clarity and
simplicity are also a great danger; they fool readers used to different manners
of speaking into ignoring the substance of the Freudian expositions, including their questionable substance. Even readers who are merely familiar with
the way in which the question of religion is customarily dealt with at German
universities could easily dismiss the work to which we refer as superficial.
Whoever is satisfied with such criticism has understood nothing of the question that guides Freud.

Political Zionism has repeatedly characterized itself as the will to normalize the existence of the Jewish people, to normalize the Jewish people. By
this self-definition it has exposed itself to a grave misunderstanding, namely,
the misunderstanding that the will to normality was the *first* word of political
Zionism; the most effective criticism of political Zionism rests on this misunderstanding. In truth, the presupposition of the Zionist will to normalization,
that is, of the Zionist negation of *galut* [exile], is the conviction that "the
power of religion has been broken" (Klatzkin, *Krisis und Entscheidung*, p. 57).[2]
Because the break with religion has been resolutely effected by many individual Jews, and *only because of this reason*, it is possible for these individuals to
raise the question on behalf of their people, how the people is to live from
now on.[3] Not that they prostrate themselves before the idol of normality; on

the contrary: they no longer see any reason for the lack of normality [*Nicht-normalität*]. And this is decisive: in the age of atheism, the Jewish people can no longer base its existence on God but only on itself alone, on its labor, on its land, and on its state. It must even as a people break with the traditions that so many individuals have already long since broken with; better the honest [*redlich*] narrowness and barrenness of civilization than the breadth and plenty that the atheist would be able to purchase only at the price of a lie.[4]

Cultural Zionism possesses the dubious merit of having mediated between political Zionism and tradition by understanding the Jewish religion, from the start, as a product of the spirit of the Jewish people. The following is a popular notion: the prophets proclaimed the most perfect morality, they posed *the* demand; this morality, this pathos, is what is essentially Jewish; after the demise of the traditional "forms," nothing prevents the same spirit from creating for itself new "forms" in *Erets Yisrael* [the Land of Israel]. The prophets, however, invoked God, who told them what to say to the people, rather than invoking the spirit of the Jewish people. Of course, the prophets' citations of the source of their words are not binding. The atheist has the perfect right, he is even duty bound, to interpret the "speech of God" as the creation of the heart of the "ones who hearken" [*Gebild des Herzens der "Hörenden"*], perhaps as the product of the spirit of the Jewish people. But he needs to be aware himself that the words he so interprets were not meant in the sense of this interpretation; unless he wants to fish in troubled waters, he must realize that his interpretation denies the original sense of the Law and the prophets; he must make this denial explicit and unambiguous. Once he comprehends *what* he denies, namely, once he comprehends that it is God he denies, then he will lose, once and for all, his appetite for the culture propagated by cultural Zionism; then he will comprehend how meager an abstraction is the "prophetic ethics" that remains after the denial of God.[5] Compared with the enormous gulf yawning between belief and unbelief, the difference between the spirit of radical socialism (which some believe they find in the Bible) and the spirit of radical antisocialism is merely the difference between two nuances of unbelief. In its argument with the non-Jewish and the anti-Zionist environment, political Zionism has always vigorously resisted the spirit of indecisiveness,[6] especially the spirit of "deliberate" indecisiveness[7] that calls itself "piety toward life" ["*Lebensfrömmigkeit*"]; hence it must [also] clearly and sharply relinquish the titles fraudulently obtained by cultural Zionism.

Given the inadequacy of Herzl's Zionism, which expressed itself most clearly in his *Altneuland*,[8] cultural Zionism had an easy position to defend. There was something convincing in the consideration that whoever affirms the Jewish people necessarily affirms its spirit, and therefore necessarily affirms the culture in which its spirit revealed itself. From the affirmation of the national culture some proceeded to the affirmation of the national tradition of the Law; among these were certainly a few who did not fully realize that this Law claims to be divine law. The believers cleared the way from their side. How often have we heard that what Judaism calls for is not belief but action, namely, the fulfillment of the Law. But what the believer may rightly demand, the unbeliever can by no means do. For what the believer praises as a hearkening and a believing that arises from doing[9] is to the unbeliever a slippery slope into belief, a numbing of conscience, and self-deception. No one can believe in God for the sake of his nation; no one can fulfill the law for national reasons. It is bad enough that even today one must still waste words on the thoughtlessness that follows this path. But can one remain standing at the affirmation of national culture? Cultural Zionism leads up to the question that is posed by and through the Law, and then it capitulates, yielding either to resolute belief or to resolute unbelief.[10]

Political Zionism, wishing to ground itself radically, must ground itself in unbelief. The argument between political Zionism and its radical opponents must be conducted solely as a struggle between unbelief and belief. This struggle is ancient; it is "the eternal and *sole* theme of the entire history of the world and of man."[11] This struggle, which had almost given out in the era of the philosophies of culture and of experience [*Kultur- und Erlebnisphilosophie*],[12] is taken up again by Freud in the previously mentioned work. Let us see what Freud wants and what he achieves.

The most Freud could achieve would be the refutation of the religious notions. At first, refutation seems conceivable: after all, according to the account of the Book of Kings, Elijah proved experimentally to the people that Baal is powerless compared with Yahweh.[13] "When St. Bonifacius cut down the sacred tree venerated by the Saxons, the bystanders anticipated a terrible event as a result of the sacrilege. It did not occur, and the Saxons accepted baptism" (p. 65). George Bernard Shaw occasionally conducted the following experiment: he lay a watch in front of himself on a table and said, if God exists and if he disapproves of atheism, let him throw a lightning bolt into the house I am inside within the next five minutes; no lightning struck. The experiment is not very persuasive; it is possible, after all, that God exists and has enough of a sense of humor to let human beings achieve felicity in their own way and to think of "blasphemy" differently from priests and public prosecutors. If God's thoughts are not the thoughts of men, and men's ways are not the ways of God, then God's thoughts and ways are not experimentally controllable; moreover, every attempt to justify directly by scientific means the denial of the existence of God is fundamentally deficient.

The insight into this impossibility is the presupposition of Freud's critique. "The reality value [*Realitätswert*] of most of them (i.e., of most of the religious doctrines) cannot be judged. Just as they are unprovable, they are also irrefutable" (p. 50). The realm of scientific knowledge is so limited that science cannot refute religion. Does this mean, however, that science is not and cannot be the judge of religion? By no means. While the critique of religion cannot shake the doctrines of religion, it can certainly shake the justifications of these doctrines.

What possibilities of justifying its doctrines are available to religion? Until several centuries ago all physicists agreed that physics was able to prove the existence of God and that [in fact] it proved it. However, this proof for the existence of God, along with all other proofs, lost the ground beneath its feet due to the developments of the last centuries. The claim that God exists may remain unrefuted: as to judging its scientific value, it is nothing but one hypothesis among many others.

The second possibility of justifying the doctrines of religion is the reliance on the authority of Scripture and tradition. This possibility, too, has become an impossibility. It is not in the least an argument for the truth of a doctrine that it is also found in Scripture, or that it is maintained by tradition. The relevant classical example is miracles. The reason why the existence of miracles cannot be proved from Scripture is that there is no guarantee whatever that the authors of the accounts of the miracles or their informants observed with sufficient accuracy and analyzed with sufficient rigor. "We know more or less in what times and by what kinds of people the religious doctrines were created" (p. 52). Religious notions stem from an age of limited scientific culture (41, 53); the scientific mind is conscious of the fact that its thought is more disciplined than the thought of prescientific humanity.

The last remaining possibility of justifying religious doctrines is the actual present experience of the believers. This way of justifying religious doctrines most corresponds to the currently regnant spirit, the positive [*positiv*] spirit; hence it is also the only [way of justifying religious doctrines] that is important and necessary to argue with.[14] The positive [*positiv*] justification of religion excludes on principle every external or mediated justification, whether by physics, or by Scripture and tradition; it relies only on what the believer sees, on what he experiences. Hence, the unbeliever appears to have no other choice than to admit: I see and experience nothing of what you, the believer, claim to see and experience; therefore, I must attempt to get along on the basis of my own experiences; you cannot call on me to depend on what you claim to see and experience. "When one has gained the unshakable conviction of the real truth of the religious doctrines from a deeply captivating state of ecstasy, what does it mean to anyone else?" (44). This, however, only makes the difficulty greater. When the unbeliever asserts that he sees or experiences nothing of what the believer claims to see or experience, does he thereby not admit that he lacks an organ, that he is blind? This charge cannot be turned against the believer: for the believer sees everything seen by the unbeliever, and he sees more. But is it not generally the case that the presumption speaks in favor of the one who sees rather than of the one who is blind, of the one who sees more than the one who sees less? This emphasis on the reliance on experience is weakened by the fact that there is also an experience of witches, ghosts, and devils. Of course, recalling Ivan Karamazov's experience of the devil, one could say that Ivan's experience tells him something infinitely *more important* and infinitely *deeper* than anything that the most admirable sciences would be able to tell him; there is very little to advance against this assessment of the inner world. But importance and depth are bad criteria when dealing with the *truth*. The most important and deepest claims of religion lose their force if God does not exist. The believers assert that they have experienced the existence of God, that they have encountered God; the unbelievers not only assert that they have not had this experience, but they also doubt the experience of the believers. What possibilities are available to the unbeliever to verify experiences that he himself has not had? The experiences of the believers are reflected in statements; these statements are, as such, determinable; the various statements are comparable; the comparative study of those statements, made by the believers in various eras, teaches us that there is a history of belief, that belief changed in an essential respect: "within these products (*sc.* the religious notions), the emphasis gradually shifts." The emphasis shifts from nature to man; "the moral [becomes] its actual domain" (26f.). To earlier generations, the power of God over nature showed itself in the miracles; the change in the attitude toward miracles is symptomatic of the change that has taken place at the core of belief. It has been noted by believers[15] that already in Scripture the emphasis is not on the *fact* of the miracle but on the *expectation* of the miracle: trust in God is not manifested by him who confirms that a miracle has happened, or who believes that a miracle has happened on hearing the accounts of others, but by him who faithfully expects the future miracle. This remark is only half accurate; it neglects the fact that, according to the meaning of Scripture, it is also very important that the miracle has happened; and between this "also very important" and becoming indifferent [to the reality of biblical miracles],[16] there is a great distance. It is no exaggeration to say that, among the believers of our age, there is little inclination to recognize the biblical miracles as realities. What does this resistance mean? The power of God over nature has lost its credibility: the claim of [the existence of] God [*Gottesbehauptung*] now holds true merely for the inner world, for the world of the heart. If that is the case, then it must be stated that the God of Scripture, the God who created heaven and earth, who not only directs the hearts of men like rivers, but who also guides natural events with a Creator's freedom, that this God is no longer believed in. What, however, are we to think of a belief in God that has changed so much? "When it comes to questions of religion, people are guilty of all sorts of insincerities and intellectual bad manners. Philosophers stretch the meaning of words to the point that they retain barely any of their original sense, they name some vague abstraction of their own making 'God,' and thus are also deists, believers in God before the entire world, who can praise themselves for having recognized a loftier, purer concept of God, although their God is merely an unreal [*wesenlos*] shadow and no longer the powerful personality of religious doctrine" (51f.).

Freud explicitly remarks (59) that his critique of religion is independent of psychoanalysis, the science he founded. The psychoanalytical explanation of religion is in fact only understandable as a task once religion has become unworthy of belief; then, however, it is necessary to explain religion, to ask why it occurred to human beings to invent a god, to cling to a god. We need not concern ourselves here with the Freudian explanation of religion, which, incidentally, can be thoroughly contested on an atheistic basis; what is important for us is the tendency that guides this explanation. Freud proceeds from the fact of human misery, from the helplessness of man vis-à-vis the dangers with which he is threatened by so-called fate, that is, by unconquered nature and by other human beings; not just his existence, but first of all his very sense of self [*Selbstgefühl*] is gravely threatened; he is miserable, he feels himself miserable. Now religion is "born from the need to make human helplessness bearable" (27). Freud sharply protests against the view that the "feeling of human smallness and powerlessness before the entire universe" be called religious: "It is not this feeling that constitutes the essence of religiosity . . . ; rather, it is the next step, the reaction to this feeling that seeks a remedy for it" (52). Religion is an illusion. This does not immediately imply that the religious doctrines are errors: some illusions also turn into truths. But the fact that the situation of man is, according to the claims of religion, just what he would be bound to wish it to be—this is what makes these claims suspect: "We tell ourselves, that it would be very nice if there were a God who is a creator of the world and a benevolent providence, if there were a moral world order and another life, but it is rather obvious that this is all just how we are bound to wish it" (53). The fact *that* religion provides comfort and help becomes the decisive objection to it. We are very much in need of comfort: this is sufficient reason to be on guard against illusions that delude us about our real situation. One can assess this critique of religion properly only if one brings to mind the structure of the critique of religion as it was constituted in previous centuries.[17] The previous critique was sustained, even swept up, by the conviction that the vanquishing of religion would be the dawn of the age of happiness, of heaven on earth; in any case, it *hoped to derive some benefit* [*versprach sich etwas*] from the demise of religion. Freud promises [*verspricht*] nothing, except insight into the real situation of man.

This, then, is the state of the struggle between belief and unbelief. Long ago it was decided that no ascent from the world to God is possible without the presupposition of belief; now it has also been decided that enlightenment about the situation of man, of man's misery, does not lead to God unless God is already presupposed. Long ago it was decided that the terribleness of belief is not an objection to belief; now unbelief has also matured enough to arrive at the insight that the probably desperate situation into which man has been brought by unbelief in no way justifies belief. Much is gained when the despair, the hopelessness, the helplessness of man, when "the misery of man without God," when the restlessness, the lack of peace, the staleness and shallowness of life without God are no longer an objection to unbelief; when it no longer seems impossible that truth and depth are opposites, that only illusion has depth.

From this [perspective] we must pose the question that is left undecided by Freud's critique. Is it—as Freud presupposes—the meaning of belief to provide comfort and aid, to give life meaning, peace, and depth?[18] Is it not in truth the case that *the* danger from which the believer hopes to be saved is beyond all the dangers that can be known to the unbeliever, that therefore belief brings just as much, and much rather, despair than comfort and help? Is it that the believer believes because, as an unbeliever, life without God appears to him hopeless, stale, and shallow, or is it not rather the case that, because he believes, he recognizes the lack of comfort, hopelessness, staleness, and shallowness of life without God? In other words, is the human misery seen and demonstrated by Freud the same "misery" that the believer knows as *the* misery? To ask in this way means to understand that the real question begins only *after* Freud's critique. But—given the recent, certainly not accidental, renunciation or (which amounts to the same) reinterpretation of the assertion of creation and the miracles, of belief in the power of God over nature—Freud's critique remains of utmost importance also for the real question.

NOTES

Source: "'Die Zukunft einer Illusion,'" *Der jüdische Student* 25, no. 4 (August 1928): 16–22. My sincere gratitude to Eugene Sheppard, who brought this essay to my attention. In "Comment on Weinberg's Critique" (see the notes there), Strauss is identified as a student member of the Jewish student corporation "Saronia." While Saronia is mentioned here as well, Strauss is now an *Alter Herr* and his residence is given as "Altona-Hamburg." In the October 1928 issue of *Der jüdische Student* appeared a critical response to Strauss's "atheistic ideology of Zionism" ("Zur atheistischen Ideologie des Zionismus," *Der jüdische Student* 25, nos. 6/7 [October 1928]: 8–13). The author, Max Joseph, subsequently published his own take on Freud ("Ist die Religion wirklich eine Illusion?" *Der jüdische Student* 25, no. 8 [December 1928]: 6-17).

1. Sigmund Freud, *Die Zukunft einer Illusion* (Leipzig, Wien, and Zürich: Internationaler Psychoanalytischer Verlag, 1927), later in: Sigmund Freud, *Gesammelte Schriften*, vol. 11: *Schriften aus den Jahren 1923 bis 1928: Vermischte Schriften* (Leipzig, Wien, and Zürich: Internationaler Psychoanalytischer Verlag, 1928), 411–66. English in vol. 21 of *The Standard Edition of the Complete Psychological Works of Sigmund Freud*, trans. James Strachey and Anna Freud (London: Hogarth Press, 1961), 5–56. The essay was a predecessor to *Civilization and Its Discontents* (1930).

2. Jacob Klatzkin (1882–1948), trained in rabbinic Judaism by his father, Elijah Klatzkin (the *shklover ilui* and "Lubliner Rav"), later studied philosophy under Hermann Cohen in Marburg (doctorate: Berne, 1912). Zionist publicist and, with Nahum Goldmann, coinitiator of the German *Encyclopedia Judaica* and of the first encyclopedic venture in Hebrew. His philosophical vitalism distanced him from Cohen (see the critical appreciation in Klatzkin, *Hermann Cohen*, 2d ed. (Berlin: Jüdischer Verlag, 1921). To Klatzkin, who was also a noted Hebrew essayist and translator, the future of the Jewish nation depended on land and language rather than on intellectual refinement or spiritual culture. *Krisis und Entscheidung im Judentum* (1921), the work cited by Strauss, is the second edition of *Probleme des modernen Judentums* (Berlin: Jüdischer Verlag, 1918).

3. The question "wie das Volk nunmehr leben soll" posed by individuals for the sake of their nation as the most urgent and inevitable question anticipates and prepares the ground for a more general formulation of the same question, namely *pous bioteon* (How are we to live?) that we find in the lecture "'Religious Situation of the Present'" (1930). The reformulation of this question into its general form signals the point at which Strauss begins to transform what he understands to be the fundamental problem of Zionism into the fundamental problem of philosophy in general.

4. It is ironic, if not uncommon in the vitalistic rhetoric of the 1920s, to speak of a "narrowness" *(Enge)* and "barrenness" *(Kargheit)* of civilization, attributes usually associated with the ghetto existence of *galut* that Zionism aims to overcome. The reference to atheism leads to the next paragraph. In his early writings, Strauss—similar to Rosenzweig in "Atheistische Theologie" (1914)—frequently criticizes Buber's cultural Zionism as a form of dishonest *(unredlich),* atheistic theology. In logical terms, typical for Strauss's argumentation in the early writings, he is interested in establishing the radically opposed presuppositions at the root of alternative worldviews that make facile attempts at "reconciliation," "synthesis," or "sublation" impossible.

5. Passages such as these can be easily misread as endorsements of Orthodox faith. Strauss, however, builds no road to such an endorsement. Instead, what he speaks of here and elsewhere is the untenability, or at least the intellectual poverty ("scantiness"), of cultural Zionism, which Strauss regards as a form of "atheistic theology" (an untenable, self-contradictory position). What he achieves in this way is an honest realization of the relative poverty of modern atheism relative to the wealth of the beautiful world of tradition that is destroyed by a modern atheism that, nevertheless, seems inevitable to him. The heroic gesture involved in this critique of cultural Zionism—that is, the gesture of staring at the open grave of a beloved—has an existentialist flavor to it (as noted by Julius Guttmann in his review of *Philosophie und Gesetz;* cf. here in the introduction). But it is important that irreconcilable opposites in the field of philosophical truths are associated with irreconcilable political opposites. More precisely, tracing seemingly equivalent and pragmatically combinable political alternatives to irreconcilable philosophical presuppositions is to clarify that, to the Zionist youth, only one political option is available that can claim to be radically "honest."

6. Literally: "limping on both legs" *(auf beiden Seiten hinken),* an idiom derived from Luther's translation of Elijah's speech on Mt. Carmel in 1 Kings 18:21. What Luther translates as "Wie lange wollt ihr auf beiden Seiten hinken?" the King James version translates as "How long halt ye between two opinions?"

7. In extension of the image of a "limping on both legs," literally *"verstehendes" Hinken,* that is, a comprehending, or knowing, limp.

8. Theodor Herzl (1860–1904), *Altneuland* (cf. Engl. *Old New Land,* trans. Paula Arnold (Haifa: Haifa Publishing Co., 1960), a Zionist novel published in 1902 describing the life of the new Jewish society in Palestine. With its emphasis on ambitious technological schemes and its utopian social vision of tolerance and harmony, *Altneuland* resembles the science fiction of Jules Verne. But its motto ("Wenn Ihr wollt, so ists kein Märchen") emphasized the feasability of this vision so powerfully that it became the motto of the entire Zionist movement. What made it the target of the criticism of cultural Zionism was the complete lack in Herzl's vision of a Jewish state of a concern with Jewish language, literature, or religion.

9. Cf. Exodus 24:7 according to the traditional Jewish translation of the phrase: "We shall do and we shall hearken."

10. Strauss shares his critical attitude toward the spiritualism embraced by cultural Zionism (especially of Ahad Ha'am) with Jacob Klatzkin, whom he cites earlier.

11. Johann Wolfgang Goethe: "Das eigentliche, einzige und tiefste Thema der Welt- und Menschengeschichte, dem alle übrigen untergeordnet sind, bleibt der Konflikt des Unglaubens mit dem Glauben. Alle Epochen, in welchen der Glaube herrschte, unter welcher Gestalt er auch wolle, sind glänzend, herzerhebend und fruchtbar für Mitwelt und Nachwelt. Alle Epochen dagegen, in welchen der Unglaube, in welcher Form auch es auch sei, einen kümmerlichen Sieg behauptet, und wenn sie auch einen Augenblick mit einem Scheinglanze prahlen sollten, verschwinden vor der Nachwelt, weil sich niemand gern mit Erkenntnis des Unfruchtbaren abgeben mag" [The real, only, and deepest theme of the history of the world and of humanity to which all other themes are subordinate remains the conflict between unbelief and belief. All epochs dominated by belief, no matter in what guise, are brilliant, elevating, and fertile for the

contemporary and posterior world. All epochs, on the other hand, during which unbelief, no matter in what guise, claims a miserable victory—and even though they may flaunt their false glory for a moment—vanish before the vantage point of posterity, for no one likes to busy himself gladly with knowledge of the infertile]. From *Noten und Abhandlungen zum besseren Verständnis des West-östlichen Divan*, quoted again in Leo Strauss, *Persecution and the Art of Writing* (Glencoe, Ill.: The Free Press, 1952), 107 n. 35. Thanks to Ken Green for identifying the source of this quotation.

12. "Philosophy of culture" *(Kulturphilosophie)* may refer to those academic philosophies that, in the mind of the younger generation, are strongly associated with Wilhelmian bourgeois culture (cf. Heidegger's verdict on neo-Kantianism in 1929 at the students' conference in Davos). "Philosophy of experience" *(Erlebnisphilosophie)* brings to mind Georg Simmel (1858–1918) and his most famous Zionist disciple, Martin Buber. Cf. Paul Mendes-Flohr, *Von der Mystik zum Dialog: Bubers geistige Entwicklung bis hin zu "Ich und Du"* (Königstein/Ts.: Jüdischer Verlag, 1979).

13. See 1 Kings 18.

14. On the "positive spirit" cf. Strauss, *Spinoza's Critique of Religion,* trans. Elsa Sinclair (New York: Schocken, 1965), 180.

15. The reference is presumably to Franz Rosenzweig, *The Star of Redemption,* trans. William W. Hallo (Notre Dame, Ind.: University of Notre Dame Press, 1985), 93–111: "On the Possibility of Experiencing Miracles."

16. The thought of this sentence is explained by what follows.

17. For the following, cf. "On the Bible Science of Spinoza and His Precursors" (1926) and the monograph *Die Religionskritik Spinozas als Grundlage seiner Bibelwissenschaft: Untersuchungen zu Spinozas Theologisch Politischem Traktat,* which Strauss completed at the same time he wrote the essay on Freud. It was published in Berlin by Akademie Verlag in 1930, as the second volume in the series of philosophical publications of the Akademie für die Wissenschaft des Judentums. The English translation is cited in n. 15 above.

18. While Strauss, the political Zionist, thinks that much can be gained for political Zionism from Freud's assertion of the validity of unbelief vis-à-vis an illusory belief, Strauss, the philosopher of religion, challenges Freud's concept of belief as too narrowly grounded in a Protestant definition of belief. This is expressed on p. 21 of "'Die Zukunft einer Illusion,'" with reference to Freud, *Zukunft einer Illusion,* 52: "Scharf verwahrt sich Freud dagegen, daß das 'Gefühl der menschlichen Kleinheit und Ohnmacht vor dem Ganzen der Welt' als religiös angesprochen werde" [Freud sharply protests against the view that the "feeling of human smallness and powerlessness before the entire universe" be called religious]. See supra, p. 207. While Freud denies this "feeling of dependence on the universe" the quality of a religious experience, his concept of religion still takes this Schleiermacherian position as the point of departure for his definition of the religious illusion. In contrast, as Strauss argues in "On the Argument with European Science" (1924) (combining a critical appreciation of Rudolf Otto's *The Holy* with Hermann Cohen's characterization of the prophetic religion), prophetic monotheism combines a heightened rationality with heightened uncanniness: "Concerning the situation in which biblical prophecy finds itself, it is characterized by the fact that preprophetic 'religion' is passionately rejected not for being 'uncanny' but precisely for being canny, for being all too canny. And the result of this *rejection* of the canny is the 'rationalism' of the prophets" ("On the Argument with European Science").

Franz Rosenzweig and the Academy for
the Science of Judaism (1929)

The actual founding document of the Academy for the Science of Judaism is the open letter "It's time . . . Ideas on the Current Problem of Education,"[1] addressed by Franz Rosenzweig to Hermann Cohen in the middle of the war.[2] The idea of the Academy was first developed in this letter. In fact, it was developed to the point that the way toward its realization could be immediately prepared. Franz Rosenzweig is the *founder* of the Academy.[3]

Franz Rosenzweig's idea, according to his express intention, was meant to be *political*. This man, who as a thinker and a scholar made such great contributions to science, was not concerned with science as something "self-evident," something that is not responsible to another, higher authority; he was concerned with Judaism. With an urgency that we cannot forget, he insisted that the norm of all science of Judaism be the responsibility for our existence as Jews. Franz Rosenzweig will always remind all those who toil for the sake of this science of their true task.

Franz Rosenzweig, a member until his death of the philosophical commission of the Academy and of the board of trustees of the Academy's Hermann Cohen Foundation, hailed the *Jewish Writings*[4] of Hermann Cohen as a "great gift" of the Academy to the Jews of Germany and the world. This work will always remain linked with Franz Rosenzweig's name: in his introduction Franz Rosenzweig has erected a monument to the greatest teacher of German Judaism. It will pass on to all future generations the memory of both these venerable men, the one who is praised and the other who praises, in a fitting unity.

NOTES

Source: "Franz Rosenzweig und die Akademie für die Wissenschaft des Judentums," *Jüdische Wochenzeitung für Kassel, Hessen und Waldeck* 6, no. 49 (13 December 1929): n.p., reprinted in *GS*, 2:363f.

1. "Zeit ists . . . (Ps. 119, 126): Gedanken über das Bildungsproblem des Augenblicks," reprinted in *Zweistromland: Kleinere Schriften zu Glauben und Denken*, ed. Reinhold Mayer and Annemarie Mayer (Dordrecht and Boston: Martinus Nijhoff, 1984): 461–81. The reference to Psalm 119:126 ("It is time to act on behalf of YHWH; [for] they have destroyed your Torah"), omitted by Strauss, is part of the original title. Rosenzweig's historical precedent in the use of this quotation is Maimonides' *Guide of the Perplexed*, where the verse serves to justify the Rambam's breach of the law not to divulge the secrets of the Torah.

2. The idea for an Academy for the Science of Judaism (Akademie für die Wissenschaft des Judentums) was initially conceived by Franz Rosenzweig in 1917 (at the Macedonian front) as an innovative institution combining scholarship and teaching, that is, a combination of free inquiry and responsibility toward the community that was to benefit from an exchange with a nontraditional scholar, just as the nontraditional scholar was to benefit in his scholarship from his responsibility toward a concrete community. The result was to be a new type of professional, the "scientific theologian" *(wissenschaftlicher Theologenstand)*. "Zeit ists . . ." was written in the form of an open letter to Hermann Cohen (addressed as "Hochverehrter Herr Geheimrat"), first published in conjunction with *Neue jüdische Monatshefte* (a journal edited, inter alia, by Cohen) and then widely reprinted. (On the background and history of the publication, see Rosenzweig, *Gesammelte Schriften* [Dordrecht: Martinus Nijhoff, 1984], 3:853.) Hermann Cohen responded with "youthful enthusiasm" to the idea and spent the last months of his life (he died in April 1918) fund-raising for the Academy. Cf. the historian Ismar Elbogen, one of the later employees of the Academy, in a 1930 obituary for Franz Rosenzweig, cited in vol. 1 of Franz Rosenzweig, *Briefe und Tagebücher*, ed. Rachel Rosenzweig and Edith Rosenzweig-Scheinmann (with Bernhard Casper) (The Hague: Nijhoff, 1979), 511f. And see Hermann Cohen, "Zur Begründung einer Akademie für die Wissenschaft des Judentums," in *Jüdische Schriften*, ed. Bruno Strauß (Berlin: C. A. Schwetschke & Sohn Verlag, 1924), 2:210–17 and cf. Cohen, *Jüdische Schriften*, 1:lxi. Due to Cohen's death and the political and economic collapse of Germany at the end of the First World War, the Academy was established on a much smaller scale: only a few researchers were supported by its stipends and none of them took upon himself the obligation, stipulated by Rosenzweig, to teach simultaneously in an adult education framework. Leo Strauss was the notable exception in that, while supported by the Academy, he taught in Kassel. See Rosenzweig, *Briefe und Tagebücher*, 1:512, 2:971, 2:1107 (the letter to Gustav Bradt, 9th of October 1926). On the Academy and its members cf. also Gershom Scholem, *Von Berlin nach Jerusalem* (Frankfurt: Suhrkamp, 1977), 189.

3. Strauss's emphasis in this obituary on Rosenzweig's founding of the Academy for the Study of Judaism is in stark contrast to the tenor of the other eulogies found in the same publication. Whereas Alphonse Paquet, Joseph Prager, and Hermann Schafft emphasize, respectively, the Jewish spiritual significance of Rosenzweig's speech-thinking for the learning instituted at the Lehrhaus (Prager), his life of faith (Schafft), reverence for his holy suffering (Paquet), and his striking beauty as a youth (Prager), Leo Strauss points out Rosenzweig's contributions to the science of Judaism and even uses the opportunity to reconnect Rosenzweig with the name of Hermann Cohen, who was widely regarded as passé. Strauss, while perhaps not being outright contrary, certainly chooses to be less sentimental than his contemporaries.]

4. Cohen, *Jüdische Schriften*. Rosenzweig's "Einleitung" is found in the first volume *(Ethische und religiöse Grundfragen)*, pp. xiii–lxiv. In the history of the interpretation of Cohen's philosophy of religion/Jewish thought, this introduction has indeed played a major, if not always helpful, role. Cf. Michael Zank, *The Idea of Atonement in the Philosophy of Hermann Cohen*, Brown Judaic Studies Series (Providence, R.I.: Brown Judaic Studies, 2000), 33–44, 165–77.

Review of Julius Ebbinghaus, *On the Progress of Metaphysics* (1931)

This Rostock University inaugural lecture develops a program that differs in two respects from the countless philosophical programs flooding the book market. It differs, first, in that it clearly does not precede the work, but grows out of it; and, second, in that it is not interested in originality. It has been a long time, to say the least, since the call for originality, and the belief in progress underlying this call, has been contradicted in such a fundamental way as is done here by *Ebbinghaus*. We are used to people showing just scorn and mockery for the belief in progress. However, we are also used to these very scorners and mockers having no qualms from the outset about raising modern reservations against the past. Since the owl of Minerva begins her flight at dusk, those who regard the present as a time of decline usually still believe that there are more possibilities of knowledge today than ever before. Those who attribute to the philosophy of antiquity or to Scholasticism a fundamental superiority over modern philosophy nevertheless routinely find them lacking in entire disciplines of modern origin, or even rediscover such disciplines in them.

Ebbinghaus renounces *all* modern objections by abandoning *the* modern prejudice, namely, the prejudice that *the* truth has not already been found in the past (p. 6f.). The condition that makes the abandonment of this fundamental modern prejudice both possible and necessary is the fact that we are "completely sold out of knowledge" [*"gänzlich ausverkauft an Erkenntnissen"*] (p. 9). The "philosophical chaos in which we live" (p. 6) reveals the presumed progress and construction as complete destruction. With this, Ebbinghaus enters into opposition in principle to what is today the most favored interpretation of the "anarchy of systems." Since anyone who thinks at all cannot avoid standing somewhere, one secures the possibility of being satisfied with this "anarchy" by "understanding" it historically, psychologically, sociologically, or anthropologically, that is, by relativizing each system with respect to the "location" [*"Standort"*] of its author; fascinated by the conditions and vicissitudes of all questions one stops—questioning. On the other hand, the few who derive from the anarchy a sharpened impulse to question are confirmed by the anarchy in their opinion that "all treasures of the past do not suffice," that one must seek *new* answers that correspond to the needs of the age (p. 7). This opinion is so attractive precisely *because* we are "completely sold out of knowledge." Is it not true that, having set out "to free the mind from all prejudice," modern philosophy has gradually destroyed all traditions and thereby helped the mind advance to freedom? Is it not, then, precisely today, especially *easy* to philosophize freely and on one's own? Ebbinghaus is of a different opinion: the freedom that is the result of the modern dissolution of all traditions is nothing but the freedom of ignorance [*Unwissenheit*], a freedom that is not altogether unbearable only if it is ready to—*learn*; specifically, if it is ready to "open the old tome,"[1] that is, to *read*, but not with "that remarkable indifference, not to say callousness, with which the previous generations read those books," but rather "with the burning interest of one who wants to be *taught*" (p. 8f.). The turn from avowed ignorance [*Unwissenheit*] to learning through reading [*lesendes Lernen*] is not natural,[2] as is shown by the position of the classical teacher of knowing about not-knowing [*Wissen des Nichtwissens*][3] with regard to learning through reading. This turn can be understood only from what is peculiar to the *presently* possible and necessary knowing about not-knowing. If it is true that "those who jump into the sea [on a rescue mission] are themselves dragged into the abyss by the weight of the rescue tools that they had assembled on the shore of the present" (p. 8), then the present has no possibility of natural or, as it is often called, "systematic" philosophizing; then the not-knowing [*Nichtwissen*] that is real in the present day is not at all the natural not-knowing [*Nichtwissen*] with which philosophizing must begin; then a long detour and a great effort are first needed in order even to return to the state of natural ignorance [*Unwissenheit*]. To use the classical presentation of the natural difficulties of philosophizing, namely Plato's parable of the cave, one may say that today we find ourselves in a second, much deeper cave[4] than the lucky ignorant persons Socrates dealt with; we need history first of all in order to *ascend* to the cave from which Socrates can lead us to light; we need a propaedeutic, which the Greeks did not need, namely, learning through reading. It is the merit of Ebbinghaus's writing that it has called attention, with fitting forcefulness, to this desideratum of all present-day philosophy.

NOTES

Source: "*Philosophie und Unterrichtswesen*, Julius Ebbinghaus, *Über die Fortschritte der Metaphysik*, [Philosophie und Geschichte, Heft 32,] Tübingen: J. C. B. Mohr (Paul Siebeck), 1931," *Deutsche Literaturzeitung* 52 (27 December 1931): 2451–53, reprinted in *GS*, 2:437–39. The review and its occasion is mentioned in a letter by Strauss to his friend Gerhard Krüger, 15 October 1931: "I now discovered a fourth man who agrees with us on the present as a second cave: Ebbinghaus. His lecture 'On the Progress of Metaphysics' contains a few quite excellent formulations; I will review the writing in DLZ." See *GS*, 2:xxix n. 40. Strauss first heard Ebbinghaus in 1922 in Freiburg while

Ebbinghaus was lecturing on "the social doctrines of the Reformation and the Enlightenment." In "A Giving of Accounts" he particularly recalls Ebbinghaus's lively presentation of Hobbes. See *Jewish Philosophy and the Crisis of Modernity: Essays and Lectures in
Modern Jewish Thought*, ed. and trans. Kenneth Hart Green (Albany: SUNY Press, 1997),
461.

1. "open the old tome": orig.: *den alten Folianten aufzuschlagen*. In his later, English
writings, Strauss uses the expression "the old books."

2. "not a natural one": the phrase *ist nicht natürlich* appears also in a 1932 lecture
manuscript (*GS*, 2:445): "Unterstellen wir also, diese Frage sei eindeutig—sie ist jedenfalls
nicht natürlich."

3. The teacher of "knowing about not-knowing" is Socrates (see the continuation).

4. The notion of a "second cave" makes its first appearance in "Religious Situation of the Present" (*GS*, 2:386–87, 389). It returns in "Die geistige Lage der Gegenwart"
(1932) (*GS*, 2:456), in *Philosophie und Gesetz* (Berlin: Schocken, 1935), 14n, 46, and
elsewhere. Cf. Heinrich Meier, *Die Denkbewegung von Leo Strauss: Die Geschichte der
Philosophie und die Intention des Philosophen* (Stuttgart and Weimar: Metzler Verlag, 1996),
21–28, 42f. Also see the introduction to this volume and cf. *GS*, 2:xxix n. 40.

The Testament of Spinoza (1932)

In their judgment of Spinoza, Europe, and Judaism along with it, passed
through stages that can be characterized summarily in the following way:
condemnation (i.e., the ban pronounced by the Amsterdam community),
followed by vindication (Mendelssohn), followed by canonization (Heine,
Hess), which was finally followed by neutrality (Joël, Freudenthal). It is obvious that in each of these epochs there were men who did not think as their
epoch did. We must mention by name Hermann Cohen who, in the year
1910, found the courage to state openly that Spinoza's "expulsion from the
community of Israel was necessary and fully legitimate."[1]

Neutrality toward Spinoza set in once one was able to admit that the
"modern worldview," whose victory was decisively aided by Spinoza's metaphysics, does not, or does not entirely, coincide with this metaphysics. But
even at this stage it was still generally maintained, and even emphasized, that
among the three great Western philosophers of the seventeenth century—
Descartes, Hobbes, and Spinoza—Spinoza was the most important one *because* he was the most progressive one. He alone had drawn certain consequences from the foundations of modern philosophy, which became fully
clarified only in the nineteenth century and which henceforth determined
the general consciousness.

Meanwhile things have reached the point where the general consciousness is determined by doubt about the "modern worldview." Regardless of the legitimacy of this doubt, it has had the effect of making the "modern worldview" no longer self-evident, so that an advanced student of this worldview is no longer held in particular esteem simply on account of such advancement. If the foundations of the "modern worldview" are being shaken by doubt, then interest necessarily reverts from its classical exponents to the men who laid the foundations of this "world view," namely, to Descartes and Hobbes. If the veneration of Spinoza is to be more than admiration for his talent or character and more than recognition of his historical effect, and if it is to apply to him as a *teacher*, then this veneration must be held in abeyance at least until the legitimacy of the foundations of modern philosophy has been decided.

We have thus begun to think of Spinoza's "radicalism" differently than the past century did. Now we see that the bold innovations of Spinoza were only consequences, rather than foundations. The fact that now gains in importance is that—compared to the significance of Descartes, Hobbes, and Leibniz—Spinoza is only of secondary significance in the history of the core sciences, that is, in the history of natural science, on the one hand, and of natural right, on the other. And the fact that Spinoza achieved more general recognition only toward the end of the eighteenth century is now also understandable: he could be accepted only at the moment when the *"querelle des anciens et des modernes"* within philosophy had been decided on the main point in favor of the moderns, and when what mattered was the restoration, for the purpose of correcting the modern idea, of certain positions of the premodern world that had been knocked over in the first onslaught; for Spinoza—who stood on the foundation of modern philosophy laid by Descartes and Hobbes—had carried along into the modern world, which he already found in existence, the ideal of life of the premodern (ancient-medieval) tradition, the ideal of the (theoretical) knowledge of God.

The (respective) position of Judaism toward Spinoza coincides with the (respective) position of Europe toward him. However, it does not completely coincide with it. Spinoza played a special role in the Judaism of the past century. When what mattered was the justification of the breakup of the Jewish tradition and the entry of the Jews into modern Europe, perhaps no better, but certainly no more convenient, reference offered itself than the appeal to Spinoza. Who was more suitable for undertaking the justification of modern Judaism before the tribunal of the Jewish tradition, on the one hand, and before the tribunal of modern Europe, on the other, than Spinoza, who,

as was almost universally recognized, was a classical exponent of this Europe
and who, as one did not grow weary of at least asserting, had thought his
thoughts in the spirit of Judaism and by means of Judaism? It is clear that, at a
time when modern Europe has been shaken to its foundations, one *can* no
longer justify oneself before *this* Europe for the sake of Judaism, nor before
Judaism for the sake of *this* Europe, supposing one still wants to do so.

The convulsion of modern Europe led to a renewed self-awareness [*Besinn-
ung*] of Judaism. This renewed awareness did not produce a change in the
assessment of Spinoza, at least not always and not immediately: Spinoza remained an authority. To be sure, one no longer needed him, or at least one
no longer seemed to need him, for one's self-assertion against the Jewish
tradition and against modern Europe. But in the exodus from the new Egypt
one saw oneself obliged to take along the bones of the man who had risen to
a kinglike position in that land and to convey them to the pantheon of the
Jewish nation, which venerated him as one of her greatest sons. No doubt
this was done in good faith. But was it right not to have asked about the last
will of the man thus honored?

But of what concern is Spinoza's last will to us if what is meant by this is
his explicit will? Even Spinoza was bound by the historical conditions under
which he lived and thought. In his age, he *had to* come into conflict with
Judaism, a conflict in which both sides were right: the Jewish community
that had to defend the conditions of Jewish existence in the Diaspora, or as
others say, the Jewish "form"; and Spinoza, who was called upon to loosen
the rigidity of the content of this "form," that is, the "subterranean Judaism,"
and thus to initiate the rebirth of the Jewish nation. Several centuries were
needed to make Spinoza's critique of the Law sufficiently flexible so that the
Law could be acknowledged without believing in its revealed character. At
the end of this development stood a generation that was free-spirited enough
to be able to accept Spinoza's critique of the Law, and that was even freer
than he inasmuch as it had moved beyond the crude alternative: divine or
human? revealed or conceived by men? When properly interpreted, not only
does Spinoza not stand outside Judaism, he belongs to it as one of its greatest
teachers.

Whoever is acquainted with Spinoza's critique of the Law knows that
this critique would not have been possible without the foundation of modern
philosophy. To be sure, in order to shake the authority of the Bible, Spinoza
also refers to certain difficulties in the biblical text. But in order to be able to
draw from these difficulties (which had been known long before him) the
consequence that the Torah was not written by Moses, and the further consequence that therefore the Torah was not revealed and hence not binding,

he had to presuppose the philosophical critique of the Law that, at least in his case, is tied to the foundation of modern philosophy. Now that this foundation has become doubtful, Spinoza's critique of the Law has also become doubtful; and accordingly, it has also become doubtful whether he should be regarded as a teacher of Judaism.

But then, must a great man whom one wishes to venerate necessarily be a great teacher? Should there not also exist, for example, great and hence venerable heretics [*Irrlehrer*]? And if this great heretic—with respect to whom, incidentally, it has not yet been established that he *was* a heretic—is a Jew, does not the Jewish nation, then, have the right and the duty to remember him proudly and gratefully?

Spinoza was a Jew. It is a certified fact that he was born and educated as a Jew. But should we mention the names of other men, perhaps of equal rank with Spinoza, who were likewise born and educated as Jews, and whom scarcely any Jew would dare to remember proudly and gratefully as a Jew? We need not mention these names, and can indeed regard the proposition as proven, that the Jewish origin and education of a great man, taken by themselves, do not give us the right to claim his greatness for Judaism. Therefore, if one disregards the fact that Spinoza was born and educated as a Jew (a fact from which perhaps not much can be concluded), and if in addition one is not satisfied with vague speculations on Spinoza's Jewish cast of mind; if therefore one wants to know clearly and distinctly where Judaism is lodged in Spinoza's thought, that is, which of Spinoza's decisive ideas bear a peculiarly Jewish imprint—then one will turn with deserved trust to those scholars who have endeavored to determine the Jewish sources of Spinoza's doctrine. A critical examination of what has emerged from these efforts leads to the following result: There is no doubt whatever that Spinoza stands in a relation of the strongest *literary* dependence on Jewish authors. Originally he came to know the philosophical tradition only through the mediation of the Jewish philosophy of the Middle Ages. But what he learned from this philosophy were insights or opinions that he could just as well have adopted from non-Jewish (Muslim or Christian) philosophy of the Middle Ages; it is the common property of the European-Mediterranean tradition. And even if it should at one point come to light that one of Spinoza's *core* doctrines, as found in his works, is found only in the work of one or another Jewish philosopher or theologian of the past, then it would still remain to be *proved* that this doctrine is actually peculiarly Jewish, and that it could not just as well have been conceived by a Greek, a Muslim, or a Christian.

"Good European" that he is, Spinoza takes from the Jewish tradition the common property of European ideas that it conveyed to him—and nothing *else.* Thus we believe we have answered the question of whether the Jew as a Jew is entitled to venerate Spinoza. Spinoza belongs not to Judaism, but to the small band of superior minds whom Nietzsche called the "good Europeans." To this community belong *all* the philosophers of the seventeenth century, but Spinoza belongs to it in a special way. Spinoza did not remain a Jew, while Descartes, Hobbes, and Leibniz remained Christians. Thus it is not in accordance with Spinoza's wishes that he be inducted into the pantheon of the Jewish nation. Under these circumstances it seems to us an elementary imperative of Jewish self-respect that we Jews should at last again relinquish our claim on Spinoza. By so doing, we by no means surrender him to our enemies. Rather, we leave him to that distant and strange community of "neutrals" whom one can call, with considerable justice, the community of the "good Europeans." Besides, we must do so out of respect, which we owe him even if we do not owe him veneration. Respect for Spinoza demands that we take his last will seriously; and his last will was neutrality toward the Jewish nation, based on his break with Judaism.

But did Spinoza leave a testament from which this very will follows unambiguously? Is the Jewish nation mentioned at all in his testament? One does not need to seek for this testament in archives that are difficult of access. It can be found toward the end of the third chapter of the *Theological-Political Treatise.*

Spinoza says: "If the foundations of the Jewish religion have not rendered the minds of the Jews effeminate [*weibisch*], then I would absolutely believe that someday, given the opportunity and human affairs being so changeable, they (the Jews) will once again establish their empire and God will elect them anew."[2] If we disregard the remark about the renewed divine election of the Jews, which, coming from Spinoza, is nothing but an empty phrase, what remains as his opinion, as his "political testament," is the neutral consideration of the possibility condition [*Möglichkeitsbedingung*] for the restoration of the Jewish state. This possibility condition is that the Jewish religion lose its power over the minds of the Jews because, according to Spinoza, this religion leads to a softening of one's turn of mind [*Verweichlichung der Gesinnung*].[3] That no state can be established in a softened turn of mind requires no proof. But Spinoza's assertion that the Jewish religion enfeebles the mind is extremely questionable; in fact, it is unintelligible. Has Spinoza completely forgotten that this religion gave the victims of the Inquisition the strength to endure the most extreme suffering? No, Spinoza has not forgotten this fact; we know this with complete certainty from his letters. He was simply of the opinion that the strength needed to endure suffering is not the same strength needed to establish and preserve a state, namely, the strength to command, without which no society can survive. And just as his teacher Machiavelli held Christianity responsible for the corruption of Roman virtue, so Spinoza held Judaism responsible for the impossibility of a restoration of the Jewish state.

It would be risky to deduce from the cited passage that Spinoza is therefore the father of political Zionism. It would be risky not so much because, as everyone knows, there is also an Orthodox, which is to say conservative, political Zionism. Rather, it is because—unlike his contemporary, Isaac de la Peyrère, who proceeded on the basis of similar presuppositions—Spinoza does not actually wish for or demand the restoration of the Jewish state: he merely discusses it. As if condescending from the height of his philosophical neutrality, he leaves it to the Jews to liberate themselves from their religion and thus to obtain for themselves the possibility of reconstituting their state.

The risk of this advice—and at this point one must recall that Spinoza makes it his business to rehabilitate Balaam![4]—becomes clear if one considers the context in which Spinoza offers it. This context is his contesting of the doctrine of the election of the Jewish nation. More precisely, Spinoza contests the proof of its election found in the fact that the Jewish nation, and no other nation, has preserved itself in spite of the loss of its state and its dispersion over the whole earth. According to Spinoza, this fact is not a miracle but largely the natural consequence of—the rites, which have separated the Jewish nation from the other peoples and have preserved it hitherto and will preserve it forever. In other words, the Jewish nation owes its present and future preservation to its Law, and thus to its religion. And should the Jewish nation now abandon this religion in order to establish its state, which, according to what has been said, it does not need, at least not for the sake of its preservation? The contradiction here is only apparent. It can be proved to be apparent even if one completely disregards the fact that Spinoza could have recommended to the Jews, or could have wished for them, the establishment of their state on grounds other than the interest in the preservation of their nation. It is clear that Spinoza distinguished between the "rites" (the "forms," as they are often called today) and the "foundations of the religion." According to his advice, the latter are to be discarded, while the former are to be retained. The foundations of the religion are that *spirit* of the Law that makes the political restoration impossible. Liberated from this spirit, the Law will not only not hamper the political restoration, but it will further guarantee the permanence of the nation, which will now have become political again. The Law as a means of national preservation, or as a form of national life—who does not know this view of Judaism! And did not Spinoza come amazingly close to it, as close as was possible in the "unhistorical" seventeenth century?

To be sure, with this difference: he still perceived an obstacle to the politicization of the Jewish nation in the spirit of the Law. And then, to be sure, with the further difference that should not be completely overlooked, which is that he voiced this view not as a Jew, but as a neutral; and he did not even voice it, but rather just tossed it off.

Should this, then, be what Spinoza's testament is about? Not in this way, not with veiled words and a weary heart, should we bid farewell to Spinoza—if, in fact, we *must* bid farewell to him as someone on whose conscience is a "humanly incomprehensible betrayal" (Cohen) of our nation. For a moment at least, we would like to disregard the popular principles on the strength of which one saw oneself compelled either to canonize Spinoza or to condemn him. It is sufficient that no one has been able to popularize him, no one has been able to turn him into small change, no one has been able to "cut him down to size." And still we ask whether we owe him veneration? Spinoza will be venerated as long as there are men who know how to appreciate the inscription on his signet ring ("*caute*")[5] or, to put it plainly: as long as there are men who know what it means to utter [the word]: *independence* [*Unabhängigkeit*].

NOTES

Source: "Das Testament Spinozas," *Bayerische Israelitische Gemeindezeitung* 8, no. 21 (1 November 1932): 322–26, reprinted in *GS*, 1:415–22.

1. Hermann Cohen, "Ein ungedruckter Vortrag Hermann Cohens über Spinozas Verhältnis zum Judentum," eingeleitet von Franz Rosenzweig, in *Festgabe zum 10jährigen Bestehen der Akademie für die Wissenschaft des Judentums, 1919–1929* (Berlin: Akademie Verlag, 1929), 59. Strauss cites this source again, and more extensively, in his preface to *Spinoza's Critique of Religion*, trans. Elsa Sinclair (New York: Schocken, 1965).

2. "Wenn die Grundlagen der jüdischen Religion die Gemüter der Juden nicht weibisch machten. . . ." Cf. Spinoza, *Theological-Political Treatise*, trans. C. Gebhardt (Hamburg: Meiner, 1955), 75: "Ja, wenn die Grundsätze ihrer Religion ihren Sinn nicht verweichlichen . . ." Cf. also Spinoza, *Theological-Political Treatise*, trans. Samuel Shirley (Indianapolis: Hackett, 1998), 47: "Indeed, were it not that the fundamental principles of their religion discourage manliness . . ." In the original: "imo nisi fundamenta suae religionis eorum animos effoeminarent . . ."

3. The phrase *Verweichlichung der Gesinnung* that Strauss uses in this explanatory paraphrase is close to the wording of Gebhardt's translation of the sentence in question. See previous note.

4. Earlier in chapter 3 of *Theological-Political Treatise*, Spinoza adduces the non-Israelite prophet Balaam (cf. Num. 22–24) to argue that, among the ancient Hebrews, legitimate prophecy was not merely thought of as an Israelite property. In Num. 22:6, Balaam's power to bless and curse are described by the king of Moab in the same terms that, according to Genesis 12:3, YHWH pronounced as a special promise to Abra(ha)m.

While the biblical narrative has Balaam bless rather than curse Israel, Jewish tradition considers him a "wicked" [*Balaam ha-resha'*] counterfigure to Abraham, representing pride and other vices. See Mishnah Avot 5:19. In a letter by Hermann Badt to Martin Buber from 4 July 1916, the "wicked Balaam" makes an appearance as well, curiously in the context of the famous debate between Hermann Cohen and Martin Buber on Zionism. See Hartwig Wiedebach, "Hermann Cohens Auseinandersetzung mit dem Zionismus," *JSQ* 6 (1999): 385.

    5. *caute* (Lat., adv.): cautiously, safely.

Index of Sources

General Index

Abraham, 94, 132, 157, 223n. 4
Academy for the Science of Judaism. *See*
    Akademie für die Wissenschaft des
    Judentums
act of faith, 70
Ahad Ha'am (Asher Hirsch Ginsberg), x, 81,
    119, 131, 82n. 6, 106n. 11, 123n. 13;
    archaeological vs. historical method,
    131; "Moses" (Hebr.), 135n. 3; on
    Moses, 131
Akademie für die Wissenschaft des
    Judentums, ix, 10–11, 43n. 55, 139–40,
    212; Hermann Cohen Foundation of
    the, 212; history of, 213n. 2; *Kor-*
    respondenzblatt, 139, 173; list of fellows
    of, 42n. 52; as a political idea, 212
Alexander of Aphrodisias, 31
Allheit (the all, totality), 95
amor Dei intellectualis, 150
Amos, 112
Amsterdam, 190
Antiochus Epiphanes, 93
anti-Semitism, 79–82, 103
apikorsut (apostasy), 127
apologetics, 139, 141, 157, 159, 161
a priori, religious, 109
Arbeiterjugend (youth wing of German
    socialist movement), 5
Aristotle, 179–81; physics, 179–80; *Politics*,
    24; as unsurpassable authority, 180
Arminians, 200n. 17
assimilation, 68, 70, 76, 79n. 5, 85–88, 94,
    96, 105n. 2, 108, 120–21

atheism, 31, 47n. 99, 64, 133, 136n. 12,
    163–64n. 12, 201–11
attributes, doctrine of. *See* God, attributes
    of
authenticity, xi
Avicenna, 24; on Plato's *Nomoi*, 44n

Badt, Hermann, 223n. 4
Baer, Fritz Jizchak, 42n. 52
Balaam, 221, 223n. 4
Balfour Declaration, 63, 127
Bandmann, Martin, 73n. 10
Baneth, Hartwig David, 42n. 52
Barth, Karl, 33, 136n. 10
being: doctrine of *(Seinslehre)*, 56–57; and
    representation, 55; and transcendence,
    78
belief, 5, 7, 15, 55–56, 60n. 6, 64; definition
    of, 55; duality of, 56; in God as a
    natural "instinct," 56; in natural reality,
    55; subject to the control of historical
    reasoning, 66; in sufficiency and in
    insufficiency, 27, 182; trivialization of,
    132; and unbelief, 203–8; as an ultimate
    certainty impervious to "argumenta-
    tion," 65
Benjamin, Walter, 23
Bergson, Henri, 107
Betar ideology (militarism), 73n. 9
Bible, 71, 108, 111; as the deposit of a
    centuries-long development, 133; as
    literature, 174. *See also* Scripture
Bible research *(Bibelforschung)*, 148

227

Democritus, 168n. 68
Descartes, René, 54, 180, 216
despair, 185, 189, 192, 208
determinism, 178
devil, the, 206
de Witt, Jan, 141, 143
dialectic theology, 136n. 10
doctrinairism. *See* French Revolution
doctrine of attributes. *See* God, attributes of
dogma, 70, 92, 110, 125–29, 130–33, 150,
    189; absence of, as a liberal Jewish
    doctrine, 95, 125; critique of, 195; of
    immortality, 190; motif of the absurdity
    of Christian, 155; as secondary to
    "religious experience," 109
dogmatics, 91
Dostoevsky, Fyodor, 69; *Brothers Karamazov*,
    206
doubt, 54, 71, 75n. 25
Dubnow, Simon, 101–6, 130–35; *Die
    neueste Geschichte des jüdischen Volkes*,
    105n. 1; *Weltgeschichte des jüdischen
    Volkes*, 105n. 1

Ebbinghaus, Julius, 214–16
egoism, 169n. 75
Einwirklichung (entering into reality), 19, 68,
    74n. 19. See also *Entwirklichtheit*
election of Israel, doctrine of the, 94, 221
Elijah, 204
emancipation, Jewish, 80–81, 86–87, 94, 96
encounter, philosophy of *(Erlebnis-
    philosophie)*, 204
Enlightenment: the age of, 86–87, 109, 112,
    148, 159, 173; critique of religion, 64,
    111, 132, 174, 186; manly attitude of
    the men of, 191; reaction against, 69;
    shallowness of, 126
Entente, the, 128
enthusiasm, 120
Entwirklichtheit (lack of reality), 19, 68, 87,
    94, 100–101n. 13
Epicureanism *(apikorsut)*, 27, 108
Epicurean type criticism/critique of
    religion. See *Kritik*
Epicurus, 189–92
epigonism, 90
Erasmus of Rotterdam, 174
Erets Yisrael (the Land of Israel), 203
eschatology, 112

essence *(Wesen)*, 56; of religion, 69
Europe, 96, 108; bourgeois-proletarian-
    Cossack future of, 90; extrication from,
    63
Ewald, Heinrich, 98
existence, 56, 111; of angels, 150; continued
    Jewish, 157; *galut*, 79; of God, 69, 125,
    132; homunculus-like, 94; national, 95;
    political, 68, 85, 93, 119; in this world
    of hatred, 104. *See also* God, existence
    of
existentialism, 47n. 99
experience *(Erlebnis)*, 19, 25, 67; philosophy
    of, 204
Ezra the Scribe, 93, 100n. 12

faculties *(Vermögen)*, cognitive, 54, 59n. 2
faith, 85, 146, 148–49, 151, 184–85; act of,
    70; denial of, 109; in the ideals of 1789,
    87; Jewish, 127; Kant making room for,
    109; loss of, 188; in national-cultural
    autonomy, 104; as obedience to God,
    148; passionate, 184; in the sufficiency
    of human beings, 184
fascism, 46n. 83
feminism, theological, 71
Fenner, Ferdinand, 98n
Fichte, Johann Gottlieb, 97, 98n
First World War, 17
Fischer, Karl, 4
Flesch, Martin, 123n. 10
Foerder, Herbert, 38n. 13
Forchtenberg (Hohenlohe), 21, 118, 121n
Frankfurt on the Main, 9, 18, 22, 38n. 13,
    57, 64–71, 121n, 122n. 6, 123n. 11,
    124, 130
Frederick II ("the Great") of Prussia, 135,
    137n. 15
Frederick Wilhelm IV of Prussia, 98
freedom, 70, 80, 103, 114, 120–21, 134,
    141–42, 175, 178, 191, 207, 215
Freies jüdisches Lehrhaus (Frankfurt), 41
    n. 10, 45, 73n. 11, 213n. 3
French Revolution: doctrinairism of the,
    86; ideals of 1789, 65
Freud, Sigmund, 202–11; *Civilization and its
    Discontents*, 209n. 1; *Die Zukunft einer
    Illusion*, 209n. 1
Freudenthal, Joachim, 216
Fritzsche, Robert Arnold, 98n

propaganda, 40n. 37
prophecy, 76, 78, 111, 131, 135, 144, 147,
152–54, 178, 181
prophetology, 24, 44n, 178–80
prophets, 7, 20, 32, 93–94, 102, 110, 133,
147, 152–54, 173, 175, 183, 190, 203.
See also religion
Protestantism, 91–92, 110, 146, 149, 155,
158, 183; cultural (see *Kulturprotestantismus*); Old Testament
scholarship of, 76; subjectivism of, 77
Proverbs, 175
Prussia, 90, 99n. 3, 105n. 4
Psalms, 133, 175
Pythagoras, 153

quaestio iuris, 79n. 3
querelle des anciens et des modernes, 217

R. Abraham ben David of Posquières
(Rabad), 154, 156, 171nn. 96, 99
Ranke, Leopold von, 99n. 4, 131
rationalism, 57, 90, 112, 191
Reaktionszeit. *See* restoration, period of
reality, 55–56, 67–69, 76, 84–85, 87, 94,
96, 102, 120, 142, 152, 205
reason, 7, 20, 23–26, 34, 55, 66, 91, 129,
142, 146, 148–51, 153, 156, 158–59,
176, 181–82, 184–85, 190–91, 194–95
reconciliation, 20, 23, 26–27, 36, 94, 133
recruitment experience. See *Keilerfahrung*
Redlichkeit. See probity
reflectiveness (*Reflektiertheit*), 26, 32, 75, 90
religion, xi, 7–8, 14, 18–20, 22, 24–25, 27,
31, 34–35, 56–57, 64, 69, 71, 76–78,
91–95, 106, 151, 158, 205, 207;
compromised forms of modern, 23;
doctrine of the "ancient," 175;
historical, 30; history of, 111–12, 157;
idealistically reinterpeted, as perhaps the
most amusing thing in the world, 109;
immanentist interpretation of, 67;
internalization of, 69; Jewish, 203; Law
as the heart of, 155; negative function
of the Jewish, 68; and philosophy, 36,
110; politicization of the Jewish, 144;
post-Enlightenment fate of, x;
Protestant, 146–47; and reason, 23;
revealed, 15, 174, 176, 178, 181–83,
185, 194; saved by the self-critique of

critique (Kant), 109; science of
(Religionswissenschaft), 107–9; state and,
19; Zionism and, 21
Rembrandt Harmens van Rijn, 160
Renaissance, 194
renaissance, German-Jewish cultural (1920s).
See German Jewry, cultural renaissance
of
Renan, Ernest, 106n. 11
representations *(Vorstellungen)*, 55
resignation, 90
restoration, period of *(Reaktionszeit)*, 69,
74n. 21
return: to cultural inwardness, 14; into the
darkness of the cave, 29; to the Gospel,
92; in Heidegger *(Kehre)*, 16; to Jewish
"content," 18; to Judaism, xi, 16, 190;
to the layer of "pure doctrine," 158; to
the level achieved by the ancients, 30;
to Maimonides, 16, 24; to the natural
conditions of the polis, 33; to the "old
books," 12; to the original, 195; to
Orthodox faith, 21; to Palestine, 85; to
the people, 68; to pre-Enlightenment
thought, 16; to reality, 19; and
repentance *(teshuvah)*, 16, 36; in
Rousseau, 48n. 118; to Scripture, 159;
to the state of natural ignorance, 215;
well-known ideology of, 119; from
words to things, 23
revelation, 32, 36, 48n. 114, 91, 109, 125–
26, 153, 176–77, 180–82, 184–86, 194–
95
reward and punishment, 191
Rickert, Heinrich, 39n. 30
right to life, 131
Rilke, Rainer Maria, 4
Ritschl, Albrecht Benjamin, 98
romanticism, 68, 99n. 4, 109
Rosenzweig, Franz, 10, 16, 32, 34, 40n. 33,
41n. 45, 42nn. 49–53, 73n. 12, 89n. 2,
117n. 22, 212–13, 129n. 7;
"Atheistische Theologie," 136n. 7,
136n. 12, 209n. 4; "Einleitung" in
Hermann Cohens Jüdische Schriften, 115
n. 5, 213n. 4; *Festgabe zum 10jährigen
Bestehen der Akademie für die Wissenschaft
des Judentums 1919–1929*, 172n. 100;
The Star of Redemption, 211n. 15; "Zeit
ists . . . (Ps. 119, 126). Gedanken über

das Bildungsproblem des Augenblicks," 212, 213 n. 2
Rousseau, Jean-Jacques, 48 n. 118
Rückert, Friedrich, 97
Ruder Verein jüdischer Studenten (Berlin), 121 n

Sabbath, 71, 156
Sachlichkeit (matter-of-factness, objectivity), 126, 129 n. 7, 142, 152
Sadducees, 195
Samuel, 131
Samuel, Sir Herbert, 63
San Remo conference, 63
Saronia (Frankfurt), 72 n. 4, 121 n
Saul, King, 131, 135, 195
Savigny, Friedrich Karl von, 99 n. 4
Schafft, Hermann, 213 n. 3
Scheler, Max, 7, 69, 75 n. 22
Schleiermacher, Friedrich Daniel Ernst, 25, 34, 48 n. 108, 58 n, 60 n. 8, 115 n. 2, 211 n. 18
Schmitt, Carl, xv n. 1, 9, 11, 13, 35, 40 n. 38, 199 n. 11; Der Begriff des Politischen, 12, 45 n. 66
Scholem, Gerhard Gershom, xv n. 4, 9, 18, 23–24, 42 n. 52, 71 n. 1, 72 n. 5, 73 n. 11; "Die blau-weisse Brille," 37 n. 4, 39 n. 21, 73 n. 8; "The Politics of Mysticism: Isaac Breuer's New Kuzari," 129 n. 5; Von Berlin nach Jerusalem, 46 nn. 83–84
science (Wissenschaft), 57, 65, 69, 87, 91, 130, 132–34, 147–48, 158–60, 173–74, 180, 217; of apologetics, 141; Orthodox misconception of, 146; and perfectibility, 27; of propaganda, 8; of psychoanalysis, 207; and religion, 205–6; of religion (Religionswissenschaft), 7, 107–14; Rosenzweig's contributions to, 212; spirit of, 39 n. 28
Scripture, 132–34, 142, 148–49, 151, 153–56, 158–59, 175–76, 179, 181, 186, 192, 206; authority of, 145, 183, 205; habituation to, 31; identification of religion and, 148; Protestant faith in, 146, 149; and reason, 190–91, 194–95; theory and, 177–78, 180, 182; as the "Word of God," 146
secularization, 86

self-preservation, 175
selicha (forgiveness), 104
Servetus, Michael, 192–94
Shaw, George Bernard, 204
Shulkhan Arukh, 32
Simmel, Georg, 123 n. 14,
Simon, Ernst, 73 n. 11, 211 n. 12
sobriety, 5, 7, 66
socialism, 67, 84, 119, 147, 203
Socrates, 11, 13, 29–30, 215
sophism, 33
Sparta, 88
Spätjudentumsforschung (Protestant historiography on postexilic Judaism), 100 n. 12
species, preservation of the, 56
Spengler, Oswald, xi
Spinoza, Baruch de, ix, xiii–xiv, 10, 12, 14–15, 20, 35, 41 n. 45, 65, 139–200, 216–23; Apology, 165 n. 22; Ethics, 146, 148–49, 152, 159, 174–75, 177; Theological-Political Treatise, 12, 139–87 passim, 222 nn passim
spirit of August 1914, the, 81
Stahl, Julius, 74 n. 21
state and church. See church and state
Stein, Arthur, 123 n. 10
Stern, Selma, 42 n. 52
Strauss, Leo, works of: "Anmerkungen zu Carl Schmitt, Der Begriff des Politischen," xv n. 1, 9, 12, 45 nn. 65–67; "Anmerkung zur Diskussion über 'Zionismus und Antisemitismus'" ("A Note on the Discussion on 'Zionism and Antisemitism'"), 79–82; "Antwort auf das 'Prinzipielle Wort' der Frankfurter" ("Response to Frankfurt's 'Word of Principle'"), 5, 18–19, 64–75, 99 n, 100 n. 13; The Argument and the Action of Plato's "Laws," 44 n; "Bemerkung zu der Weinbergschen Kritik," ("Comment on Weinberg's Critique"), xv n. 4, 8, 20–21, 64, 118–24, 209 n; "Biblische Geschichte und Wissenschaft" ("Biblical History and Science"), 20, 22, 130–37; "Cohens Analyse der Bibel-Wissenschaft Spinozas" ("Cohen's Analysis of Spinoza's Bible Science"), 139–72, 197 n. 3; "Cohen und Maimuni," 44 n; contributions to Der Jude, 10; contributions to Moses

General Index 237

separation of philosophy from, 182;
Spinoza's, 183; traditional, 125;
Zionism and, 87
theophany, 79n. 7, 133, 171n. 90
theory, 177–82, 186; of attributes, 111; and
blessedness (beatitudo), 177; distinction
between motive and, 186; as the
fulfillment of striving for self-preservation, 175; of knowledge (Erkenntnis-
theorie), 58; of mythology, 114; political
(Staatstheorie), 142–43; radicalism of, 35;
religion and, 184–85; Zionist, 9
Thomism, 34
Thurneysen, Eduard, 136n. 10
tolerance, 95
Tolstoy, Leo, 106n. 11
Tönnies, Ferdinand, 123n. 14
Torah, the, 126, 189, 195; battle against the
rule of, 128; as the deposit of a
centuries-long development, 133;
Mosaic authorship of, 107, 218;
submission of the Jewish people to, 125;
tension between theory and, 177
Tower of Babel, 33, 125
tradition, 69–70, 77, 90, 95, 108, 110–11,
119–20, 129, 131–32, 135, 156, 158–
59, 176, 188–91, 195, 203, 205, 214–
15, 217–19; the beautiful world of,
160
transcendence, 109, 111; of God, 57, 151;
of the Ought, 114; of reality, 55; of the
religious object, 78
Treitschke, Heinrich von, 100n. 12, 103
Trinity, doctrine of the, 155; criticism of, as
shittuf (mixing), 75n. 24
Troeltsch, Ernst, xi, 7, 115n. 2
truth, 69, 92, 109, 125, 134, 147, 150–51,
177, 184, 188; Aristotelian and
Cartesian conceptions of, 180;
availability of perfect, 180; and being,
56; is in the beginning, 194–95; and
depth are opposites, 208; faith in
Scripture as the norm of, 149; and
genuineness, 195; and the historical
religions, 57; and illusion, 207; the
Jewish concept of, 131; lovers of, 189;
modern prejudice concerning the, 214;
as the norm of itself and of the false,
159, 174; of reason and of revelation,
91, 181; of religious doctrines, 205–6;

of Scripture, 178–79, 183; and untruth
in politics, 83
Turkey, 63, 128
turning, 16–17, 29, 76; to the truth, 195

unbelief. See belief
uncanny, the, 65, 112–13. See also canny,
the, and the uncanny
universalism: of the Christian enlightenment, 86; of Judaism, 107–8, 112–13
Unreflektiertheit (lack of reflectiveness), 26,
75. See also reflectiveness
untruth. See truth

value, 95–96; judgments and the rhetoric of
radical opposites, 26; knowledge
(Erkenntniswert), 54; of moderation, 34;
numinous, 78; oppositions of, 151; of
the political as distinct from the moral
and the religious, 34; reality (Realitätswert), 205
values, 15, 17, 20, 75, 93; of argumentation
and formal politicism, 65; of critique
and argument, 7, 19; German-Jewish,
67; of liberalism, 18; universal crisis
of, x
Vedic religion, 114
Verne, Jules, 210n. 8
Vernunft (reason), 54, 59n. 3, 168n. 69. See
also reason
Vienna, Congress of, 74n. 21. See also
restoration, period of
virtue, 87; Christianity and the corruption
of Roman, 221; of courage, 34; of
intellectual Redlichkeit, 24–25; as its own
reward, 151; of modesty, 33; of probity,
the will to work, and frugality, 91
virtues, hierarchy of, 47n. 104
vitalism, 60n. 6, 73n. 10, 116n. 10, 209
n. 2
Voltaire (François-Marie Arouet), 132,
137n. 15

Wahrnehmung (perception), 54
Wandervogel, 3–4, 10, 72n. 5
Weber, Max, xi, 7, 15, 26, 39n. 28
Weinberg, Hans, 21, 119–21; "Zionismus
und Religion," 46n. 87
Wellhausen, Julius, 93, 119; Prolegomena zur
Geschichte Israels, 123n. 12